D1570594

COGNITIVE and AFFECTIVE GROWTH: Developmental Interaction

CHILD PSYCHOLOGY

A series of volumes edited by **David S. Palermo**

OSHERON ● *Logical Abilities in Children*
Volume 1 *Organization of Length and Class Concepts: Empirical Consequences of a Piagetian Formalism*
Volume 2 *Logical Inference: Underlying Operations*
Volume 3 *Reasoning in Adolescence: Deductive Inference*
Volume 4 *Reasoning and Concepts*

FREEDMAN ● *Human Infancy: An Evolutionary Perspective*

DE PALMA AND FOLEY (EDS.) ● *Moral Development Current Theory and Research*

KLAHR AND WALLACE ● *Cognitive Development: An Information-Processing View*

SMITH AND FRANKLIN (EDS.) ● *Symbolic Functioning in Childhood*

HAITH ● *Rules That Newborn Babies Look By*

SHAPIRO AND WEBER (EDS.) ● *Cognitive and Affective Growth: Developmental Interaction*

FIELD, SOSTEK, VIETZE, AND LEIDERMAN (EDS.) ● *Culture and Early Interactions*

KUCZAJ (ED.) ● *Language Development: Syntax and Semantics*

COGNITIVE and AFFECTIVE GROWTH: Developmental Interaction

edited by

EDNA K. SHAPIRO
Bank Street College of Education

EVELYN WEBER
Wheelock College

LEA LAWRENCE ERLBAUM ASSOCIATES, PUBLISHERS
1981   Hillsdale, New Jersey

Lawrence Erlbaum Associates, Inc., Publishers
365 Broadway
Hillsdale, New Jersey 07642

Library of Congress Cataloging in Publication Data
Main entry under title:

Cognitive and affective growth.

The chapters in this volume are based on papers
presented at a conference sponsored by Wheelock
College and Bank Street College of Education, June 1978.
  Bibliography: p.
  Includes index.
  1. Cognition in children—Congresses.   Emotions
in children—Congresses.   3.   Child psychology—Con-
gresses.   I. Shapiro, Edna Kaufman.
II. Weber, Evelyn.   III. Bank Street College of
Education, New York.   IV. Wheelock College.
BF723.C5C555   155.4'12   80-29690
ISBN 0-89859-092-2

Printed in the United States of America

Contents

Preface   *vii*

Conference Participants   *ix*

Conference Commentary   *1*

PART I: THE EVOLUTION OF THE DEVELOPMENTAL–
         INTERACTION POINT OF VIEW   *7*

  1. The Evolution of the Developmental-Interaction View   *9*
      Barbara Biber

PART II: INTERRELATIONS BETWEEN COGNITION AND
          AFFECT: THREE VIEWS   *31*

  2. Developmental Concepts of Cognition and Affect   *33*
      Jan Drucker

  3. Cognitive-Affective Interaction:
      A Concept that Exceeds the Researcher's Grasp   *47*
      Herbert Zimiles

  4. Perspectives on Theory: Another Look
      at the Developmental-Interaction Point of View   *65*
      Margery B. Franklin

PART III: RECIPROCAL RELATIONS
           IN THE FIRST YEARS OF LIFE   *85*

  5. The Reciprocal Role of Social and Emotional
      Developmental Advances and Cognitive Development
      During the Second and Third Years of Life   *87*
      Sibylle K. Escalona

6. Perspectives on Interactional Research   97
    Leon J. Yarrow

PART IV: QUESTIONING THE ROLE OF
         DEVELOPMENTAL STAGE THEORY   109

7. Developmental Stage Theory
    and the Individual Reconsidered   111
    Edna K. Shapiro and Doris B. Wallace

8. Stage Theory and Curriculum Development   132
    Evelyn Weber

PART V: THE NATURE AND DEVELOPMENT OF
        GENDER DIFFERENCES   145

9. Gender Differences in the Nature of
    Premises Developed About the World   147
    Jeanne H. Block

10. The Child's Construction of Gender:
    Anatomy as Destiny   171
    Dorothy Z. Ullian

PART VI: THE DEVELOPMENT OF CHILDREN'S AWARENESS
         OF INTRAPSYCHIC PROCESSES   185

11. What Children Understand of Intrapsychic Processes:
    The Child as a Budding Personality Theorist   187
    Robert L. Selman

Author Index   217

Subject Index   223

Preface

The common theme that unites the contributors to this book is their commitment to an integrative view of developmental phenomena, one that highlights the relationships among different aspects of development and the reciprocal nature of relations between people and their environments. The articles are based on papers presented at a conference called to explore what we have called a developmental-interaction point of view—an approach to developmental psychology and education that stresses these interactive and reciprocal relations.

It is becoming commonplace to express discomfort with recent preoccupation with cognition, a preoccupation that has led to a narrow, even exclusive, focus on cognitive phenomena at the expense of other aspects of development. Currently there are many signs of renewed attention in theory and research to social and emotional development and their interrelations with cognition. At the same time, there has been a new appreciation of the importance of contextual influences, and of the interdependency of individuals and their environments. The pursuit of an integrative view of development seems particularly timely.

The conference that led to this work was initiated to bring together a group from diverse professional backgrounds who share certain basic assumptions but view development from different perspectives. The goal of the conference, as of this volume, was to foster interchange and the elaboration of an interactionist view. The group represents several disciplines concerned with developmental phenomena—cognitive psychologists, developmental psychologists, educational and curriculum specialists, clinicians. Some are primarily devoted to research, others to practice. In spite of different orientations, they can be said to be working within the same family of ideas.

The group was kept small intentionally so as to allow for extended discussion of issues. The issues confronted here are not likely to be resolved by any single set of papers; the collection is offered as a contribution to a view of development that honors its complexity.

The conference, jointly sponsored by Wheelock College and Bank Street College of Education, was held at and hosted by Wheelock College in June 1978. We wish to express our gratitude to President Gordon Marshall of Wheelock for his generous support. After initial consultations with Barbara Biber, the conference was planned and organized by Edna Shapiro and Herbert Zimiles of Bank Street College and Lydia Gerhardt, Elizabeth Ann Liddle, Evelyn Weber, and Nancy Wyner of Wheelock College.

Chapters in this book have benefited from the comments of conference participants. A capsule sampling of ideas expressed in discussion at the conference is presented before the individual chapters. We are grateful to all the participants for their thoughtful contributions to the proceedings and to this work.

Edna K. Shapiro
Evelyn Weber

Conference Participants

LOUISE BERMAN, College of Education, University of Maryland
BARBARA BIBER, Research Division, Bank Street College of Education
JEANNE H. BLOCK, Institute of Human Development, University of California at Berkeley
JAN DRUCKER, Department of Psychology, Sarah Lawrence College
SIBYLLE K. ESCALONA, Rose Fitzgerald Kennedy Center, Albert Einstein College of Medicine, Yeshiva University
MARGERY B. FRANKLIN, Department of Psychology, Sarah Lawrence College
LYDIA GERHARDT, Graduate School, Wheelock College
ELIZABETH ANN LIDDLE, Graduate and Undergraduate Schools, Wheelock College
FRANCES MINOR, School of Education, New York University
PATRICIA P. MINUCHIN, Department of Psychoeducational Processes, Temple University
ROBERT L. SELMAN, Judge Baker Guidance Center and Graduate School of Education, Harvard University
EDNA K. SHAPIRO, Research Division, Bank Street College of Education
MARGUERITE SMITH, Infant Development Unit, Solomon C. Fuller Mental Health Center
BERNARD SPODEK, College of Education, University of Illinois
DOROTHY Z. ULLIAN, Department of Psychology, Wheelock College
DORIS B. WALLACE, Research Division, Bank Street College of Education
EVELYN WEBER, Graduate School, Wheelock College
NANCY WYNER, Graduate School, Wheelock College
LEON J. YARROW, Child and Family Research Branch, National Institutes of Child Health and Human Development
HERBERT ZIMILES, Research Division, Bank Street College of Education

COGNITIVE and
AFFECTIVE GROWTH:
Developmental Interaction

Conference Commentary

Edna K. Shapiro
Bank Street College of Education

Evelyn Weber
Wheelock College

The conference group was just about the right size to be able to sit around a rather large square table, and the discussions after each paper were lively, sometimes heated. Although the talk was taped, we are not presenting the proceedings. Experience tells us that such reports seldom convey the intellectual or emotional enthusiasm that marked the original occasion—like jokes, so hilarious when spontaneous, but leaden when retold. Yet many interesting and provocative ideas were expressed that did not find their way into the papers, and it seems to us that it would be unfortunate to recycle the tapes without attempting to extract at least some of them. Our goal in this sampling is rather like trying to pick the nuts and raisins out of the cake. We trust that our selection honors the intent and meaning of the participants.

On rereading the discussions we find several themes that cut across the content of the papers, and we have organized this summary in terms of those emergent themes. Note please that almost all comments are paraphrased and taken out of context; we have made no effort to follow the sequence of the discussion as it actually occurred. We have also omitted content that is covered in the chapters in this volume. The six themes are: concern with a historical perspective on psychological and educational thinking, relations between cognition and affect, and between theory and practice, a concern with the values that have influenced and that underlie psychological and educational theory and practice, and the need to consider development in context. Finally, the implications for research was a theme that threaded through all discussions.

The group was struck by the fact that many participants independently had turned to the past. Taking a *historical perspective* seemed to offer a way of anchoring current formulations and research paradigms, and also a possible guide in the search for new constructions. Sibylle Escalona said it was only by "iron self-discipline" that she had not looked back. She went on to suggest that the desire to take a historical perspective may be more than an acknowledgment that our present ideas and techniques are far from meeting our goals; it may also bespeak a more serious application of ideas about development to ourselves as a discipline, seeing that issues of continuity and discontinuity and successive phases are relevant to the development of theory, as well as of persons. The retrospective look can be humbling, for we find that ideas are continually being rediscovered. Bud Spodek remarked that, although participants kept returning to the history of ideas, no one went beyond the history of psychology to the broader social and intellectual history that has both shaped and limited psychological inquiry. Doris Wallace pointed to the peculiar separation of developmental psychology from fields with which we might assume overlap, social psychology for one.

Barbara Biber talked about historical changes in the concept of education and the role of women in our society. The encouragement of less boy–girl differentiation has a long tradition, at least in certain schools, and grew out of the early feminist movement. The idea that education could alter or weaken stereotypic behavior was an innocent effort at manipulation, but value laden, and oriented toward promoting greater equality for women. The issue of the denial of possibilities for women was taken as primarily social and political. Now we seem to be getting closer to understanding its psychological ramifications.

Because a central idea of the conference was concerned with relations between *cognition and affect,* it is not surprising that there was considerable discussion of what we mean by these terms, and what forms the relationship might take. Should we try to define the terms? We could take the easy road to a dictionary definition; trying for a psychologically sound and precise definition seemed premature, and impossible. More simply, how shall we talk about them? Does talking about cognition and affect imply separation? Escalona said that the vocabulary of "domains" suggests separate territories. It might be more helpful to think of cognition and affect as dimensions or facets of a single experience or event. Some raised the question of why we stay with these terms if they are not useful, definable, or practical. Jan Drucker turned the question around to ask, Why haven't we abandoned them? Reason and emotion have been thought of as polarities for centuries, and there is something phenomenologically compelling about the distinction. Margery Franklin suggested that, although most of us do not view cognition and affect as being separate in life, they can be distinguished theoretically, and we all have a notion of what we mean. The solution was pragmatic: not to define terms, but to try to sharpen our ideas and clarify our categories through discussion.

One of the initial goals of the conference was to elaborate and refine the concept of cognitive–affective interaction. It was noted that interaction implies effects in both directions and, further, that interaction is only one form that the relationship may take: Cognition and affect may be parallel systems, or there may be fusion. Leon Yarrow remarked that we need also to distinguish interactional relationships from other kinds of relationships in which several variables may act together to enhance or moderate an effect. It is indeed possible that all these forms of relation between cognition and affect are true at different times, in different circumstances, and may vary also with developmental level. When we speak of reciprocal relationships, are we saying that they are simultaneous? sequential? that influences may extend over time?

Dorothy Ullian pointed out that we have an articulated structural theory of cognitive development, but no comparable theory of emotional development. Is the course of affective development like that of cognitive development? It may be following a false track to search for parallel developmental lines. Jeanne Block reminded us that a number of different terms are used to refer to affect—emotions, feelings, states, moods; they are not interchangeable, but they are not clearly differentiated. Beyond this, we need to consider children's understanding of emotion, which reflects how they comprehend experience.

Another theme that recurred throughout the discussion had to do with the relation between *theory and practice* or, as Franklin put it, theory and realization. The practice with which we were most concerned was educational practice, inasmuch as this was a meeting of psychologists and educators. But there was also talk about clinical practice, and the similarities and differences in how theory is used in both educational and therapeutic settings. As Bob Selman said, theorists, especially Piaget and Freud, do not have just one theory, but a number of theories, at the least, a metatheory and a clinical theory. Although some seemed to talk in terms of moving from theory to practice, there was general consensus that in this relationship too, one needs to think in reciprocal terms—that one makes inferences from theoretical statements, and also that observations from practice need to be juxtaposed against theoretical statements. In fact, it is essential to go in both directions, to work both ways. Connecting theory with what happens in educational or clinical settings can be salutory also because it helps to keep our thinking from getting too involuted. Escalona said that practical decisions and actions are not based on but are informed by theory, and noted that the issue is not simply how far from reality the theory is, but how developed the theory is. Theories in the social sciences, including those in developmental psychology, are not so highly developed that we should feel constrained about raising questions when our appraisal of situations we observe seems not to mesh with theoretical statements.

Selman noted that there is a growing awareness of the need to distinguish between competence, which is a theoretical abstraction, and performance, which is observable behavior.

The way one conceptualizes the relation between theory and its utilization depends also on the particular aspects of theory one uses to inform practice. As Franklin said, the translation of Piagetian concepts to educational practice has been focused primarily on operativity, which is very different from thinking about, for example, the development of children's understanding of intrapsychic processes. In the latter, the focus is on children's experience of their own lives and other people in their lives. And Frances Minor observed that the meaning that children give to phenomena is at the heart of the developmental–interaction point of view, for it is there that cognitive and affective aspects are merged.

Some participants questioned whether theory might not sometimes serve as a repressive rather than a liberating force—an especially important question in the classroom context where the teacher has considerable power, and the children are not voluntary participants. Spodek said that, given the power situation in most classrooms, it made him uneasy when teachers use therapeutic models. Biber commented that this is a problem of long standing in educating teachers. She would put no limit on how much understanding of inner processes a teacher should have. The challenge is for the teacher to be able to use her knowledge wisely and with delicacy, to be sensitive to the dangers of the superficial and intrusive. There is no prescription for how to do this. Drucker pointed out that we need to distinguish between educational and therapeutic interventions and the kind of change that is brought about by educational or by therapeutic means. She remarked that what is true for the teacher and for parents is also true for the clinician and probably for anyone who interacts with children; there is a constant tension between a clearly differentiated view of children's needs and multiple facets of their functioning and what one does at any given moment. The goal is to make it a productive tension.

Another thread had to do with the *values,* explicit or implicit, that underlie psychological theory. The developmental–interaction point of view is based on a particular value system that informs the image of what education should be. Nancy Wyner added that both psychological theory and educational practice are influenced by the values of the political system in which they are embedded.

Louise Berman pointed out that the kinds of images of persons the educator holds reflect values. When we look at a classroom, we have to realize that, although individuality may be a value, no one thinks that any kind of individuality can emerge; only certain forms of individuality are allowed in any specific classroom. In another connection, Spodek remarked that the individual has to be involved in the means and ends of his own education. How is knowledge generated and how is it verified? For example, does he know that something is true or right except by having the teacher tell him that it is so? Spodek noted that such questions form part of the set of values that relate to the liberal tradition.

Many statements reflected the interest current in psychological thinking on viewing the *individual in context.* Patricia Minuchin asked, how can we think about and study development, even when complexly defined to incorporate affective, cognitive, and interpersonal aspects, how can we talk about it as a bounded unit? If one takes a systems point of view, it is almost meaningless to talk about the individual without dealing with the context. And if you add to that the need to take change into account, you add another level of complexity. Yarrow noted that when we talk about context, we are talking at many different levels—the political–social context, the cultural context, the geographic, the context of the American middle-class family; or the immediate environment, the personalities of the parents, the characteristics, sensitivities, and vulnerabilities of the child.

Here, as with other content, *implications for research* were explored. Dissatisfaction with limited cause–effect formulations and narrow experimental methods, and the desire for more imaginative forms of inquiry were general. How to do and interpret research, given the concept of reciprocity of different processes and the demand to take context into account, was the issue. Herb Zimiles remarked that sometimes our expectations were unrealistic, that one should not expect to find perfect consistency in research findings nor, for that matter, does one expect to find it in ordinary behavior. Yarrow reported that in a study he and his colleagues are doing of the home environment, they have the technology that permits them to record a mass of data, in sequence. When it is time to analyze, however, they still have to face the question of where to start the sequence and where to end it.

In working with very young children, Escalona noted that variability in affective state or the momentary situation has more potential for creating developmental disequilibrium than with older children or adults. Marguerite Smith made the point that sometimes you can understand what has happened only in retrospect, which makes it important to do longitudinal studies. As an example, she told about a blind baby she had worked with who had a new sibling when he was 20 months old, and had a very painful separation from his mother; the child was clearly depressed, unhappy, and disruptive while she was in the hospital. It took him 2 or 3 months to overcome his anxiety about her leaving. The next year, there was another baby. Now the child was 3, and much more confident, but above all, he had well-developed language. During the second separation he could express his sorrow saying, "Where are you mommy?" or "I love you darling, come home." He recovered from that separation in a very short time. Was it the ability to express his feelings in language, or that he had already had one separation experience, or that he was older? Or all of these? We still have to make inferences, but knowing about the earlier episode influences the interpretation.

Selman asked Escalona about her observation of the baby who crawled away and then, discovering that the mother was not there, "behaved as if the mother had left the baby." Can one say that the child, when it walks away at 18 months, feels as though the mother has abandoned it? Is that a testable hypothesis? Escalona, like Yarrow, thinks we ought to make the effort at least to imagine what goes on in the head. But it would be entirely wrong to say, "He or she *feels* that"; it is, however, important to say his or her behavioral response is *as though*. Selman also noted that, when we talk about reciprocal interaction, we need to think about how issues in the child's development raise conflicts for the parent, which would lead us to a theory of adult ego development in parenting.

To end here is artificial, although it reflects the unfinished-business quality of the discussions themselves. Lydia Gerhardt thought it regrettable that so little attention had been paid to the role of physical and motor development. Several noted that we had dealt with only a narrow portion of the developmental span, for the most part, very young children and the adults who interact with them.

The goal of the conference was to provide an opportunity for the exchange of ideas among a group of knowledgeable professionals sympathetic to an integrative approach to understanding developmental phenomena. It is only occasionally that there is any intensive cross-referencing of communication across disciplinary boundaries. We have tried to represent some of the flavor of the interchange when such a group comes together. The nature of the thematic concerns and the level of discussion attest, we believe, to a commitment to grapple with rather than to ignore or retreat from the intricacy and interdependence of developmental phenomena.

THE EVOLUTION OF THE
DEVELOPMENTAL-INTERACTION
POINT OF VIEW

In 1964, when Barbara Biber wrote about the relationship of early childhood education and philosophical issues, she posed two central questions:

What can early education do to lead the young, groping mind toward the kind of intellectual potency that is represented by the capacity to deal analytically and synthetically with the ever-widening world of objective knowledge and personal experience? How can the young child experience the deep, creative involvement in his early encounters with the world of things, problems, and ideas that will insure against superficiality and indifference and lay the groundwork for an attitude of commitment to hopes and ideals for man's progress?[1]

Her approach to these questions was both developmental and interactive, integrating affective and cognitive aspects and demonstrating a willingness, on the part of the educator, to deal with complexity.

Here Biber turns to the value system inherent in a developmental-interaction point of view, and the relation between such a system of preferred values and the kinds of

---

[1]Biber, B. Preschool education. In R. Ulich (Ed.), *Education and the idea of mankind.* New York: Harcourt, Brace & World, 1964, p. 86.

7

curricula designed for children. She sees this view as generating a continuing search for the nature of experiences that can promote optimal development of individuality while, at the same time, remaining congruent with images of an improved society. Taking a historical perspective, Biber describes both change and constancy in the values and means of achieving them.

1 The Evolution of the Developmental-Interaction View

Barbara Biber
Bank Street College of Education

The developmental-interaction view, as currently stated, represents a perspective on the relation between development and learning that has evolved over several decades and is, as it should be, in the process of change and reformulation as new knowledge and insights become available (Biber, 1977b; Franklin & Biber, 1977; Shapiro & Biber, 1972).[1] In the following presentation I attempt to: (1) make the issues of values within this framework explicit; (2) trace the history of this viewpoint in education; and (3) denote the psychological theories with which it is compatible and interactive. Before tracing the course of thinking and experience that led to the contemporary conceptualization, it is useful to begin with a capsule definition of the developmental-interaction view in current usage, as given by Shapiro and Biber (1972):

Developmental refers to the emphasis on identifiable patterns of growth and modes of perceiving and responding which are characterized by increasing differentiation and progressive integration as a function of chronological age. Interaction refers, first, to the emphasis on the child's interaction with the environment—adults, other children, and the material world—and, second, to the interaction between cognitive and affective spheres of development. The developmental-interaction formulation stresses the nature of the environment as much as it does the patterns of the responding child. . . .
It is a basic tenet of the developmental-interaction approach that the growth of cognitive functions—acquiring and ordering information, judging, reasoning, prob-

---

[1]This approach has served as a perspective for analysis in a book addressed to parents (Cohen, 1972); in a study of deprived and middle-class children in Israel (Krown, 1974); and in a review of research literature about the middle years of childhood (Minuchin, 1977).

lem solving, using systems of symbols—cannot be separated from the growth of personal and interpersonal processes—the development of self-esteem and a sense of identity, internalization of impulse control, capacity for autonomous response, relatedness to other people [pp. 59–60, 61].

A Basic Value System

This brief statement refers to a viewpoint that has evolved from a system of preferred values concerning the relation of the individual to society. For us at Bank Street, it has remained consistent over more than 50 years. As is to be expected, the concepts of the nature of experience, school experience in particular, that is supposed to support acceptance and internalization of the values has changed substantially in response to advances in conceptualizing the course of growth processes and in understanding the dynamics of the motivational system.

Looked at historically, this viewpoint developed as both an educational philosophy and a design for practice, resting on a body of preferred values with respect to human behavior. We have had a degree of confidence, not as great now as it once was, that a selective kind of experience in school not only influences the formation of the individual value system in the years of growing toward maturity, but also maintains some viability in the choices made in the adult world of conflicting values (Biber, 1972).

We have related practice to theory, revising practice according to changing theory of learning and growth processes, but always within the parameters of the preferred educational and social goals and values. It is generally recognized now, more than formerly, that psychological theories are also value invested. In our Bank Street history, we have worked toward internal consistency among values, learning–teaching practices, and psychological theories of motivation and development. It has become clear that only certain theories can both support and stimulate certain educational designs.

If we look at our statements of the developmental–interaction viewpoint with the eye of the educator who must build the substance of the educational experience selectively, the guidelines are incomplete or, perhaps, open-ended. We assumed, but did not specify nor describe, how our underlying values shape the nature of the socializing process and influence the curriculum—the programming, the settings, the behavior codes, and the selection of instructional methods. This is especially true with reference to the first definition of "interaction," which speaks for emphasis on the child's interaction with the environment—adults, other children, and the material world. It can be maintained that the term "interaction" itself is an educational or curricular directive, in contrast to learning programs in which the child's role is essentially passive. But, beyond the general concept of "interaction" there are underlying values that determine a school's selection, emphasis, and interpretation of the substance of the learning experience. The statement referring to "interaction," as it stands, could legitimately include educational designs of contrasting values. We did not intend that. What follows is a brief review of the Bank Street value base in formation. A subsequent section contains a description of how changing insight into the developmental process has required change in the educational perspective, even while the value base remains constant.

In the broadest sense, the basic value system is an amalgam of ideas about social change, processes of maturing, and selection of preferred learning-teaching strategies. There is a rationale for the relation between the educative process and the experiences designed for children, on the one hand, and a system of preferred values, on the other. Projected developmentally, a system of values embraces three psychological domains: the nature of individuality, the quality of relations between persons, and the relation between the individual and the society in which he or she lives.

Our preferred value system is grounded in the humanist position on the importance of human beings from two perspectives—individuality and social potential. This general proposition generates a complex and continuing search for what kind of educational experience promises optimal development of individuality and what images of society shall be the template for designing the social dynamics of a classroom.

The dimensions in which goals of education are conceptualized reflect underlying values. They bespeak the extent to which the educational process is geared to a short-term accomplishment agenda or, by contrast, to a long-term developmental perspective. As examples of the latter, I find in the history of Bank Street statements of goals at different periods that reflect the different uses for which such statements were intended. For example, one formulation takes a perspective that is adapted to relating educational goals to concepts of positive mental health (Biber, 1961). One of the goals, "positive feeling toward the self," is defined, in part, as enjoyment of one's own powers as a sensing, feeling, thinking being; another, "relatedness to people," includes the capacity to relate to others as individuals relatively free from group stereotyping; and "relatedness to environment" includes positive, motivated connectedness with the contemporary world of processes and ideas.

Another later statement is more focused on expressing similar goals in terms of salient developmental processes with illustrations of the learning experiences that are the necessary foundation. Here, the goal "to nurture self-esteem and self-understanding" includes, in addition to self-acceptance, the ability to identify with one's origins—as a member of a sex, a family, an ethnic or racial group; the goal "to encourage differentiated interaction with people" includes, in addition to relating to others as nonstereotyped individuals, the capacity to communicate with others, express feelings and ideas. In this formulation, the concept, relatedness to environment, appears as ability "to sustain curiosity about the world" as part of the more general goal of strengthening commitment to and pleasure in work and learning (Shapiro & Biber, 1972).

The differences in the definitional content between these two formulations do not obscure what is common between them. They represent educational goals that are sensitive to the general humanist priorities. In both, albeit with some changing emphasis, the self, the interpersonal process, and the person in relation to the larger world scene beyond the school are included in the educational agenda.

From this perspective, the nurturing of individuality to its optimal potential is the foundation for the personal value system in formation. The educational experience is designed to provide gradually a reciprocal relation between individual fulfillment and socialized experience so that the moral implications of the school community are built not on principles of sacrifice, compromise, and denial, but rather on the psychological interchange of sources of gratification expressed through balancing the experience of satisfying the self with yielding it—rather, exchanging it—for the pleasures of social mergence. Only a certain kind of curriculum, where there is opportunity for more collective than competitive enterprise, supports that process. In our perspective, it is assumed that this movement between the self and the social can be considered an appropriate developmental step toward a value system that attempts to integrate what is good for the individual with what is good for mankind. I put it in these words once: "Fulfillment of the individual alone, even by ambitious criteria of psychological health and realization of potential, does not constitute a system of values. . . . The worth of the individual becomes the cornerstone of a value system only when fulfillment of the individual, abstracted from personal right and privilege, culminates in a universal concern for everyone else's individuality [Biber, 1964, p. 75]."

How one arrives at the formation of a value system that serves human beings, individually and collectively, is a major challenge to those value-conscious educators who represent discontent with the way things are. This has been a challenge to Bank Street, reflected in research programming and educational ideology, throughout its history. The expression of position changes from time to time, in response to changed modes of thinking about how values are established and how they might be influenced, in particular, through the medium of the quality of experience in school.

We have consistently, however, in theory and practice, expressed opposition to the dominant built-in pressure of established education toward conformism of behavior and thought within the context of an authoritarian personal and social system. We have questioned methods that attempt to treat value education as a separate and distinct curriculum area. We have had deep concern for school situations where moral maxims are verbalized, held up to children as models for their behavior in the very situations where there is flagrant violation of what is being spoken. Unfortunately, these are prime lessons to children in how to mistrust. From another perspective, there are the more recently developed methods for processing moral development through the course of cognitive maturing with the assumption that conceptual insight will have important influence on behavioral decisions (Kohlberg & Turiel, 1971). The incorporation of value teaching in school curriculum accelerated in the decade of the seventies and was accompanied with great differences of opinion as to method (New York Times, March 4, 1980).

From our point of view, the separation of "value education" from the total educational milieu bespeaks insufficient recognition of the interweaving of the complex components of the learning experience. This position has taken different forms in the course of years. In the earlier period, the statement of the interaction principle was filtered through concepts and images of educational programming. The vision was described as "educating the 'whole child'—releasing the powers and expanding the freedom of action of children in their learning years while developing them as thinking, rational problem solvers and providing them with experience in maintaining satisfying interpersonal group relations" (Biber, 1977b; p. 423). In the contemporary statement, the principle of interdependence is expressed in psychological dimensions—the growth of cognitive functions interacting with the growth of personal and interpersonal processes. The principle of interaction does not define the choices intrinsic to a given value system. It behooves those who adhere to such a system to define what choices are made, what learning–teaching processes are preferred as being consistent with and supportive of the value perspective.

The basic attitudes and values that are to be given priority are expressed in choices of alternative teaching methods, in the criteria for what constitutes a positive learning–teaching milieu, and in the nature of sanctions against what is not acceptable. The educational goals are formulated in terms of stimulating major developmental processes in the direction of selected values of optimal functioning. The processes that are learning oriented are integrated with images of positive personal and interpersonal functioning. Thus, the concept of *competence* includes, beyond quality of performance, the individual's perception of himself as someone able to overcome obstacles, master confusion, and solve problems. This is an expected outcome to the extent that the school has provided productive modes of interchange and suitable challenge. The sense of *individuality*, of individual identity, is formed, differentiated, and internalized to the extent that a curriculum plan provides for autonomous functioning—opportunities to make choices, develop preferences, take initiative, risk failure, and set an independent course for problem solving. In the early years, the quality of school life is such that the child sees himself naturally as having a voice to question, to doubt, to contradict. This is the foundation for expecting and being able, in later years, to sustain autonomy of judgment and be less dependent on external symbols of approval and ingroup acceptance. By our humanistic code, we have to turn from realized, autonomous individuality to the *socialized* self. This calls for a code and a program that sponsor ongoing relations of mutuality in play, work, talk, argument, sympathy, where pooling of ideas and cooperative activities replace the highly charged focus on the symbols of individual success. From active interchange through a variety of modes of communication and joint enterprise, awareness of other individuals' uniqueness is generated in ways that can be assimilated as a source of enriched experience rather than a target for competitive conquest. A fourth dimension deals with *integration* as a goal in contrast to compartmentalization of functions or experience. This dimension is conceived as a process of synthesis, a bringing together of seemingly disparate realms of experience. It refers to the merging, the counterpoint of personal and interpersonal experience, the level of new meanings derived from experience in which thought and feeling are conjoined, where self-feeling and empathy are interactive. It is in this integrative process that we usually find the fullest expression of creative potential (Biber, 1977b).

Coming closer to classroom imagery, it is possible to see the learning environment as one in which the child, according to Franklin and Biber (1977), is the:

> major actor, so organized that he can gain a sense of his own competence through the experience of *autonomy*. . . . His ways of . . . reconstructing experience are valued for *aesthetic qualities* and expression of *feeling* as well as for evidence of cognitive mastery. There is a wide latitude for varied personal interaction on many levels since the social climate is not rigidly stratified. . . . The teacher is looked to not only as a guide for penetrating the how and why of the external surround but also as a willing, dependable resource for dealing with fear, loss of direction, anger, or loneliness. . . . When it is successful, the child finds strength and pleasure in creating order through his expanding thought processes, from sharing depth of feeling with teachers and children, and from re-creating symbolically the meanings—real and fantasied—that are of the greatest moment to him [p. 24].

Perhaps, in a small way, this brings our brief statement referring to "emphasis on the child's interaction with the environment—adults, other children, the material world" closer to the reality of the child's experience.

There is, then, a basic assumption in this approach, namely that these preferred values, embedded in the school goals and experienced in the modes of learning and interchange, will be internalized and, further, that these values will influence the modes of relations that the individual establishes in the world.[2] A more realistic assumption is that they will have some degree of influence even when they come into conflict with contrary family and out-in-the-world value systems. In a larger perspective, we can hope that this kind of experiencing of an egalitarian, democratic, social system in the years of schooling, if widely realized and implemented, could be a force for effecting social change. It is on this plane that the Bank Street ethos is obviously closely related to John Dewey's philosophy. In our time, as was also true in Dewey's era, applying the demo-

---

[2]See Franklin and Biber (1977) for discussion of this issue in relation to the Bereiter and Engelmann program.

cratic ethos to education is not the dominant trend. It runs counter to other trends in contemporary life that are reflected, for example, in the adoption of educational techniques that deal with the learning process through methods of behavior change and claim to be value free. This contention and the associated disregard of the values implicit in the use of such methods has been argued.

An Educational Perspective in Support of the Democratic Process

Dewey's philosophy and its projection into the theory and practice of education in the early decades of the twentieth century provided new hopes and images for a changing society anchored in a commitment to revolutionize the goals and methods of the established educational system. After so many years and so many volumes of exegesis on his thinking, it is refreshing to turn to his own formulations (Dewey, 1938/1963), where he tried to counteract misinterpretations of his theory. The concept of freedom intrinsic to his educational philosophy was being turned gradually into a dogma of rebellion instead of weighing past values in terms of which might and which might not contribute to a regenerative present.

He decried the tendency to reject indiscriminately the practices of the older education and, in so doing, to:

> make little or nothing of organized subject matter of study; to proceed as if any form of direction and guidance by adults were an invasion of individual freedom, and as if the idea that education should be concerned with the present and future meant that acquaintance with the past has little or no role to play in education [Dewey, 1938, p. 22].

Do we hear an echo in our time in the educational protest movement of the 1960s?

Dewey's colleague, George Counts (1932), advocated a more decisive role for the school, well beyond the function of enlarging students' "acquaintance with a changing world." He asked the educational profession to become active in sponsoring the forward movements in our society, to: "make certain that every progressive school will use whatever power it may possess in opposing and checking the forces of social conservatism and reaction [p. 24]." The schools were to be the instruments of a new vision for society. It was Counts' vision of a changed society as well as Dewey's image of a changed school that, in the 1930s, motivated many of the members of the Bank Street College community and their colleagues in the City and Country School.

Translated into school terms, this image becomes one of active involvement of children and teachers; an open atmosphere of social interchange; of freedom to initiate and pursue lines of individual interest; a program including varied experience inside and outside the domain of school; of learning through ongoing interactions with things, people, ideas; of acquiring symbolic skills in the functional contexts in which they are used. There was a new paradigm for the learning process—thinking and questioning, doing and testing—the prescribed mode of the scientist. Motivated by the pleasure and meaningfulness of their studies and activities, it was expected that children would manage their impulses without arbitrarily imposed restraints and together generate an informal, cooperative minisociety—basic experience for how to live in and improve the encompassing adult democracy. It was a radical image in contast to the conventional American school of the early twentieth century, though there had been other radical images of learning and education earlier and in other places.

This new image of the dimensions of school experience was, as is to be expected, interpreted and enacted in different ways by the educational innovators of the twenties and thirties who associated themselves with the progressive education movement and undertook to enact the Deweyan philosophy. There were certain common features in the programs that were developed but also major differences in qualities and emphasis in enactment.

We are familiar with the basic learning-by-doing paradigm and the prime value placed on finding methods that would nurture each child's individuality and given potential for learning. The experiences stimulating the program offered not only a new richness of experience in an extended environment, but offered varied modes for absorbing, expressing, and reorganizing experience. In all, opportunity for self-initiated reexpression of experience in language, in play, in construction, in art was valued, especially to the degree that, once given the materials and the necessary surround, the children could reorganize their experiences to new levels of insight and understanding. The necessary surround included opportunity to talk and exchange doubts and wonder with other children and teachers in a new learning atmosphere, and for the older students to discover what others have thought in the world's recorded knowledge. The pleasure of expression, the intimate interactions among the children, the relaxation of experiencing authority without anxiety all contributed to a positive, enjoyed learning atmosphere.

The major thrust of this early period came from Dewey's image of a new kind of school, a world where young children could be active questioners and experimenters. The dimensions of new freedom to be attained through full development of thinking and reasoning powers appealed to certain early educators more than to some others for whom the new freedom was more prized when expressed meaningfully through the expressive media. The weighting of different programs in different schools reflected these basic differences.

An outstanding early, fully documented study describing the mode and the rationale for stimulating thinking in the early years of childhood was written by Harriet Johnson (1928/1972).[3] In working with 2-year-olds, she documented the

---

[3]This program was the base on which the program for the education of young children, one of the major Bank Street College activities, was built.

progression from early sensorimotor, manipulative activity to the capacity to deal symbolically with experiences and illustrated a desirable role for the teacher, both in stimulating the process and being aware of when the child was not ready. The natural interchange with the children in caring for them or talking with them about their play offered the opportunity for stimulating perceptions of difference, seeing objects in terms of functions, using the child's questions to help him find his own answers, and creating mutual enjoyment of the "whyness" of the interchange.

Stimulation of thinking—called "relationship thinking" by Lucy Mitchell (1934/1964) and others—was part of a method. It was described by Biber (1977a) as: "a systematic effort to create a learning environment in which conceptual organization of elements of experience . . . would be continuously and naturally stimulated as part of the child's encounter, physical and symbolic, in the course of his active response to his environment [p. 45]." The concept of what constitutes the learning environment was extended to include the world beyond the school walls. Understanding the "work processes" carried by machine and man was stimulated through exploratory trips and encounters. This experience was coordinated with subsequent discussion and reading, graduated in complexity according to developmental level. The contemporary Bank Street opposition to methods that turn to systematic exercises, extrapolated from meaningful experience, as the way of reinforcing cognitive processes has had deep roots. Instead, the modes of questioning, explaining, deducing, generalizing, hypothesizing were and are integrated with varied experiential stimulations.

This was also the period, the twenties and thirties, in which the progressive schools built their program for the early years around carefully planned play activity. The children were free to relive and rethink their experience symbolically, projecting their conceptual insights into a sphere of physical and symbolic objects and space. The imaginative organizing and reorganizing of the relationships projected was the children's input into the process but, in these schools, the teacher perceived and supported the play experience as a mode of thinking, a natural medium for generating further questions as well as expressing relationships that had already been mastered. The teacher saw her role as providing the next level question in the form of inquiry, or perhaps by offering an added symbolic figure as a stimulant to more elaborated conceptualizing, mindful always of the degree of the children's readiness to step ahead with the thinking process. At this stage of generalizing the teaching-learning process for the younger children, according to Biber (1977a) three principles were formulated: "(1) Play is a basic mode for thinking in early childhood; (2) An important aspect of the teacher's role is to exploit the ongoing daily encounters, physical and social, as material for stimulating thinking processes; and (3) the cognitive search for relationships should be stimulated through providing varied, multiple opportunities for the children's direct, active contact with the people and processes of their environment [p. 47]."

From several sources, during this period, the new mood of criticism of traditional education broadened to include concern with emotional processes and personality formation. "Understand the whole child" developed new directives to understand how emotions condition the way children use the experience that any school provides. In 1930, there were at least two conferences (Faris, 1930; Washburne, 1930) dealing with the relation between disturbance at home and behavior in school, asking school people to look under the surface of children's behavior. In the same decade, some school people, from their direct experience with children, were impressed with the extent to which this new mode of school life liberated not only the mind, but the inner person, expressed in greater self-confidence and freedom from the debilitating fear of failure (M. Johnson, 1939). There were other progressive school people, interested in applying the concepts of burgeoning psychoanalytic theory to the educative process, who were also aligned with Dewey's philosophy but whose curriculum and school climate were adapted to the concept that socialization depends on individual resolution, a recognition of the complexity of the subjective inner life and its place as the foundation for fundamental social adaptation (Naumberg, 1928). These were early voices leading toward the principle of cognitive-affective interaction.

An Enlarged Perspective from Developmental and Psychodynamic Psychology

The movement toward a cognitive-affective interaction position matured gradually over several decades. The perspective of the total educational process changed in response to concepts from psychodynamic psychology of changing drives, energies, and conflicts at different stages of development. It changed in response to increased knowledge from developmental psychologists on the complex course by which cognitive functions change and mature. The movement of thought by psychologists of those persuasions were paralleled by that of educators who chose to continue and develop the ethos of the progressive school movement by incorporating and applying new insights into human behavior and the developmental process. Some of the newer insights came from the laboratory and the couch; some came from educators' analyses and reflections on the life of the classroom. From these several sources, the parameters of knowledge relevent to the educative process were extended well beyond the perspective of the early progressive school movement. What matters is that, in our own era, there is more joint inquiry, more pooling of educators' insights from the complex totality of a learning environment with psychologists' findings from studies that analyze rather than mirror the reality of the classroom.

The interdependence of cognitive and affective experience and growth, as a postulate, influences our perceptions and interpretation of the learning process. When we think of the learning process as being fundamentally active, we refer to patterns of exploration, manipulation, and investigation, to a basic drive and available energies to fulfill curiosity with the expectation of knowledge gained. Learning, perceived as subjective experience, encompasses, in addition, varying degrees of sense of competence, of confidence in being able to initiate a course of inquiry or of stimulation in the face of the unknown. The weightings of these and other components of the learning experience depend on the qualities of the learning environment provided. Similarly, the concept of the course of development as comprising an invariant sequence of stages characterized by cognitive shifts from global to differentiated, from concrete to abstract thinking, and from concrete operational to thinking in terms of logic and principles is a basic construct for educational planning. But this sequence needs to be understood also in terms of the changing drives, shifting patterns of affiliation, and stage-specific conflicts that enter into the vitality of the cognitive processes.

The interest in spontaneous play in relation to the thinking processes that characterized the Harriet Johnson Nursery School in the twenties and generated a "why and wherefore climate" in the successive years of the City and Country School has lasted through the years (Pratt & Deming, 1973). But the perception of play as a mode of thinking and feeling, of reasoning and catharsis, reflects the expansion of psychological theory and a broader perspective on play dynamics.

The dramatic play experience is now understood as serving a dual function in the developmental process. Play activities continue to take shape in the form of verbalization, manipulation, construction, plot invention, and role portrayal, incorporating reproductions and distortions of reality even as, with maturity, portrayals become increasingly realistic. In those terms we continue to value it as a medium by which young children gain new cognitive control over nascent conceptual content and are stimulated to pursue the dilemmas they encounter in their own productions and reproductions. In addition, we now perceive and value free play as an opportunity afforded the young child to express and act out, in this symbolized form, the wishes, fears, longing for strength, pleasures, and pains of the inner self. In this free play process, we see the opportunity for synthesizing the subjective and objective aspects of experience, with the term ''free'' representing the opportunity in early childhood to be relieved from pressures in traditional forms of education, to be realistic and logical as early as possible. Further, this opportunity to relive and externalize symbolically those parts of the subjective life that are conflict laden and could not be faced without the shield of a symbol such as that provided by the play process is recognized and valued as therapeutic in the total developmental process.

As the children mature, the spontaneous ''playing'' of the early years evolves toward more structured, socialized forms of dramatic enactment, involving a ''cast'' of characters. Decisions, undertaken by the children themselves, about what the playing shall be about, where it shall lead, who shall take which role, and what to use as the media of representation involves a complex process. To be carried through successfully, this requires children in the primary years to forgo self-fulfilling, egocentric projections and the distortion of reality to meet inner needs or wishes. This more mature form of "free" play builds on more empathic sensitivity to the flow of others' feelings and thought and the readiness to engage in and even enjoy the adaptive modes that are necessary for creating and acting out relatively complex play schemes that satisfy others' perceptions and wishes as well as one's own. Whereas the group play content and action reflects the dominant realism of this stage of development, the experience for the individual child is part of the open-ended search for identity. In Levinger's words (1956): "He is striving and growing through a series of roles, to find out who he can be some day, to hold on to what he was before, and in his dramatic play, to deal with . . . unresolved questions of the nature of the world, himself and others [p. 30]." Obviously, in order for this kind of dramatic play to support the growth processes of this stage of development, it is important that the teacher know how to add to the knowledge adventure the children initiate and, at the same time, be sensitive to the individual intrapersonal processes that are activated and projected in response to the relative openness of the play-making experience.

The importance of the identification process has been recognized in the use of the "free" dramatic forms in connection with the social studies curriculum— where the conceptual mastery of information, including the perplexities and contradictions that are involved in understanding distant social reality, is projected through the portrayal of its meaning from the sphere of personal reality. There are plays in which the enactment symbolically controls incipient social danger. In 1945, a sixth grade class in a New York City school created and enacted a play that began with a family talking about the atomic bomb. In the fourth scene, Lisa Meitner, at a moment of insight, is helped to escape from the SS guards who have come to arrest her. In the last scene, Einstein is writing to the president to support development of the atomic bomb project (Mitchell, 1950). There are other plays that offer an individual child an extension of the self through identifying with people of other eras. "It was a poignant experience to me as a teacher," Charlotte Winsor writes, "to watch a girl whose classroom role was a minor one, and who, as she enacted the part of Joan of Arc, seemed to grow in stature herself, seemed to be accepted by the group as a growing person, and came through her experience—her social studies experience—a bigger person, at least for the time being, in the eyes of the group and in her own eyes [Winsor, 1957; p. 399]."

Looked at comparatively, the dramatic play form of fusing personal and impersonal meanings in reorganizing experience is radically different from traditional educational modes. The contrast lies in valuing elemental aspects of life experience as primary material for learning in contrast to educational designs where personal, individual meanings are neglected or stripped away for the sake of making progress toward depersonalized generalization and abstraction.

Among other methods that provide opportunities for processing experiences from the spheres of both thinking and feeling is the group discussion period, led by the teacher, open to child-initiated review of experience, expression of quandaries, and planning the course, individually or as a group, for finding answers and alternative modes of searching for the answers. In this method, there is a dialogue between the children and the teacher that allows for free movement of thought—offering facts, disagreeing, and analyzing what sounds confusing. But there is also the dynamics of the personal interchange among the children—the experience of affiliation through verbal agreement or isolation through its opposite, the management of the impulse to conquer through verbal annihilation, or the primary pleasure of establishing the social self as a voice to be heard by others while sensing, at the same time, how opinions are part of one's private self.

From the curriculum design, one can find multiple instances of how the guiding of the learning adventure exploits the advantages of incorporating emotional responsiveness with intellectual processing. There is, for example, the practice of exploration of the environment surrounding the school, aimed at encouraging sensitivity in a broader surround—experience for arousal of wonder, capacity for making discriminating observation, varied exposure to the miracles of technology. It is important to be aware of the resonating emotional experience of such learning adventures by which, for one child, watching a steam shovel is material for identifying with strength whereas, for another, it becomes a traumatic image of his fear of destruction.

Similarly, the discovery approach, namely, the emphasis on explorations and independent pursuit as the preferred method for gathering knowledge and gaining insight, in contrast to didactic teaching methods, has wider relevance than its definition as a cognitive style (Biber, 1967). It obviously stimulates autonomous functioning in an important life sphere, giving the child the personally felt experience of his initiative and his own powers of pursuit of answers to the unknown. As a changing forefront in curriculum design, this approach has had educator (Mitchell, 1944) and psychologist (Bruner, 1961) protagonists. But the importance of taking into account the subjective aspects of the discovery experience, the transformations that take place between intake and output, the recognition of autoplastic as well as alloplastic processes has been argued by Jones (1968) and others.

Recognition of the inseparability of the objective and subjective components in learning experiences requires adaptation of the teaching role to complement this insight. All teaching strategies are directed toward some form of mastery as a target of learning. Insight into the subjective components requires that the selection of method be weighed in consideration of what might be called side effects—influence of the simultaneous noncognitive components on the learning experience.

Teachers' awareness and exploitation of noncognitive factors amplifies the learning experience. For example, a teacher utilizes the reading of a story about firemen to clear up the young children's lack of mastery of the concept of multiple roles—they do not seem to perceive the firemen as being also daddies. Instead of giving a didactic explanation, the teacher, knowingly, makes room for one of the children to answer the question: "Is a fireman a daddy?" from his own experience (his father is a fireman). The teacher's "side effects" goal, in a social relations perspective, is to help children establish mutually supporting roles and also to see each other, as well as teachers, as sources of information.

The narrowing influence of didactic teaching style and/or dominant concern for cognitive maturing is reflected at all stages and in varied kinds of subject matter. Instruction and evaluation of children's creative products in terms of adherence to external reality bespeaks lack of recognition of creative products as the expression of an integrative process in which individuals, at all stages, find symbolic ways of dealing with both logical and alogical aspects of experience. Another illustration is the teacher's insight into the 10-year-old whose composition reads: "The Condor is a very huge bird. It's eyes and nose is more sharper than ours. If it is flying through the air and smells a dead animal it circles down, down, and down. . . . As soon as it spies it's pray it glides. . . ." On one level, the teacher is satisfied with how much her emphasis on use of language to express meaning has been absorbed by this child. But she is interested, further, to understand how much this story of the Condor, its final flight to its nest, and its feast on the captured "pray" by a child from an underprivileged family may parallel the self-comforting themes of young dramatic play. The misspelling has its time but it can wait a bit.

These few illustrations may have served to identify the basic principles underlying the educational process, namely, the importance of recognizing the emotional processes associated with methods that are directed toward intellectual mastery and of adapting choice of method to both planes of psychological reality. What seems to have come together in this later phase is the earlier ideal image of a curious, creative, problem-solving, socially sensitive individual and the contemporary interest in the life of feeling, the condition of the self, the inner processes and opportunity for personal integration of meanings and purposes in both spheres.

The Psychological Theory Substrate

It may be interesting to shift focus from the changes in educational method that are associated with educators' deepening insight into child behavior to the parallel changing perspectives among psychologists during the last few decades. The educators (represented here within Bank Street ideology) number a small proportion of the educational profession in the national scene with, as already indicated, a particular defined ideology and a methodology deduced therefrom. Nor do the psychologists being considered represent the whole profession; there are no behaviorists among them. Obviously, the range in both cases is limited to a mutually compatible sphere of values and a common preference for dynamic rather than static concepts with a willingness to, even a pleasure in, facing rather than evading complexity.

Over the years there were many voices from the field of psychology that influenced the evolution of the developmental-interaction point of view. But the diversity can be disciplined into three groupings that differ from each other in the dimensions of psychological functioning considered most central to understanding the nature and the course of individual and environmental interaction.

In one group, I place those who contributed most significantly to understanding development in terms of the individual-environment interaction systems that place central importance on the qualitative change from stage to stage in the course of the maturing cognitive process (Piaget, Werner, Kamii, Weikart, Lavatelli). Another group took a position against what has been considered a too narrow perspective of human functioning as represented in formulations that were concentrated on study of cognitive processes (Isaacs, Sanford, R. M. Jones, Zigler, MacKinnon, Barron, G. Murphy). A third group contributed primarily to analysis of psychodynamic processes and the underlying motivational systems that have a determining influence on behavior, thus supplying another framework for portraying and analyzing the developmental stage sequence and the processes of individualization (Hartmann, Rapaport, White, Erikson, Werner, Barron). Brief reference to examples selected from each of these groups, all of which have seemed essential to our Bank Street educational theory and practice, illustrate how the complexity of guiding the educational process calls for integrating more than any one perspective of psychological functioning.

Maturing Cognitive Capacities.   Though not intended as such, developmental theory as formulated by Piaget and Werner has had a major influence on educational theory and experimental programming. At the center of this general viewpoint is the concept of an "active organism" and the corollary view that: "man creates his knowledge, that knowledge results from the transformation of material that occurs as psychological structures are brought to bear vis-à-vis the 'materials' of the world [Franklin & Biber, 1977; p. 11]." Other well-known basic concepts are directly relevant to educational design—development conceived as successive patterns of functioning characterized by relatively stable organization; successive stages representing qualitatively different cognitive structures as the basic learning apparatus; the changing modes of organizing experience from the early presymbolic stage to representational thought, from prelogical thinking to logical construction.

The implications from this concept of the developmental process to educational theory and practice have had two different pathways. One has been gradual, represented by early interest of those educators for whom understanding of cognitive process—the thinking mode—had old roots and who found it deeply stimulating to turn to Piagetian formulations for new insight, beginning with the publication of his earliest work on the language and thought of the child (Piaget, 1926). For these educators, these new insights could be coordinated with the system of theory and practice deriving originally from Dewey. Kohlberg and Mayer's (1972) integration of Deweyan and Piagetian thought is, in a sense, a theoretical analysis of a movement of educational change. By contrast, the planned construction of educational designs conceived of and emanating directly from Piagetian concepts was a later development. Not surprisingly, there was great difference of opinion as to which applied system was truest to the basic theory (Kamii & DeVries, 1976; Lavatelli, 1970; Weikart, Rogers, Adcock & McClelland, 1971).

At the level of educational practice, inheritors of the progressive school movement find substantial congruence between their established practice and more recent inferences for program that have been articulated by Evans (1971) as derivatives from Piagetian theory. The principles Evans names call up images of long-established practice that conform to and illustrate his categories. Speaking in the first person, Biber (1977a) writes, referring to Evans:

> For his "active self-discovery," I see well-equipped situations with open schedules and an honest invitation to explore. For "inductive learning experience," I see experiences planned outside the classroom, such as trips and the Socratic-style group discussions that follow, for "novel experiences facilitating stage-relevant thinking operations accommodated to the child's intellectual style," I see a group of four-year-olds taking a new route through the building to their play roof, internalizing the experience of alternative means to a common end. For "enriched concrete sensory experience," I see the easels, the clay boards, the musical instruments, the gerbil nibbling in his cage. For "symbolization in manipulative play and aesthetic experience," I see the complex block structures, the dress-up materials, the house play corner. For the "sharing of viewpoints," I hear the teacher calming a fight between two children as each presents her case verbally to the other while at the same time helping them find an acceptable way to deal with conflicting impulses [pp. 50–51].

The parallelism between what has been established at the level of educational application and what is being projected as originating in Piagetian theory is worth recognizing at the same time that we appreciate the major advances in the theory of cognitive maturing, which has been illuminated by the work of Piaget and Werner and the other psychologists who have continued to make theoretical and experimental contributions to this salient aspect of human functioning.

Cognitive, Affective, And Social Interaction. There is little question that cognitive–developmental theory has been and will continue to be valued appropriately for its contribution of added knowledge and insight into a prime area of human functioning. Considerable criticism, however, has been focused on failure to recognize that it offers only a partial paradigm of complex human behavior and does not take account of the complex reality represented in inter-action of cognitive and affective factors. It could be maintained that this vast complexity needs to be studied in its separate parts if any substantial mastery is to be attained. Even so, critics ask for awareness of this restriction, especially because application to practice, as in education, can suffer from any given era's preoccupation with some selected aspect of function to the neglect of others.

Susan Isaacs, herself both researcher and practitioner, worried about this problem in the thirties (1930, 1933) and pointed to the need for separating her data—discovery, reasoning, and thought in one volume, hostility, guilt, and sexuality in another—even while her prime purpose was to trace the interdependence of these functions. Sanford (1967) was concerned with the same issue and attributed the separation of the intellectual from the rest of personality to educators and their reluctance to be involved in anything but the intellect. He, too, took the position that: "Cognition, feeling, emotion, action, and motivation are easily separated by abstraction, but no single one of these can function independently of the other [p. 79]."

One well-documented analysis of how a cognitive-interaction approach can be integrated into a curriculum project is presented in Richard Jones' (1968) critique of the social studies curriculum, *Man: A Course of Study,* developed by Bruner (1966). He argues for making positive use of the emotion aroused by viewing a disturbing film on the Netsilik Eskimo life pattern. Emotional arousal can serve to deepen learning once the children have had the opportunity to express and share their feelings and anxieties with the group and integrate this personal experience with perception and analysis of a strange culture and its disturbing elements. Conversely, failure to allow for the expression and working through of aroused emotion undercuts the potential for learning.

In the seventies, Zigler (1973) was a strong voice for recognizing the influence of social and emotional factors on total cognitive development: "Children are much more than cognitive automatons," he wrote during the period when his leadership in the Office of Child Development influenced the guidelines for Head Start centers and other preschool operations.

The creative reorganization of experience is a central area of interest to those engaged in penetrating the interplay of cognitive and affective experience. In the early progressive movement, creative activities claimed an important place in the curriculum. In addition to the satisfaction children experienced in the opportunity to use paint, language, music, and dramatic invention according to their own idiomatic forms of representation, these activities were valued as equally important to the maturing of thinking processes through the symbolizing, organizing, and reorganizing of the perceived relationships of direct experience. Later, through systematic study, the concept of the nature of intellectual functioning involved in creative activities was differentiated to include divergent thinking processes and transformation of experience such as are involved in tendencies to play with ideas, to sense ambiguities, and to see patterns underlying surface confusion or contradiction.

Other studies perceived the essence of creativity as a synthesis of rational and nonrational, subjective and objective processes. Whereas one investigator (MacKinnon, 1962) advocated closer attention to nonintellectual factors "intimately associated with creative talent," another (Barron, 1958) took a more psychodynamic view, seeing the disposition of the creative person to integrate diverse stimuli as related to the degree to which the person is in contact with irrational elements in his own inner system. Suggestions for furthering creativity experience in school programs came from psychologists. Gardner Murphy (1964) argued against the trend to separate thought processes from the impulsive and motivational life of the child: "the learner must not be deprived of the riches of his impulsive life, and the teacher must be the quickener of that impulse life through which thought can grow [p. 158]."

Conflict Resolution and Ego Functioning.   That brings me to the aforementioned psychodynamic perspective from which the course of development is conceptualized in terms of changing drives that dominate successive periods, and resolution of conflicts inevitably associated with the socializing, maturing processes as well as those at an instinctual level. The redirection of psychoanalytic thinking toward the study of ego functioning represented in the contributions of Hartmann (1939/1959) and Rapaport (1958) generated new ways of evaluating the differential influences of modes of rearing and educating children.

In White's (1959) revision of analytic theory, ego functions are seen as largely autonomous and learning takes place primarily through action and its consequences. There is a given tendency to be active and produce an effect on the environment based on independent energies not related to conflict-induced tensions. Knowledge is gained, reality tested, and adaptive patterns established through exploration, manipulation, and investigation, yielding pleasure in fulfilling impulses toward the active role. Ego strength derives from two sources— competence and sense of competence. Objectively, competence encompasses all the modes of interacting effectively with the environment at all developmental levels. Subjectively, the sense of competence, the fruits of action, represents the cumulative inner sense of one's ability to be effective. Maintaining this subjective sense of competence becomes the important nucleus of motivation for further engagement with the environment and leads, in a cycle, to new levels of competence.

The psychodynamic perspective (Erikson, 1950, 1959) is represented in the image of developmental sequence as a succession of changes involving stage-specific conflicts and alternative modes of conflict resolution that reflect the quality of interaction with the salient life figures and the expectations and demands of the larger society. In the early years, these conflicts belong to the instinctual sphere. Primitive nascent feelings of belonging to another person collide with new fears of loss. Separation is felt as permanent loss when cognitive systems are bound to immediacy of time and space. Giving up of things that have been lovingly assimilated to the self must be resisted to save the wholeness of the self. Anger released at another resonates within the self when self and other do not yet belong to two distinct universes.

With maturity, the ego functions—the ability of the organism to perceive, learn, remember, think, move, and act—become increasingly important in regulating instinctual drives and are generalized into ways of dealing with reality that are, in turn, stage specific. So, for the middle years, we are familiar with the maturing processes represented in the drive to become competent in the world of ideas and activities beyond what has been family generated, as well as the need to establish rules as means of control and to replace fantasy with cognitive-derived reality. In this conceptualization, the healthy evolution of these forward-moving drives is influenced by the nature of the resolution of conflicts particularly active during this developmental stage—the ambivalence of dependence-independence motivation, the shift from conflict with to identification with the parent of the same sex, the sacrifice of yielding subjective impulse to requirements of socialized functioning. For the educator who needs to understand not only the sequence of cognitive maturing but also the nature of forces that interact with cognitive functioning, this conceptualization of psychosocial maturing adds a needed dimension.

Especially significant to the educator is Heinz Werner's (1957) concept of stage sequence in terms of developmental heterogeneity. Progress from stage to stage represents, as in other formulations, advancing capacity to operate on different levels according to requirements of the situation. But in Werner's view, the sequence is more additive than replacing, and maturity, especially creativity and flexibility, is a function of the capacity to continue to utilize primitive as well as advanced operations. This perspective matches Barron's (1958) view of creative productivity as being related to the survival of irrational elements in the mature system.

An effort to consolidate a psychological position based on a preferred philosophical system and values for human functioning was expressed in a paper by Reese and Overton in 1970. They present the basic premises of Werner, Piaget, and Erikson as belonging together as a common-based *Anschauung* of human behavior—what they call a "world view" underlying a consistent "family of theories." They use the term, "family of theories," to designate those theories that are compatible with each other, in this case, an organismic model of human functioning by which change, accepted as given, is conceptualized in terms of levels of organization, processes are more significant than products, and experience has a greater influence on development than does specific training. Their analysis of the internal consistency within these theoretical perspectives is a valuable conceptual contribution (see Franklin, this volume).

Similarly, the position has been taken in this chapter that, for understanding behavior in school and for comprehensive educational programming, the principles and perspectives of three internally consistent systems are needed as the rationale and foundation for the total design. In this presentation, I have used Bank Street ideology and practice to illustrate how an educational perspective has been integrated with the premises of developmental and psychodynamic theory, how the socialization process is stimulated through a defined group ethos, and how building curriculum is expected to traverse the in-school and beyond-the-school worlds of experience.

A value-oriented educational program has educational and developmental goals that are related to ideal images for each of us separately and all of us together, as a society, in school and beyond. In reality, the goals are never fully achieved. That calls on us for further rethinking of the totality of the learning experience—continued inquiry as to how and whether theory and research corroborate and illuminate what has been learned empirically, for active search for what can be generated and stimulated by new theoretical paradigms, and for further rethinking and renewed experimental adventure in the educational design.

REFERENCES

Barron, F. *Creative person and creative process*. New York: Holt, Rinehart & Winston, 1958.

Biber, B. Integration of mental health principles in the school setting. In G. Caplan (Ed.), *Prevention of mental disorders in children*. New York: Basic Books, 1961.

Biber, B. Preschool education. In R. Ulich (Ed.), *Education and the idea of mankind*. New York: Harcourt, Brace & World, 1964.

Biber, B. A learning-teaching paradigm integrating intellectual and affective processes. In E. M. Bower & W. G. Hollister (Eds.), *Behavioral science frontiers in education*. New York: Wiley, 1967.

Biber, B. The "whole child," individuality and values in education. In J. R. Squire (Ed.), *A new look at progressive education*. ASCD Yearbook. Washington, D.C. Association for Supervision and Curriculum Development, 1972.

Biber, B. Cognition in early childhood education: A historical perspective. In B. Spodek & H. J. Walberg (Eds.), *Early childhood education: Issues and insights*. Berkeley, Calif.: McCutchan, 1977. (a)

Biber, B. A developmental-interaction approach: Bank Street College of Education. In M. C. Day & R. K. Parker (Eds.), *The preschool in action: Exploring early childhood programs* (2nd ed.). Boston: Allyn & Bacon, 1977. (b)

Bruner, J. S. The act of discovery. *Harvard Educational Review*, 1961, *31*, 21–32.

Bruner, J. S. *Toward a theory of instruction*. Cambridge, Mass.: Harvard University Press, 1966.

Cohen, D. *The learning child*. New York: Pantheon, 1972.

Counts, G. S. *Dare we build a new social order?* New York: John Day, 1932.

Dewey, J. *Experience and education*. Lecture to Kappa Delta Pi, 1938. New York: Macmillan, 1963.

Erikson, E. H. *Childhood and society*. New York: W. W. Norton, 1950.

Erikson, E. H. Identity and the life cycle. *Psychological Issues*, 1959, *1* (1).

Evans, E. D. *Contemporary influences in early childhood education* (2nd ed.). New York: Holt, Rinehart & Winston, 1971.

Faris, E. The child's emotions. Foreword to *Proceedings of Midwest Conference on Character Development*. Chicago: University of Chicago Press, 1930.

Franklin, M. B., & Biber, B. Psychological perspectives and early childhood education: Some relations between theory and practice. In L. Katz (Ed.), *Current topics in early childhood education* (Vol. 1). Norwood, N.J.: Ablex, 1977.

Hartmann, H. *Ego psychology and the problem of adaptation*. New York: International Universities Press, 1959. (Originally published, 1939).

Isaacs, S. *Intellectual growth in young children*. London: Routledge & Kegan Paul, 1930.

Isaacs, S. *Social development in young children*. London: George Routledge & Sons, 1933.

Johnson, H. M. *Children in the nursery school*. New York: Agathon Press, 1972. (Originally published, 1928.)

Johnson, M. *Thirty years with an idea*. New York: Teachers College Press, 1939. Unpublished thesis.

Jones, R. M. *Fantasy and feeling in education*. New York: New York University Press, 1968.

Kamii, C., & DeVries, R. Piaget for early education. In M. C. Day & R. K. Parker (Eds.), *Preschool in action* (Second ed.). Boston: Allyn & Bacon, 1977.

Kohlberg, L., & Mayer, R. Development as the aim of education. *Harvard Educational Review*, 1972, *4*, 449–496.

Kohlberg, L., & Turiel, E. Moral development and moral education. In G. Lesser (Ed.), *Psychology and educational practice*. Chicago: Scott Foresman, 1971.

Krown, S. (In collaboration with M. Many). *Threes and fours go to school*. Englewood Cliffs, N.J.: Prentice-Hall, 1974.

Lavatelli, C. S. *Piaget's theory applied to an early childhood curriculum*. Boston: American Science and Engineering, 1970.

Levinger, L. Dramatic play—an intellectual and creative process. In *Imagination in education*. New York: Bank Street College of Education, 1956.

MacKinnon, D. W. The nature and nurture of creative talent. *American Psychologist*, 1962, *17* (7).

Minuchin, P. *The middle years of childhood*. Monterey, Calif.: Brooks/Cole, 1977.

Mitchell, L. S. Research on the child's level: Possibilities, limitations, and techniques. *University of Pennsylvania Bulletin*, 1944.

Mitchell, L. S. *Our children and our schools*. New York: Simon & Shuster, 1950.

Mitchell, L. S. *Young geographers*. New York: Basic Books, 1964. (Originally published, 1934).

Murphy, G. Non-rational processes in learning. In R. Gross & J. Murphy (Eds.), *The revolution in the schools*. New York: Harcourt, Brace & World, 1964.

Naumberg, M. *The child and the world*. New York: Harcourt Brace, 1928.

Piaget, J. *Language and thought of the child*. New York: Harcourt Brace, 1926.

Pratt, C., & Deming, L. The play school. In C. B. Winsor (Ed.), *Experimental schools re-visited*. New York: Agathon Press, 1973.

Rapoport, D. The theory of ego autonomy: a generalization. *Bulletin Menninger Clinic*, 1958, *22*, 13–35.

Reese, H. W., & Overton, W. F. Models of development and theories of development. In L. R. Goulet & P. B. Baltes (Eds.), *Life-span developmental psychology: Research and theory*. New York: Academic Press, 1970.

Sanford, N. The development of cognitive-affective processes through education. In E. M. Bower & W. B. Hollister (Eds.), *Behavioral science frontiers in education*. New York: Wiley, 1967.

Shapiro, E., & Biber, B. The education of young children: A developmental-interaction approach. *Teachers College Record*, 1972, *74*, 55–79.

Washburne, C. The teacher and the emotional life of the child. In *Proceedings of Midwest Conference on Character Development*. Chicago: University of Chicago Press, 1930.

Weikart, D., Rogers, L., Adcock, C., & McClelland, D. *The cognitively oriented curriculum: A framework for preschool teachers.* Washington, D.C.: National Association for the Education of Young Children, 1971.

Werner, H. The concept of development from a comparative and organismic point of view. In D. B. Harris (Ed.), *The concept of development.* Minneapolis: University of Minnesota Press, 1957.

Winsor, C. B. What are we doing in social studies? *Forty-fifth Annual School Men's Week Proceedings.* Philadelphia: University of Pennsylvania Press, 1957.

White, R. Motivation reconsidered: The concept of competence. *Psychological Review,* 1959, *66.*

Zigler, E. Project Head Start: Success or failure? *Learning,* 1973, *1.*

INTERRELATIONS BETWEEN COGNITION AND AFFECT: THREE VIEWS

The developmental-interaction view has taken it as axiomatic that cognition and affect are intimately interrelated. On the one hand, much of psychological theory and research has treated these aspects of human functioning as separable and separate; indeed the term cognitive–developmental epitomizes this separation. On the other hand, the assumption of interrelationship has a long and honorable history. Each of the chapters in this section deals with concepts of affect and cognition, and possible ways in which they may be interrelated in psychological theory construction and research.

Jan Drucker places the argument in the context of the history of dichotomous thinking, from the myth of Phaedrus to Riegel's dialectical psychology. She questions the heuristic value of considering cognition and affect as separate paired systems and offers a beginning reconceptualization, taking the concept of differentiation as an organizing principle.

Herbert Zimiles points to the paradoxical fact that, although many psychologists accept the idea that cognition and affect are interrelated, few do systematic research that elucidates the nature of the relations. He reviews the fate of the concept of cognitive–affective interaction in psychological research and then examines research that takes up the question from different points of view. He sees the experimental research tradition as a barrier to the study of the complexity of the interrelations of affect and cognition.

Taking the developmental–interaction point of view as her focus, Margery Franklin explores the nature of psychological theory and theory development. She has devised new and provocative ways of thinking about and classifying psychological theories, and criteria for combining theoretical constructs to form a coherent system.

2 Developmental Concepts of Cognition and Affect

Jan Drucker
Sarah Lawrence College

> *The Heart is the Capitol of the Mind -*
> *The Mind is a single State -*
> *The Heart and Mind together make*
> *A single Continent -*
>
> Emily Dickinson

Interest in the domains of human functioning residing in the Heart and Mind extends far back in our history and transcends the traditional theory, terminology, and methodology of psychology. Poets and philosophers, playwrights and preachers have all explored the nature and influence on human life of reason and passion, or cognition and affect. This chapter explores some of the issues, historical and contemporary, in the formulation of psychological theory as it addresses the specific questions of the interrelatedness of cognitive and affective functioning. Whether these domains ought to be conceptualized as separate, if interacting, and what their course of development entails are themselves to be taken as questions open for examination and debate. A developmental account of these matters needs to be responsive to the increasing emphasis being placed by both research and theory on the antecedents, emergence, and early development of a whole range of psychological phenomena. In briefly reviewing some of the approaches that have been taken to these conceptual issues, and highlighting the considerations I see as needing to be further addressed, I inevitably leave out much important history and many contributors. It is my hope, however, that my comments may further the investigation and articulation of a differentiated but fundamentally integrative developmental view—a step toward a map of that elusive "single Continent."

DICHOTOMIES AND DIALECTICS

The dichotomous mode of thinking, involving an antithesis between two poles, has occupied a substantial place in the history of the human intellectual endeavor. Marx was much interested in the propensity of human beings to think dichotomously, seeing it as a reflection of the "bourgeois ideology," presenting a serious impediment to social science model building. Discussing this (Hegelian) analysis, Ollman (1976) has written:

> Probably the most distorting and least recognized of all such abstractions are the basic dichotomies such as fact–value, cause–effect, freedom–necessity, nature–society, and reason–feeling, in which people organize their everyday thoughts and experiences. With each half grasped as independent and the direct opposite of the other, things are taken to be either one or the other—nothing is both. To be sure, these dichotomies are themselves abstracted from the conditions and activities of real people. As modes of thought, they clearly reflect lives that are artificially broken up into times for thinking and times for feeling, into a place for working and a place for living, into ways of knowing and ways of judging and so on [pp. 231–232].

Although it is well understood that young children employ dichotomous analysis at its most unbending (aspects of the world are seen as all good or all bad, etc.), the implications of this observation for a developmental line of modes of thought that might culminate in a transcendence of such dichotomies has been insufficiently explored—a point to which I return in the following.

Prologue: The Mind–Body Question

Perhaps the first major dichotomy to be subjected to rigorous exploration was the question on which the Greek philosophers founded the work of psychology—the consideration of evidence and logical arguments for and against the doctrine of a relative separation of mind and body. This question, as framed, remains an important one for philosophy, though some modern psychologists, influenced by the findings of the biological sciences in regard to brain structure and function, are shifting the weight of their inquiry to the search for models and data that might lead to a more sophisticated and differentiated view of the interrelationships of soma and psyche. Current questions center on the relevance of the fascinating information emerging from such disciplines as neurophysiology and anatomy, for our considerations of behavior and experience, our models of the mind and the developmental process, and, indeed, our philosophical view of the nature of human beings.

Some of those who pose and attempt to answer such questions view the physical as an underpinning of the psychological—and speak in terms of the biological *bases* of behavior and experience. Others seek *interrelationships,* as exemplified by concepts of, for example, psychosomatic illness. For still others, *parallelism* is the best way to conceptualize mind–body relationships. Piaget (Fraisse & Piaget, 1963) wrote of the importance of the task of understanding the relations of conscious reactions and organic structures, and he felt optimistic about the complementarity of differing approaches within psychology: "these two orientations, organicist and deductive, are in no way contradictory, but rather complementary . . . the more exact neurology becomes the more it will need deductive models [p. 190]." Piaget hoped for an isomorphism between implicative systems of meanings and the causal systems of the material world, which would eventually make possible a like isomorphism between the models of these phenomena.

Freud, too, was involved for a time in the active exploration of physiological bases of psychological phenomena and models linking the two, and though he abandoned the attempt to delineate such a theory himself, a number of contemporary psychoanalysts are again beginning to think about the implications of biology for their theory and practice. For example, McLaughlin (1978) has explored the concepts of primary and secondary process mental functioning in the context of recent neurophysiological findings. Although he warns of the pitfalls such comparisons may hold, McLaughlin feels there is a degree of "fit" between central psychoanalytic concepts and a division of labor between hemispheres of the brain. He makes a point, however, that is worth bearing in mind as we consider various dichotomous concepts of human functioning: "so clear a division . . . probably represent[s] oversimplifications that do not account adequately for the rich capabilities for fusion and synthesis that are reflected in human behavior. It may be that the two different modes in their interrelationship . . . produce . . . a new dimension or perspective that is more than the sum of the parts [pp. 245–246]."

However mind and body are to be conceptualized—interrelated, isomorphic, synergistic—model builders need to guard against the automatic assumption of a dichotomy, to examine the potential limitations and injustice to the phenomena such an assumption may entail, and to explore various models of interrelationship, as this chapter begins to do in relation to cognitive and affective functioning. They need, further, to be on guard against the perennial tendency to move too rapidly and simplistically from research findings, in any branch of scientific inquiry, to theory, and, especially, practice in any other. On the other hand, such complex issues need to be considered in the illuminating light of cross-disciplinary discourse, and the dangers of parochialism are equally to be avoided.

Reason and Passion

One facet of the mind–body question explored almost from the beginning was the association of reason, or thought, with the immaterial "mind," however conceptualized, and passion with the physical "body." The dichotomous, antithetical, often adversarial concept of these aspects of life has continued to focus debate through the ages. Although it was Socrates who focused attention on the psyche as the seat of moral and intellectual faculties, and thus more important than the body, it fell to Plato to articulate and defend the nature of the psyche. Most relevant to the discussion at hand is Plato's allegorical myth, from the *Phaedrus,* as cited by Guthrie (1960):

> the composite nature of the human soul is symbolized by the picture of it as a winged chariot in which a human charioteer, representing the reason, drives a pair of horses, one high-spirited and naturally inclined to obey the charioteer, the other bad and disobedient. These represent the brave side of human nature including strength of will, and the bodily appetites respectively. Once long ago the chariot made its way round the very rim of the Universe where it could contemplate the eternal verities, but the restive plunging of the bad horse brought it down and immersed it in the world of matter and change [pp. 97–98].

Aristotle took issue with some aspects of Plato's concept (and may have established the first integrative position on the subject) when he held that the psyche must be conceived as a unity, although possessing perhaps various faculties or powers, differentiated by their functions. With a finely honed appreciation of the extent to which the questions we ask determine the kind of answers we are likely to find, he offered methodological advice that is well taken today. In *De Anima* he asked how one could best pursue knowledge of the soul. "To attain any assured knowledge about the soul is one of the most difficult things in the world. . . . In the case of each different subject we shall have to determine the appropriate process of investigation. . . . Again, which ought we to investigate first, these parts or their functions, mind or thinking, the faculty or the act of sensation, and so on? [McKeon, 1947, pp. 145–147]."

These speculations about the nature of the psyche, and indeed these questions about how to study it, have continued to characterize psychological inquiry in the intervening centuries, directly at times, as in the heyday of trait psychology, more indirectly at others. However, assumptions about the dichotomous nature of reason and passion are to be found in literature, political theory and strategy, and the arts as well as psychology and philosophy. The adversarial view of thinking and feeling, often coupled with the notion that the human being is a weak creature whose reason can easily be overcome by passion, assumes that the two are in constant battle for the control of behavior, always pulling in opposite directions, as did Plato's horses. Alexander Pope (1751) put it succinctly: "The ruling passion, be it what it will/The ruling passion conquers reason still [p. 31]."

Much of the debate has tended to take on a moral tone—to center on value judgments about reason and passion. Consider the opposite utopian visions of absolute freedom of indulgence of impulses, and of rationality, self-discipline, and intellectual discourse as espoused by Emerson and fellow New England Transcendentalists. Whether one takes a basically Calvinist view of the inherent evil of passion needing to be overcome through education and reason, or an idealized Rousseauean one—and each of these oversimplified world views has had contemporary counterparts in extremes of educational theory and practice—the antagonistic dichotomy is maintained. Most views have been based on the assumption that passion is there first, residing from birth in the body, and reason develops only gradually, dependent on environmental input and eventually gaining sway over passion. However, even given a more impartial estimation of thought and feeling as equally central to the human experience, one is left with the need to conceptualize these apparently separate and opposite phenomena.

The Dialectic Alternative

I have referred in the foregoing to Marx's view of the limitations of dichotomous thinking, and the intervening discussion has further addressed the misuses of such an approach to reason and passion. The notion of entirely separate, competing systems of cognition and affect is intrinsically antithetical to a holistic view of human functioning. A truly integrated view, it seems to me, must make provision for an intimately interactive, even inherently relational concept of psychological processes. The Marxian solution to this problem was to conceive of phenomena in terms of a *dialectic* in which entities are defined only in their interrelation, having no existence apart from the development of relations among them.

As Engels (1935) wrote: "When we reflect on nature, or the history of mankind, or our own intellectual activity, the first picture presented to us is of an endless maze of relations and interactions, in which nothing remains what, where and as it was, but everything moves, changes, comes into being and passes out of existence [pp. 26–27]." Conceptualizing a continuous tension between the burgeoning process of what is to come and the relatively static nature of what has been, this mode of analysis points to an inherent conflict in man and society between opposing tendencies to fixity and to change and takes the analysis of the transformation of relations as the most powerful conceptual tool. Explanation in such a system always has to do with the clarification of relationships.

The implications of this analysis for the present discussion may be summarized as follows: Human beings exist in a relational context; aspects of their functioning that appear to be static are in fact to be thought of as continually in flux, whereas *those that appear to be separate are to be thought of as differentiated only in relation to each other*. This suggests that if we experience thinking and feeling as separate we must understand this distinction to be based only on their dialectic relation and to be a temporarily instituted, static one, artificially disembedded from the ongoing flow of psychological functioning and experience.

Such an analysis has indeed been applied to some developmental phenomena by Riegel (for example, 1976) and colleagues who have articulated the "dialectic of human development," part of a dialectical psychology that studies action and change, the ceaseless flux of human life. However, as a developmentalist, I must take issue with a central aspect of Riegel's interpretation and application of Marxian principles, logical and internally consistent though it may be. Riegel argues against Piagetian and any other developmental theory that makes provision for stable organizations in the process of development or emphasizes the theme of equilibration. Any analysis that rejects the need to conceptualize patterning, relative stability, and cohesiveness of psychological functioning will not serve our purpose. The data of development require us to construct a theory that allows for pattern as well as flux, temporary structuralization as well as evolution, emergent organizations as well as continual incremental change, however relational a framework we posit for these processes. The challenge would appear to be to encompass the helpful concept of dialectical relations within a broader analysis of development. Cognitive and affective functioning present the ground for such a challenge, and the centrality of the idea of differentiation in early development may provide the theoretical and empirical means for such an analysis.

DIFFERENTIATION IN DEVELOPMENT

Despite the fact that in the course of development we come to the point of distinguishing and labeling "thinking" and "feeling," there are no moments of pure thought existing outside of an ongoing emotional climate within the thinker nor, romanticized interpretation notwithstanding, of pure feeling, moments without cognitive content. Once language and language-organized modes of thought develop they become shaping influences on our construction of experience, except in moments of extreme regression, and perhaps to some extent even then. Although one could arrange various experiences on a continuum in terms of the relative weight of significantly active cognitive and affective processes, the shift in proportions is always just that, a relative matter. Compare, for example, a temper tantrum to doing a crossword puzzle. The distinction made by the subject is thus never a complete one, though even fairly young children seem to find it a congenial one to make.

A similar difficulty in the categorization of situations, behavior, and experiences into cognitive and affective can be seen from the vantage point of the observer. Many of the kinds of variables that psychologists are currently addressing in the attempt to describe and conceptualize the consistency of individual functioning over time are presented as stylistic dimensions underlying and influencing both cognitive and emotional behavior but in themselves defying categorization as either. Infant observation, too, has yielded a number of dimensions, on various levels of abstraction, from observation—temperamental differences, patterning, activity level, drive and ego endowment, perceptual acuity, responsivity, motor maturation, mood, tension arousal, and discharge modes, attributes of the organism that seem inappropriately designated cognitive *or* affective. That they ultimately interact in organismic systems that carry out various functions serving cognitive and affective processes seems a useful way of thinking about such dimensions. It seems likely, however, that both the experience and the functions of cognition and affect, to whatever extent they are differentiated later, are not much differentiated in early life.

The relative undifferentiation of the infant and the centrality of progressive differentiation (and complex integration) to the process of development are fundamental concepts of the three major theories of development. Freud (here I include those who have importantly contributed to Freudian developmental theory), Werner, and Piaget, despite their important differences of aim, method, and explanatory concepts, all emphasize differentiation and the related idea of the emergence during development of qualitatively new structures and functions. The consideration of how differentiation and subsequent hierarchic integration (most thoroughly and elegantly posited by Werner) takes place is a central task for developmental psychology, and cognitive and affective functioning are vital domains for such exploration. The implications of the concept of differentiation for the present argument are briefly summarized in the following:

1. *Differentiation is both a process and a product of development.* Theorists assume that during development the organism becomes more differentiated in function, and perhaps structure, because behavioral indices of less global, more specific, less diffuse, more patterned functioning can be seen, even during earliest infancy. At the same time, there is evidence that the infants and children themselves are progressively differentiating aspects of their experience.

2. *Major advances in differentiation in the various domains of the child's life can frequently be seen to occur at about the same time.* For example, the "hatching" period described by Mahler, Pine, and Bergman (1975), characterized behaviorally by new social interactions with the world, seems to correspond to advances in perception, cognitive organization, and new levels of behavioral patterning as described by other workers. Similar confluences of developmental progressions seem to signal periods of significant psychological integration during the second and third years, between 5 and 7 years, and so on (Shapiro & Perry, 1976.) Although the exploration of such nodal points in development is itself an important task, the significance for the issue at hand lies in the support such observations lend to the dialectical viewpoint: Differentiated systems in the maturing organism seem to develop in relation to each other and complementarity of function may well emerge through such a process.

3. *Many aspects of infant behavior and patterns of functioning appear to defy categorization as "cognitive" or "affective."* Yet they would seem to play

important roles in the determination of the nature, effectiveness, and interplay of what will come to be a given child's cognitive and affective functioning. If we conceptualize the neonate as an organism only slightly differentiated, those behaviors and integrations that can already be seen to function in patterned and organized ways can be understood as prerequisites to and influences on what will later become the differentiated cognitive *and* affective, social and intrapersonal functioning of the child. Such factors seem to play an important role in the development of individuality.

4. *Research investigations into the nature of differentiation of many sorts in the course of early development should be a high priority; likewise, the interrelated attempt to conceptualize the specifics of differentiation and integration in development, in such a way as to account for both stability and change in organismic functioning, must be emphasized in developmental theorizing.* The implications of the search for such a developmental model are intriguing, and there are many beginning formulations and areas of research that might form the basis for such work. In an interesting article on the nature of drive–defense relationships and the ways they become structuralized in development, Pine (1970) conceives of structuralization as the association of certain ideas with certain experiences, a notion that allows for a degree of consistency over time, always within a set of dynamic relations. A similar idea is articulated by Biber and Franklin (1967) when they delineate the developmental process as involving: "qualitative shifts or changes in the individual's means of organizing experience and coping with the environment [p. 11]."

In short, I am proposing that in seeking to understand the relative structuralization of *relations,* both within the psychic functions of the child and between the child and aspects of the environment only gradually perceived by the child, we move toward a model conceptualizing relative stability as well as continual change, subjective experiences of differentiation as well as externally evident structural and functional differentiation. There are some intriguing and potentially rich implications of such a position for research directions.

One of the first areas for exploration along these lines could be the very dichotomies Marx illuminated, the ways in which the infant and young child begin to make distinctions and the development of more complex behavioral organizations but also of relational thinking over time. It is possible that such an approach might lead to somewhat new ways of looking at domains of experience relatively ignored and/or inaccessible up to this point, and to new ways of defining problems and asking questions. For example, the delineation of timetables and patterns of differentiation of infant functioning in regard to affective states and children's later awareness and articulation of them would be a valuable addition to our current knowledge.

However, one of the most fruitful potential areas for study would seem to be the various isomorphisms in the emergence of dichotomous views of self and other, real and not real, thought and feeling, and like polarities over time. Metaawareness—how children come to make conscious distinctions among these pairs of concepts, to articulate them, and to employ them in various spontaneous ways—is a largely unexplored but crucial domain in this regard. Likewise, the emergence and development of the ability to transcend or modify dichotomous thinking, to grasp relations, multiplicity of meaning, and determination, and other subtleties deserve careful study.

From another point of view, one would want to continue to explore those stylistic issues already proving so intriguing from the standpoint of longitudinal studies of organized sets of relations among psychic functions. Certainly this would provide a context for the close examination of the balance between change and relative stability in the development of given infants and children (see Escalona, 1968, and Murphy & Moriarty, 1976, for fine examples of related studies). Of course, in the vigorous pursuit of both the notion of dimensions of experience and development that underlie or contribute to both cognitive and affective functioning, and the synthetic and integrative tendencies that make them possible, it is important not to replace one dichotomy with others endowed with the same pitfalls. Complex theory and imaginative methodology are necessary to do justice to complex human phenomena.

INTEGRATIVE FORMULATIONS

The call for a more sophisticated, interactionist position has been heard from various directions for a long time. In 1670, philosopher–mathematician Blaise Pascal wrote: "The heart has its reasons, which reason knows nothing of. . . . We know the truth not only by the reason but by the heart [1965, pp. 343–345]." G. K. Chesterton (1911) took this one step further: "Nothing sublimely artistic has ever arisen out of mere art, any more than anything essentially reasonable has ever arisen out of the pure reason [p. 8]." In contemporary psychology there is increasing evidence of attempts at integration in both concepts and studies of cognitive and affective functioning. The developmental-interaction point of view, to which this volume is devoted, is the result of major synthetic and integrative attempts by those opposed to artificial dichotomization and dedicated to the concept of the "whole child." Biber and her colleagues have made important contributions to educational philosophy and practice as well as developmental theory, drawing on the thought of Dewey, Freud, Werner, Piaget, and Erikson. The growing influence of such thinking on theory and research is clear from this volume and the growing literature addressed to various sorts of interaction of psychological processes as well as of individual and environment.

An interactionist position both reflects and contributes to the subtlety and richness of our conceptualizations about the developmental process. As Franklin (this volume) clarifies, a cognitive–affective interaction point of view can lead to research on the effects of one of these factors on the other, often in complex and reciprocal ways, or to the search for underlying dimensions of experience and growth that may be reflected in both cognitive and affective domains. The growing body of work on temperamental differences and related variables is a good example of the latter, as is an interesting study by Olesker (1978). Examining some cognitive and perceptual capacities, measured by standardized tests, as well as social–emotional ones observed naturalistically, Olesker found major confluences of developmental progressions and suggested a substratum of functioning reflected in each of these areas in an interactive process.

Despite these promising approaches to the conceptualization and investigation of cognitive–affective interaction, a common thread they share with most traditional work on the topic is the assumption of separate and internally unified entities or systems that can then be examined in terms of a dynamic or functional interaction. Even some of those who are most associated with inquiry into either cognitive *or* affective functioning have taken a theoretical position that assumes interaction. A prime example is Piaget (1969), who has emphasized the development of a particular type of cognition, yet who seems to espouse an interactionist view; for instance: "We have assumed that affective decentring is a correlative of cognitive decentring, not because one dominates the other, but because both occur as a result of a single integrated process [p. 26]."

Although these approaches have served as important correctives to earlier, more narrowly defined views of human functioning, thorny developmental questions remain. To what extent are cognitive and affective functioning to be conceived as separate, if intertwining? If separate, are they to some extent equivalent, even parallel in developmental lines, and in the role they play in the total functioning of the person? Most importantly in the present discussion, are they to be considered as standing in human mental and behavioral life as a *pair* of phenomena—whether in antithesis, dialectical differentiation, complementarity, or other interaction?

There probably would be general agreement among diverse theorists and researchers that it is helpful to think of cognition and affect as at least somewhat separate systems within psychological functioning as a whole and to examine their developmental courses, functions, characteristic vicissitudes, and interactions with other organismic and environmental factors without assuming parallelism. Yet it is not clear that it is either sensible or heuristic to consider them as intrinsically, inevitably paired systems. It may well have been this pairing, within psychology, that added to and helped to entrench the antithesis already established in other intellectual and common cultural traditions. At this point, contributions to alternative concepts may further thinking and exploration that transcend the limitations of such pairing.

A natural starting point for the reconceptualization of the necessity of pairing cognition and affect is the positing of one system as underlying, secondary to, or otherwise related to the other in a nonequivalent way. de Riviera's (1977) proposition for a "structural theory of the emotions" and Doyle's (unpublished) consideration of affect as a response to cognition are thoughtful contributions along these lines. Within the psychoanalytic tradition a comparable attempt is made by Schur (1969), who redefines affective experience so as to include a cognitive component, drawing on Freud's similar, yet not identical and often varying ideas about thinking and affect. I believe that this kind of work stands in the same relation to more usual psychoanalytic formulations (for example, Rapaport's [1960] view that: "Affect and idea are thus conceived of as complementary and alternative drive representations [p. 26]'') as de Riviera's and Doyle's thoughts do to tradition in cognitive psychology. Understanding that all cognition has an affective context as all affect has a cognitive component has been an important advance in much current thinking about these issues.

Another approach that contributes to the elimination of unnecessarily dichotomous thinking grows out of the consideration of the *functions* served by a given piece of behavior or developmental process. The concept of multiple function and the related notion of overdetermination, familiar to psychoanalysts, has potentially much broader applicability to a range of developmental phenomena (Drucker 1975). That any given developmental process or achievement will serve both cognitive and affective functioning and be produced by them is a point of view that should prove important for the framing of an integrative approach to both theory and research. Likewise, the investigation of the specific functions of particular faculties (see, for example, Franklin, 1977, on the functions of language in play) focuses attention on a level of inquiry and a mode of analysis that does not require the usual dichotomous view of cognition and affect.

Finally, the most important new directions may start from a reconceptualization of the basic cuts to be made in psychological theory. In a very early publication, Heinz Werner, just beginning to articulate what would become the organismic–developmental theory so rich and yet so relatively unexplored by mainstream psychology until recently, proposed what he called a table of concepts on a genetic basis. In this highly condensed paper, Werner proposed that concepts are abbreviations for whole ranges of ideas and that: "apart from what is called the intellect—which is none other than the senses refined by conscious will—one can discern two fundamental functions: (1) outer and inner sensation; (2) feeling. Both can be the stuff of ideas. Thus, on the one hand, there are sensory concepts, and on the other hand, emotional concepts [1911/1978, p. 9].'' Although Werner went on to discuss many aspects of mental life he did not, to my knowledge, specifically pursue the idea of affective concepts to any great extent. Yet by comparison with Piaget, whose references to affective schemata were not central to his view of the development of intellectual functioning, Werner's later work on symbolization and other central mental phenomena continues and builds upon the kinds of assumptions about functioning evident in this early paper. Further, whereas Piaget speaks to an underlying common basis and a presumed parallelism in the development of cognition and affect, Werner is suggesting that he sees perception and feeling as in some ways "paired" phenomena, each playing a role as input to the material of cognition. I am struck by the fertility of such a notion and the potential utility of this as an alternative formulation to the cognitive versus affective dilemma.

I see, further, a potential meeting ground of Wernerian and psychoanalytic-developmental theory in addressing such issues. Within the psychoanalytic framework, the role of language and thought are beginning to be increasingly actively explored by those who carefully glean from Freud's tantalizing comments on the subject the basis for a psychoanalytic theory of cognitive development. Understanding that thinking and feeling have both drive and ego aspects is a starting point. The delineation of the role of language and thought in organizing experience is an area deserving further exploration, toward which Noy's (1979) most recent paper, taking as its focus the separate but interrelated development of the primary and secondary mental processes, is a careful, complex, important contribution.

These avenues, growing out of different traditions, inevitably carry with them not only different concepts of mental functioning but different domains of phenomena addressed and different methodologies. They may nonetheless prove to be compatible and pioneering contributions to the evolution of an integrative developmental theory of cognition and affect, as well as of other central processes, that breaks away from traditional dichotomies and places all phenomena within a larger and comprehensive view of human functioning.

SOME FINAL THOUGHTS

In the preceeding pages I have attempted to review and critique briefly the dichotomous concepts of thinking and feeling that have characterized not only formal psychological research and theory but also the literary and philosophical traditions of Western society and their commonsense articulations. The Marxian analysis of the societal context of such polarities, their individual psychological manifestations, and their pervasive and negative effects, is helpful in offering an alternative, dialectical mode of conceptualizing cognition and affect. The utility of the organizing principle of differentiation, and potential theoretical and research approaches to the questions that arise from such a consideration have been briefly explored. Many have been seen to share the assumption that cognitive and affective functioning are somehow paired, whether in antithesis or not.

My review of these issues, incomplete as it is, has convinced me that although important steps have been taken toward a new conceptual framework, much work remains to be done. The forging of a theory that accounts not only for both stability and continual change over the course of development but also for the possibility of varying kinds of interactions among organismic systems and functions is indeed a challenge. That such a theory should also account for the individual's *experience* of his or her own mental functioning as well as behavior, and for both general developmental trends and individual differences in that experience and its articulation may seem nearly impossible. Yet this is what a comprehensive developmental theory seeks to achieve.

This quest becomes particularly meaningful when one considers certain kinds of phenomena that raise the issue of experience with great force and poignancy. Some of de Riviera's subjects, asked to describe their experience of emotions, reported: "The emotions are red and yellow threads which, interwoven with the ordinary whites and grays, add color to enrich the cloth [of my life]. . . . [another person replied:] Why, I'm not like that at all. My life, like the world, is filled with mountains, plains, swamps and deserts; the emotions are winds which pick me up from a swamp and deposit me on a mountain top or set me in a desert [1977, p. 123]."

It is my hope that some of the distinctions and proposals set forth in this chapter may be helpful in the task ahead. Certainly the bases for interesting and fruitful integrations of cognitive- and psychoanalytic–developmental theory around issues such as cognitive and affective functioning are increasingly apparent. Drawing on them, and pursuing imaginative research, we may be better able to conceptualize and detail the developmental process by which people come to experience their lives in complex ways, to articulate that experience, to differentiate it from that of others, and to be aware of their own thoughts and feelings and take them as objects of contemplation.

ACKNOWLEDGMENTS

Conversations with Gertrude Baltimore, Susan Engel, Barbara Fields, Ray Franklin, Nancy Kaplan, Wendy Olesker, and Jeannette Stone have contributed in important ways to this paper. I am, above all, grateful to Margery B. Franklin, valued friend and colleague.

REFERENCES

Biber, B., & Franklin, M. B. The relevance of developmental and psychodynamic concepts to the education of the pre-school child. *Journal of the American Academy of Child Psychiatry,* 1967, *6*(1), 5-24.

Chesterton, G. K. *A defence of nonsense.* New York: Dodd Mead, 1911.

de Riviera, J. A structural theory of the emotions. *Psychological Issues,* 1977, *10* (4, Monograph 40).

Doyle, C. Current concepts of emotion: A paradigm-shift in the making? (Unpublished).

Drucker, J. Toddler play: some comments on its functions in the developmental process. *Psychoanalysis and Contemporary Science,* 1975, *4,* 479-527.

Engels, F. [*Herr Eugen Duhring's revolution in science*] (Translated by E. Burns, edited by C. P. Dutt). New York: International Publishers, 1935.

Escalona, S. K. *The roots of individuality.* Chicago: Aldine, 1968.

Fraisse, P., & Piaget, J. *Experimental psychology, its scope and method. Vol. 1, History and Method.* New York, Basic Books, 1963.

Franklin, M. B. *The functions of language in play.* Read before the National Association for the Education of Young Children, Annual Meetings, Chicago, Ill., November, 1977.

Guthrie, W. K. C. *The Greek philosophers.* New York: Harper & Row, 1960.

Johnson, T. H. *The complete poems of Emily Dickinson.* Boston: Little Brown, 1960.

Mahler, M. S., Pine, F., & Bergman, A. *The psychological birth of the human infant.* New York: Basic Books, 1975.

McKeon, R. (Ed.). *Introduction to Aristotle.* New York: Modern Library, 1947.

McLaughlin, J. T. Primary and secondary process in the context of cerebral hemispheric specialization. *Psychoanalytic Quarterly,* 1978, *48*(2), 237–266.

Murphy, L. B., & Moriarty, A. E. *Vulnerability, coping and growth.* New Haven, Conn.: Yale University Press, 1976.

Noy, P. The psychoanalytic theory of cognitive development. *Psychoanalytic Study of the Child,* 1979, *34,* 169–216.

Olesker, W. Cognition and the separation–individuation process. *Psychoanalysis and Contemporary Thought,* 1978, *1*(2), 237–267.

Ollman, B. *Alienation: Marx's conception of man in capitalist society.* Cambridge, England: Cambridge University Press, 1976.

Pascal, B. [*Pensees*] (Translated and edited by H. F. Stewart) New York: Pantheon, 1965.

Piaget, J. *The psychology of the child.* New York: Basic Books, 1969.

Pine, F. On the structuralization of drive–defense relationships. *Psychoanalytic Quarterly,* 1970, *39*(1), 17–37.

Pope, A. *Moral essays.* Edinburgh: James Reid, 1751.

Rapaport, D. *The structure of psychoanalytic theory: A systematizing attempt. Psychological Issues,* 1960, *2* (2, Monograph 6).

Riegel, K. The dialectics of human development. *American Psychologist,* 1976, October, *31*(10), 689–700.

Schur, M. Affects and cognition. *International Journal of Psychoanalysis,* 1969, *50,* 647–655.

Shapiro, T., & Perry, R. Latency revisited: The age 7 plus or minus 1. *Psychoanalytic Study of the Child,* 1976, *31,* 79–105.

Werner, H. *Developmental processes* (Edited by S. S. Barten and M. B. Franklin). New York: International Universities Press, 1978.

3 Cognitive-Affective Interaction: A Concept that Exceeds the Researcher's Grasp

Herbert Zimiles
Bank Street College of Education

The construct of cognitive–affective interaction occupies a strangely contradictory position in current psychological theory and experimentation. In their conversations, many psychologists frequently refer to it as though it were axiomatic. When speaking of the complexity and subtlety of cognitive functioning, they allude in a matter-of-fact way to the existence of the interaction between thought and emotion as though it were one of the most salient defining features of the nature of cognition. At the same time, when one examines the voluminous research literature in cognition, there is hardly a reference to the concept and scant acknowledgment of its importance. The ways in which aspects of thought and emotion influence each other are seldom subjected to systematic study.

In effect, two different paths of discourse on the topic have evolved: (1) an intuitive, overarching perspective that takes the construct for granted; and (2) a research literature that hardly acknowledges its existence. Given the powerful empirical bias of American psychology, it is the rapidly growing research literature that is the more dominant force. The aim of this chapter is to create a framework of greater acceptance for the construct by considering various ways in which it intersects with current lines of research. Beginning with an overview of how the construct has been treated by various theoretical approaches and research priorities of the past, I then identify areas of current research and theory that either explicitly or implicitly touch upon this interaction.

A BRIEF HISTORICAL OVERVIEW

As may be expected, the concept of cognitive–affective interaction has been dealt with very differently by different schools in psychology. It owes much of its recessive position to the fact that psychology has been dominated by the behavioristic tradition. During the middle decades of this century, American psychology struggled to achieve maturity by ridding itself of mentalism. Calling for an end to reliance on convenient fictions that allude to invisible internal states as explanatory concepts, such theorists as Guthrie, Hull, and Skinner reduced the complex processes of learning and thinking to an analysis of mechanical linkages between visible stimuli and responses governed by the laws of association and conditioning.

The principle of cognitive–affective interaction was invoked as one means of resisting the purge of mentalistic thinking. Because the affective system was less amenable to behavioral analysis and was somehow grudgingly acknowledged to have an interior apparatus, by pointing to the linkage between thought and feeling, psychologists were able to reassert the importance of internal states in understanding how people think. Thus, the concept of cognitive–affective interaction served to define an ideological position as well as to express a set of specific hypotheses regarding the nature of the relation between thought and emotion.

The gestalt psychologists of the thirties and forties provided a more doctrinaire basis for opposing the associationism of behaviorism. While studying problems that illustrated the role of perceptual organization and cognitive synthesis in problem solving, gestalt psychology served as a haven for the mentalistic thinking rejected by behaviorism. But, for the most part, the problems that were studied were unrelated to the affective life of the individual.

Probably more relevant and, it would now seem, of greater enduring influence was the work of Heinz Werner (1948). Werner's extraordinary synthesis of observations and findings in the diverse fields of anthropology, animal behavior, psychopathology, and neurology led to a theory that described development in terms of increasing differentiation of parts and increasing centralization and hierarchization of modes of functioning. Werner's organismic psychology was so full of hyphenated terms that the concept of cognitive–affective interaction was hardly conspicuous. In describing the syncretic quality of primitive organization, Werner repeatedly refers to the blending of affective and cognitive elements. Without dwelling on the issue per se, the concept of cognitive–affective interaction was fundamental to his theoretical framework. Toward the end of his career, Werner, in collaboration with Wapner (Werner & Wapner, 1952), developed sensory–tonic field theory as a means of explaining the role of the organic condition of the perceiver in perceptual experience.

Although Werner worked to develop and refine his system of theorizing within the framework of academic psychology, the sphere of thought that gave the most direct articulation to the concept of cognitive–affective interaction was the psychoanalytic movement. It would not be inappropriate to describe psychoanalytic theory as a body of ideas that is primarily concerned with the relation between thought and emotion. One of the cornerstones of psychoanalytic theory, Freud's distinction between primary and secondary processes, concerns the manner in which the ego, with its capacity for ordered thinking and reality orientation, monitors the intrapsychic forces that produce fantasies and dreams.

At the same time that academic psychologists in the 1950s were skeptically examining evidence purporting to indicate that perceptual processes are mediated by emotional factors, the psychoanalyst Ernest Schachtel (1959) asserted as a basic theoretical premise in his treatise on development the distinction between *autocentric* and *allocentric* modes of perception, that is, between subject-centered and object-centered perception, between perceptual experience based on how the person feels and that based on the characteristics of the object to be perceived. Far from questioning the validity of the primary/secondary process concept, psychoanalysts were pressing for its further refinement. For example, in the volume honoring David Rapaport, two of his closest associates, Gill and Holt, both chose to write on elaborations of the concept of primary process (Gill, 1967; Holt, 1967). Notwithstanding the wealth of evidence assembled by psychoanalytically trained observers—the dreams, hallucinations, delusions, thought disorders, amnesias, and other forms of aberrant thought that have been understood in terms of their emotional significance—efforts to study such phenomena systematically in the laboratory have been relatively rare and have been met with skepticism and disinterest by many academic psychologists. It is as though a group of scholastics is engaged in bitter debate over whether there is really a reddish fluid that flows inside the body, while in the next building a group of hematologists is conducting a seminar on recent advances in the physiology of vascular systems.

Although there were theoretical currents that supported the concept of cognitive–affective interaction during the post-World War II era, the psychology laboratories of the universities that generated the data that filled the research literature remained dominated by a behavioristic psychology of learning. As the behaviorists began to consolidate their control of academic psychology, they attempted to broaden their viewpoint and extend their sphere of influence. The work of Miller and Dollard (1941; Dollard & Miller, 1950), especially, signaled an effort to extend the range of applicability of rigorous and parsimonious behavioristic theory. As part of this expanded outlook, many learning laboratories turned to the study of the effect of anxiety on conditioning and verbal learning (Sarason, Hill & Zimbardo, 1964; Taylor & Spence, 1952) but these efforts remained embedded in the narrow experimental and theoretical paradigms that gave birth to them. They were never put forth as a new commitment to examine the nature of cognitive–affective interaction.

Perhaps the most sustained interest in problems pertaining to cognitive–affective interaction by academic psychologists was shown by post-World War II social psychology. Sherif's (1935) early demonstration of group influence on perception of motion using the autokinetic effect paved the way to a variety of studies demonstrating the influence of group pressure on judgments and beliefs. Among these were a series of investigations concerned with the effects of prestige and suggestion on judgment and preference (Asch, 1951). Building on advances made in wartime studies of propaganda, research in communication and persuasion (Hovland, 1954) examined how characteristics of the communicator, the communication, and the audience (i.e., factors that were for the most part affect laden) influenced the acquisition and retention of information. On a different but related track, the study of the authoritarian personality and other personality-related aspects of ethnic and religious prejudice explored the role of emotional needs and conflicts in the formation of interpersonal perceptions (Adorno, Frenkel-Brunswik, Levinson, & Sanford, 1950). All the aforementioned studies had in common the idea that seemingly rational and objective thought processes could be shown to be influenced by subjective, affective factors.

Most dramatic of all was the effort to demonstrate that emotional needs and values had a decisive influence on perceptual behavior. Pointing to studies that indicated that drive states, attitudes, and values influenced the nature of perceptual experience, Bruner and Postman (1948) distinguished between "autochthonous" or structural and "behavioral" or motivational determinants of perception. As often happens with such efforts to break new ground, the issues raised by this wave of experimentation became mired in an endless methodological quibble. As people grew tired of the controversy, they noted that virtually all the evidence pertaining to what came to be known as "perceptual defense" dealt with marginal levels of perceptual activity and, therefore, began to question its overall significance. Interest in the issue subsided. Most of the research provoked by the controversy was primarily concerned with correcting methodological flaws in previous work; it contributed little to a theoretical examination of cognitive–affective interaction. If anything, these studies demonstrated how resistive to experimental verification are hypotheses regarding the influence of internal states on aspects of cognitive functioning. In his incisive review of this train of thought and exploration, Floyd Allport wryly commented (1955): "If we were to entertain such questions too seriously, we might seem to be challenging our confidence in our mental stability. (p. 39)" Perhaps because these studies were largely conducted by social psychologists, most were primarily directed at demonstrating that social and emotional phenomena were indeed powerful influences on the nature of psychological functioning. However, such data were seldom viewed as calling for a basic revision in theory of cognitive functioning.

As already indicated, it was in the world of dynamic psychology that the connection between thought and emotion was taken for granted. While social psychologists were struggling to demonstrate the reality of perceptual defense phenomena, clinicians were routinely using clients' perceptual responses to semistructured stimuli as a basis for identifying emotional needs and conflicts. The projective hypothesis of Lawrence Frank (1939) is predicated on the assumption of cognitive–affective interaction.

Academic psychology took a dramatic turn in the early 1960s when it began to reexamine the work of Piaget. Why Piaget's concern with reflective thought and conspicuously mentalistic forms of theoretical speculation came to be received so warmly at that point is difficult to explain, but with it came a legitimatization of cognition as a sphere of research. This trend was reinforced by Bruner's rephrasing and adaptation of Piagetian theory to fit an information-processing approach to the study of cognition. Ulric Neisser's formulation of a cognitive theoretical framework in 1967 helped to call attention to the fact that even the simplest perceptual responses required inner processing and interpretation. However, the main outcome of the Piagetian renascence was that cognitive psychology turned to a focus on logical thinking. The huge volume of Piaget-related research that ensued has contributed little to an understanding of affective influences on cognition. The concept of cognitive-affective interaction has not flourished during the recent wave of research in cognition. Once more, as in the days of learning theory, the focus of research seems directed at clarifying the nature of newly defined elementary processes. Speculation regarding the interaction between different classes of variables is suspended until the ever-elusive basic facts are established.

DIMENSIONS OF THE PROBLEM

The elusiveness of the nature of cognitive-affective interaction stems from the fact that it takes many forms. Its multifaceted character comes into focus when one examines the variety of ways in which thought and emotion interact, as they do, for example, in the following issues and topics: affect as a driving force, the disabling effects of cognitive-affective interaction, the need to know as part of the affective system, the self-concept and ego functioning, cognitive style and cognitive dispositions, social cognition, and sex difference. The relation of these topics to cognitive-affective interaction is discussed in this section.

Affect as a Driving Force

Preferring to define the affective system in biological rather than mentalistic terms, the early behavioristic work in learning theory described the role of drive states as that of fueling the learning process. Miller and Dollard (1941), for example, distinguished between the drive state that impelled the organism to respond and the cue that gave direction to the response. It was only gradually acknowledged that drive states could be cue producing and that there were other affective states that were not necessarily biologically grounded that could also impel the organism to learn. For the most part, however, the early work in learning theory attempted to circumscribe the role of affect and to make clear distinctions between the function of affect and of cognition. The drive state provided the impetus to learning but was seldom viewed as influencing the nature of the outcome.

The simple model promoted by behaviorism did little justice to the complexity involved. The nature of the need can have an overriding effect on how and what is learned as well as how much is learned. Consider the following example: If we are presented with a detailed map of a particular city, we will give it a glance and set it aside. It is an item full of information that is unlikely to generate interest or foster substantial learning. But if we are visitors to that city intent upon moving about and exploring, we will treat the map as a compelling object and proceed to master its content. The example demonstrates that huge variations in the vigor and thoroughness of learning can be produced by changing a nonbiologically derived need state of the learner. The variation in cognitive functioning has to do with how and what is learned, as well as how much is learned; the nature of the cognitive performance is shaped by the need state, not merely activated by it.

Whereas in the above case it is the actual content of the material to be learned that meets a compelling need, in other instances it may be the symbolic significance of the material to be learned or the symbolic significance of accomplishing the learning that is need satisfying. The intricacy and subtlety of such incentives to effective cognitive behavior is revealed by some observations made long ago by Lois Murphy. In a volume entitled *Emotional Factors in Learning* (Murphy & Ladd, 1944), she analyzed case studies of how emotional factors influence the learning experiences of college students. Murphy sought to understand the dynamic factors that define individual patterns of educational experiences. In discussing how different ways of relating oneself to the world of activity and thought affected the quality of learning, she noted the following examples:

> One student has a ''drinking-in'' orientation, another has the will to master or accomplish, or to acquire the power of expertness; others want something to do, their interests appear to function as a release, providing an outlet, a ''giving-out'' experience. In contrast are those who have possessive feelings about education, a need to amass learning [p. 158].

In these comments, Murphy suggests that how people learn, what they learn, and why they learn reflects and serves a complex, personality-related system of emotional needs.

The affect system is not merely a necessary condition for learning, an independent driving force, but rather an interactive element that, in addition to setting off the learning process, contributes to its scope and character by steering and monitoring the cognitive performance.

The Disabling Effects of Cognitive—Affective Interaction

Another widely held view of the impact of emotion on thought is that of an intrusive, undermining influence. Paradoxically, such an idea is the obverse of the notion of affect as a goad to cognition. Especially by those who regard intellectual behavior as functioning in machinelike fashion, the influence of emotion on thought is seen as a force that deflects the perfectly ordered vehicle from its projected course. Although the image of cognitive functioning upon which such a model is based may be faulty, evidence for the disabling effect of emotion on learning and thinking abounds.

In examining how this question has been dealt with, one is struck by the strikingly different theoretical positions and levels of inquiry that have been applied to this set of problems. While experimental psychologists were relying exclusively on self-report inventories to assess anxiety for the purpose of examining its effect on simple learning tasks, clinicians with much greater access to detailed information of their clients' emotional lives had devised more elaborate theoretical frameworks for describing how various psychopathological trends could adversely affect intellectual functioning. Rapaport's (Rapaport, Gill, & Schaefer, 1945/1976) classic work on diagnostic testing provided a comprehensive, interpretive scheme for differentiating various forms of affective disorders on the basis of patterns of variation in performance both within and among subtests of intelligence. Despite the absence of experimental verification, Rapaport's system has served as a handbook for clinicians concerned with diagnostic testing. Much richer and more incisive, and at the same time more difficult to pin down and substantiate, is the interpretive system that guides the assessment of cognitive functioning and affective themes in projective test performance. Whether evidence drawn from psychopathology regarding the influence of affect on thought reveals something about the nature of cognitive–affective interaction among normal people will probably remain a subject for continuing debate.

Another level of clinical functioning that bears even more directly on the relation of emotion to thought is to be found in the rapidly growing field concerned with learning disabilities. Its label tells us that we are again dealing with pathology. But learning disability phenomena fall on a different continuum, one that can less easily be dismissed as being irrelevant to what is loosely defined as the realm of the normal. Although many forms of specific learning disability are thought to have a neuropsychological base, de Hirsch (1977) has described how the emotional life of a growing child may contribute to the formation of a learning disability and how it also influences remediability. In outlining the interacting forces that affect a child's scholastic effectiveness—inherent endowment, vulnerability to stress, level of neurophysiological maturation, developmental status (perceptual, cognitive, linguistic, and interpersonal), emotional climate of the home, the social environment that has in part shaped the child, and the educational measures that have thus far failed—she capsulates a theory of cognitive–affective interaction.

Some of the difficulties of documenting the complex interaction between emotion and thought in the normal range of functioning are illustrated by a study undertaken by the author (Zimiles & Konstadt, 1962). Interested in demonstrating that some lapses in cognitive functioning may be symbolically related to an area of emotional conflict, we conjectured that an incapacity to spell may represent a disguised and displaced unwillingness to accept rules. In order to test this hypothesis, a scale was developed purporting to measure resistance to authority's demands, and we examined the relation between scale scores and spelling ability. The correlation between scores was in the expected direction but not very high. It remains to be seen whether the comparatively low relationship found between these variables reflected poor validity of the scale that had been constructed or a failure of the underlying hypothesis.

It may be observed from this brief discussion that the manner in which emotional factors interfere with cognitive performance is itself a complex, variable phenomenon that requires further differentiation. Emotional factors vary in the degree of specificity of their adverse effect, ranging from a generalized disability involving a band of content or an array of related tasks, to a highly specific impairment owing to a particular traumatic history or the affective significance of a given element of information or task to be learned. A more important dimension of the problem is the nature of the mechanism that inhibits cognitive performance. Explanatory constructs vary as a function of the level of analysis and theoretical posture favored by the investigator. In their molecular stimulus–response analysis of serial learning and conditioned response acquisition, Taylor and Spence (1952) invoked a competing response explanation of the adverse effect of anxiety. On the other hand, Rapaport et al. speak of the loss of ego control required for efficient attention and concentration that adversely affects rote memory, arithmetic reasoning, and other aspects of mental functioning. Clinicians will often point to the impaired self-esteem of people that predisposes them to dampen their efforts to succeed for fear of experiencing failure, thereby producing the very failure they were attempting to avoid and further damaging their self-esteem. In many situations it is the symbolic significance of successful cognitive functioning that is viewed as the critical dynamic factor. Successful cognitive performance may represent conformity to (generalized or specific) authority about which the learner is conflicted, or it may entail acting out competitive, aggressive impulses that are expected to evoke retribution, or it may arouse expectations that the demonstration of self-reliance and competence that is evinced by effective cognitive functioning will lead to the loss of precious dependency relationships. Thus, the disabling impact of affect would appear to be mediated by a variety of interfering mechanisms: anxiety-produced competing responses that interfere with the formation of new stimulus–response linkages, impaired attentiveness and concentration stemming from a loss of ego control, fear of failure that induces more failure, resistance to the real or symbolic authority demands entailed in a learning situation, fear of retribution for aggression symbolically expressed in the act of learning, fear of the loss of a dependency relationship resulting from the demonstration of cognitive competence.

The Need to Know as Part of the Affective System

Is the impulse to explore and be curious part of the innate human motivational system or do these patterns emerge in the service of other affective needs? And, irrespective of the origin of this impulse, is it meaningful to differentiate people in terms of their need to know? Harlow (1950) was one of the first experimenters to suggest that the opportunity to explore is intrinsically motivating, that exploratory behavior may be impelled not only by the practical need for information, but is in itself gratifying. Berlyne (1960), in conducting some of the pioneer work in this field, has coined the terms "specific" and "diversive" curiosity to distinguish between patterns that have a particular informational objective and those without a specific aim.

In an effort to examine the usefulness of differentiating children in terms of their variations in curiosity, Maw and Maw (1972) have reported a series of studies of fifth-grade children whom they categorized as low or high in curiosity. They found reliable differences between them in creativity, self-concept, response to verbal absurdities, and a variety of other measures. The correlational design introduced ambiguity. Is it possible that the conceptual framework employed by the teachers and peers whose ratings identified the high- and low-curiosity groups overlapped with the content of measures used by Maw and Maw to identify correlates of curiosity?

In a study that compared the functioning of exploratory and cautious children in first-grade open classrooms, Minuchin (1976) found more differences between the groups in their social behavior than in indices of intellectual inquiry. The exploratory/cautious distinction was not predictive of many patterns of classroom behavior. Clearly, more work is needed to identify the dimensions of the exploratory–curious dimension, work directed at measuring this attribute with greater precision, establishing its stability and coherence, and demonstrating its relation to other dimensions of psychological functioning. In the meantime, the question of whether it is appropriate to regard exploratory behavior and curiosity as stable and coherent need systems that have a measurable influence on patterns of cognitive development must be left in abeyance. The degree to which such need systems are inborn and an intrinsic property of the species is even more difficult to ascertain.

The Self-Concept and Ego Functioning

One aspect of the concept of cognitive–affective interaction concerns self-related ideas and feelings—self-knowledge and self-concept. Data regarding the nature of the self and ideas about the self are amassed by the growing child. The growth of the self-concept calls upon the child's integrative skills; it is mediated by the workings of the child's cognitive apparatus. At the same time, the content of this accumulating body of knowledge, ideas of self-worth, bear directly on the emotional system of the individual.

Although exactly what is meant by the concept of the self, its hypothetical structure and function, and its salience as an explanatory construct varies widely among psychologists, it has been a principal organizing construct for Gordon Allport (1955), for Kelly in the psychology of personal constructs (1955), for neo-Freudians, and for a great many others. It is also a concept of great relevance to the developmental–interaction point of view, whether it is defined as a collective body of ideas that a child has about himself or herself that affects specific choices and levels of aspiration, or as a stabilized, summative estimate of self-worth.

Several aspects of the self have been distinguished: (1) the strength of the self; (2) the valence of the sense of self; and (3) understanding and knowledge of self. Strength of self refers to the wholeness and coherence of an individual's sense of being, the sense of identity. The concept of valence deals with evaluative attributes that define the self, with special emphasis on the sense of worth. If we regard all psychological experience as being sifted through the self and, in turn, as being assimilated to influence the sense of self, then the dimensions of both salience and valence are pivotal. Although these two aspects of the self are different, and the dynamics of their development involve overlapping but also distinctive factors, they have in common the fact that they both deal with ideas that have substance and are at the same time intimately associated with feeling. It is, then, a sphere of intensive interaction between thought and feeling, a situation in which the two feed each other.

Still another aspect, not independent of but quite different from the others, is the accessibility of the sense of self—the degree to which ideas about the self are available to be used in making various decisions. Degree of self-knowledge and self-understanding would appear to have both cognitive and affective antecedents. Affective factors that deal with the acceptability of the self will surely influence the degree of accessibility of the sense of self. At the same time, self-knowledge and self-understanding are also shaped by the cognitive environment. It may be speculated that an environment that calls for the utilization of self-awareness, one that enables the individual to draw on one's own framework and own perceptions and beliefs should lead to a progressive increase in self-knowledge and self-understanding. Similarly, it may be surmised that the more that information about the self is communicated to the child, the more references there are to the self in interacting with the child, the greater will be the clarity and sharpening of self-knowledge. In sum, principal features of the self-system—the solidity of the self, the sense of self-worth, and its accessibility to the individual—call for the focus of thought on feelings and ideas, which lie at the core of an individual's affective system.

Defined in overlapping, sometimes even identical terms, with that of the self, the concept of the ego, and especially that of ego-functioning, usually refers to the monitoring and ordering of the environment for the purposes of self-preservation and self-enhancement. Because ego-functioning is concerned with integrative levels of psychological functioning, it represents a level of analysis that deals with the interaction between thought and feeling.

One of the leaders in the study of integrated levels of functioning has been Lois Murphy. During an era when the field has been largely concerned with elementaristic ways of describing behavior, she has remained steadfastly committed to identifying major axes of psychological organization. The conceptual framework for ordering coping mechanisms presented in the most recent report of the Topeka project, *Vulnerability, Coping, and Growth* (Murphy & Moriarty, 1976), once again indicates the degree of differentiation and refinement of description achieved by her analytic categories. The degree of overlap between cognitive and affective attributes, and the manner in which the distinction between these attributes tends to get blurred when they are sensitively and comprehensively described, is illustrated by Murphy's system. For example, among the attributes listed under cognitive capacities are: receptivity to environmental cues, moods, qualities, enjoyment of fine nuances of sensation, and freedom from inhibitions or rigidity in thinking. Correspondingly, under the affect cluster we find: enjoys newness, discovery. The first phase of the major longitudinal study conducted in Topeka was guided by Escalona (1968; Escalona & Heider, 1959). Her continuing studies of infancy (see Escalona, this volume) shed light on the beginnings of psychological organization by demonstrating the emergence of early patterns of individuality that serve as the cornerstone of subsequent forms of integrative functioning.

Efforts to capture the essential characteristics that are involved in arriving at a summative assessment of integrative functioning and emotional well-being, as White (1959) formulated them in his examination of competence and effectance, have most often been conducted by those attempting to define "positive mental health." Brewster Smith (1959) and Marie Jahoda (1958) have made major contributions to this area, and Norma Haan (1963) has provided a conceptual framework for assessing ego functioning in adults.

An important development in the evolution of psychologists' concern with cognitive-affective interaction is Jane Loevinger's effort to assess ego development (1976). Because of her expertise as psychometric methodologist and critic, there are grounds for expecting Loevinger to deliver some valuable maps of the terrain and to lure other methodologically oriented researchers into the study of complex functioning. Loevinger's work offers the greatest hope for reducing the gulf between the methodologically oriented elementarism of the research world and the clinicians' efforts to understand complexity.

Cognitive Style and Cognitive Dispositions

One of the most promising, but not yet fulfilled efforts to describe and measure cognitive-affective interaction has been the study of cognitive style. Cognitive style refers to a characteristic mode of cognition that is closely interwoven with aspects of an individual's temperament and personality. Although it is defined in terms of distinctive patterns of cognitive functioning, it is a form of cognition that is thought to be dynamically related to aspects of impulse control and affective expression.

In his review of varieties of cognitive style reported in the research literature, Messick (1976) indicates the wide range of phenomena that have been investigated within this framework. In addition to Witkin's comprehensive studies of field dependence/independence (Witkin, Dyk, Faterson, Goodenough, & Karp, 1962; Witkin, Lewis, Hertzman, Machover, Meissner, & Wapner, 1953), there have been noteworthy investigations of such attributes as conceptual style, breadth of categorizations, leveling/sharpening in memory, reflectiveness/ impulsiveness, risk taking/cautiousness, sensory modality preference, and convergent/divergent thinking. Few of the foregoing distinctions have been substantiated by systematic empirical study, that is, have presented consistent evidence that the hypothesized distinctions hold. Seldom are the data most parsimoniously explained in terms of the construct of stylistic variation.

Originally conceived as a theoretical mechanism for penetrating to the more complex interrelations between thought and feeling, the concept of cognitive style has suffered from the fact that it has, for the most part, been studied within a methodological framework that regards cognitive functioning in much simpler terms—as an array of independent, univocal traits. Investigators of cognitive style have adhered to methodological conventions that render difficult their basic commitment to the study of complexity. For example, they have acquiesced to the adoption of a nomothetic framework in measuring their phenomena when such a constraint would seem to be antithetical to the basic premises of such work. In addition, in order to encourage the use of their concepts and measures, many investigators have devised brief measures to serve as indices of the phenomena they are attempting to study. Such brief measures belie the complexity that the work was originally designed to clarify. For these and other reasons, the study of cognitive style remains a potentially fruitful but not yet fully realized strategy for viewing cognitive functioning organismically.

Different from but related to characteristics studied under the rubric of cognitive style are those attributes that influence the effectiveness of cognitive functioning but are not part of what might be termed a person's cognitive apparatus. Such behavioral attributes provide the context and support for cognitive functioning but are not part of the information-processing system. However, because they may have a decisive effect on cognitive competence, they have been termed "cognitive dispositions" in an effort to capture their ancillary function (Zimiles, 1972). We may include among these such characteristics as autonomy, individuality, inquisitiveness, perseverance, and resourcefulness.

This incomplete roster of supporting behavior patterns points to a substratum of cognitive functioning, to the behavior systems that mediate effective cognition. These dispositions have important affective components; they are shaped by the child's social and emotional experience. They are the soft elements in the cognitive system, parts that function less mechanically and precisely.

It may be that by assigning a label to these attributes or otherwise according them greater recognition, they will become more available for use as explanatory constructs. For example, in attempting to understand the differential impact of different school experiences, perhaps the principal distinguishing features of contrasting approaches to education lie not in the amount of academic knowledge acquired, as implied by our heavy reliance on achievement tests to evaluate educational programs, but in the distinctive patterns of cognitive dispositions that are fostered.

Social Cognition

A counterpart to the idea that the growth of the self-system calls upon the child to integrate feelings about information as well as thoughts about feelings is the notion that the child's interactions with other people whom he or she regards as essential to his or her well-being become the occasion for profoundly important information processing and ordering. Whereas, traditionally the study of cognitive development has been largely confined to children's understanding of inanimate subject matter or with emotionally neutral events, it has only recently been recognized that a great deal of the child's commerce with the outer world involves interpersonal behavior. Most situations encountered by children are ones in which the content of the thought processes and problem-solving activities are relationships with other people. Such events call for ordering, understanding and, to some extent, predicting the behavior of other people.

The social nature of cognitive content often renders it more compelling. Especially when the very young child is interacting with parents or caretaking figures, the need to understand and predict behavior may seem to the child to be a matter that takes on life-and-death proportions. These social events, with the sense of urgency assigned them by the child, present a special opportunity for cognitive mastery. It may be speculated that such occasions are the time for the formation of basic schemata—of the permanent object, perceptual constancy, principles of transivity, conservation, classification and seriation, and other logical structures. The child's early perception of the mother becomes the basis for object permanence and constancy. At later ages, the child's relation to family and peers—the observed regularities in behavior of significant persons, the ability to understand and predict their likes and dislikes, judgments and preferences—presents situations in which the child is especially motivated to learn. The need to "figure out" behavior, defend, and befriend are occasions that call for conceptual functioning regarding the relations among events. They entail the differentiation of complex cues and the detection of regularities in complicated forms of behavior. Most workers in the growing field of social cognition (Chandler, 1976; Shantz, 1975; Youniss, 1975) tend to emphasize how these phenomena help to reveal the nature of social development and the special problems they pose for cognitive functioning. In light of the special meanings that must be associated with ideas and knowledge about people, it would seem more fruitful to focus on the cognitive aspects of such interactions.

Of special interest in research often subsumed under the heading of social cognition is Martin Hoffman's theoretical analysis of the development of altruism (1975). He attempts to show that the child's developing interpersonal perception and role-taking skills interact with the affect experienced when witnessing another person in distress to form an altruistic motive. He marshals evidence for the existence of an independent altruistic motive. Hoffman describes manifestations of empathic distress, the condition that forms the base for altruistic thinking. He also speculates on the influence of training in role taking on the development of altruism. In effect, Hoffman describes the development of altruistic behavior as a gradual integration of emotional reactions to distress with the child's developing cognitive sense of others. His theoretical conception directly invokes the concept of cognitive–affective interaction.

Sex Differences

The study of sex differences, especially those in cognitive functioning, should be included in this overview of useful concepts and promising research trends. In addition to identifying methodological pitfalls in conducting such work, Jeanne Block's incisive reassessment of the research literature (1976; also see Block, this volume) has helped to bring to the surface more differences between the sexes than at first seemed apparent. Because there is scant evidence to indicate that sex differences in cognitive functioning are inborn, and much to suggest that they result from distinct patterns of socialization, and because the socialization processes that constitute the antecedents to sex differences tend to be powerful, stable, and coherent, and their greatest impact is likely to be on affective dimensions of psychological functioning, the investigation of sex differences in cognitive functioning would appear to be an extremely promising arena for studying cognitive–affective interaction.

CONCLUDING COMMENTS

Originally planned as a means of coming to terms with the concept of cognitive–affective interaction, this chapter has barely taken the first steps of such an exploration—reviewing how the concept has tumbled about, decrying its limited acceptability to various theoretical approaches, and examining some of the contexts in which it has been and is now being studied.

This brief exploration of the realm of cognitive–affective interaction reveals that it impinges on a wide variety of important areas of research. However, the concept of cognitive–affective interaction is almost never directly confronted. It is as though investigators have avoided acknowledging the depth of complexity they have knowingly and courageously agreed to explore. A large part of the problem lies in a paradoxical methodological dilemma that tends to undermine efforts to study complexity. The tools and methodological frameworks available to researchers have been fashioned by a tradition that has been concerned with simplifying and consolidating. Faced with an almost impenetrable complexity, psychologists turned to a strategy of quantifying, limiting, and reducing. There gradually evolved a methodology and a methodological framework geared toward generating lean and efficient research. It made sense to begin by attempting to disentangle and tease apart. The requirements of unidimensional scaling and the development of such quantitative methods as factor analysis were geared toward identifying elements, measurable building blocks.

A curious, understandable, but not necessarily logical methodological orientation that accompanied the commitment toward basic ordering and simplification was the conviction that measurement procedures should be relatively brief and uncomplicated. They should be easy to administer and short in duration so that they could be widely used and relatively inexpensive in terms of personnel and time required of them. The criteria of easy repeatability and efficiency of measurement (somehow confused with objectivity of study), arbitrarily and prematurely invoked, placed still more serious limits on the complexity and depth of investigation that could take place.

Contributing further to the adoption of a narrow perspective has been the researcher's preference for the experimental method. Although ensuring greater precision, the experimental method is largely limited to the simple case. It calls for an independent variable that can be manipulated easily over a range of values that can be described quantitatively, or at least one that varies discretely. As a result, most research in cognitive functioning is concerned with such manipulable attributes as characteristics of the stimuli to be learned. Because the emotional state of an individual cannot be assessed quantitatively and cannot be manipulated by the experimenter, it is much less often studied.

Heir to such a tradition, the psychologist who wishes to move beyond the level of elementarism and simplicity that formed the foundation of current methodology is faced with an armentarium of methods and procedures that were not geared to penetrate the thickets of complexity. At the same time, the standards and criteria for evaluating research have been established to correspond to the commitment to certainty and simplicity. Not only do investigators lack the tools to investigate complexity with thoroughness and incisiveness, they are stymied by a set of standards for evaluating research that are not friendly to their aspirations. There is then a process of double accommodation required of the investigator of complexity. He needs to adapt his research blueprint to the constraints of a methodology devised to study much simpler problems, and he must frame his study and his findings in a mode that meets the standards of acceptability established for research geared to achieve different objectives.

The net effect is to stultify the study of complexity. It is not surprising, then, that efforts to study cognitive–affective interaction have faltered. The study of complex problems has been forced into a mold that was made to deal with simple forms of behavior. Once, when David Rapaport was introduced as the main speaker of an august interdisciplinary conference in psychiatry, he began by noting that he had found it so difficult even to discipline himself that it seemed utterly out of the question for him to try to *inter*discipline himself. In the same way, psychologists encounter so much difficulty in simply identifying and measuring the basic parameters of affect and of cognition that it seems impossible for them to explore productively the interrelation between two such largely unknown quantities. And yet it may be that the interactionistic properties of these entities are among their basic defining traits and that a thorough understanding of each cannot be achieved without dealing with their interrelation.

REFERENCES

Adorno, T. W., Frenkel-Brunswik, E., Levinson, D. J., & Sanford, R. N. *The authoritarian personality.* New York: Harper, 1950.

Allport, F. H. *Theories of perception and the concept of structure.* New York: Wiley, 1955.

Allport, G. *Becoming: Basic considerations for a psychology of personality.* New Haven, Conn.: Yale University Press, 1955.

Asch, S. E. Effects of group pressure upon the modification and distortion of judgments. In H. Guetzkow (Ed.), *Groups, leadership and men.* Pittsburgh, Pa.: Carnegie Press, 1951.

Berlyne, D. E. *Conflict, arousal, and curiosity.* New York: McGraw–Hill, 1960.

Block, J. H. Issues, problems, and pitfalls in assessing sex differences: A critical review of "The Psychology of Sex Differences." *Merrill–Palmer Quarterly,* 1976, *22* (4), 283–308.

Bruner, J. S., & Postman, L. Symbolic value as an organizing factor in perception. *Journal of Social Psychology,* 1948, *27,* 203–208.

Chandler, M. J. Social cognition and life-span approaches to the study of child development. In H. W. Reese (Ed.), *Advances in child development and behavior* (Vol. 11), New York: Academic Press, 1976.

de Hirsch, K. Interactions between educational therapist and child. *Bulletin of the Orton Society,* 1977, *27,* 88–101.

Dollard, J., & Miller, N. E. *Personality and psychotherapy.* New York: McGraw–Hill, 1950.

Escalona, S. K. *Roots of individuality: Normal patterns of development in infancy.* Chicago: Aldine, 1968.

Escalona, S. K., & Heider, G. M. *Prediction and outcome: A study in child development.* New York: Basic Books, 1959.

Frank, L. K. Projective methods for the study of personality. *Journal of Psychology,* 1939, *8,* 389–413.

Gill, M. M. The primary process. In R. R. Holt (Ed.), *Motives and thought: Psychoanalytic essays in honor of David Rapaport.* New York: International Universities Press, 1967.

Haan, N. Proposed model of ego functioning: Coping and defense mechanisms in relation to I.Q. change. *Psychological Monographs,* 1963, *77,* 1–23 (Whole No. 571).

Harlow, H. F. Learning and satiation of response in intrinsically motivated complex puzzle performance by monkeys. *Journal of Comparative and Physiological Psychology,* 1950, *43,* 289–294.

Hoffman, M. L. Developmental synthesis of affect and cognition and its implications for altruistic motivation. *Developmental Psychology,* 1975, *11,* 607–622.

Holt, R. R. The development of the primary process: A structural view. In R. R. Holt (Ed.), *Motives and thought: Psychoanalytic essays in honor of David Rapaport.* New York: International Universities Press, 1967.

Hovland, C. I. Effects of the mass media of communication. In G. Lindzey (Ed.), *Handbook of social psychology* (Vol. 2). Cambridge, Mass.: Addison–Wesley, 1954.

Jahoda, M. *Current concepts of positive mental health.* New York: Basic Books, 1958.

Kelly, G. A. *The psychology of personal constructs.* New York: Norton, 1955.

Loevinger, J. *Ego development: Conception and theories.* San Francisco: Jossey–Bass, 1976.

Maw, W. H., & Maw, E. W. Differences between high- and low-curiosity fifth-grade children in their recognition of verbal absurdities. *Journal of Educational Psychology,* 1972, *63,* 558–562.

Messick, S. Personal styles and educational options. In S. Messick (Ed.), *Individuality in learning.* San Francisco: Jossey–Bass, 1976.

Miller, N. E., & Dollard, J. *Social learning and imitation.* New Haven, Conn.: Yale University Press, 1941.

Minuchin, P. *Differential use of the open classroom: A study of exploratory and cautious children.* Final Report to the National Institute of Education # NE-G-00-3-0018, 1976 (Temple University, Philadelphia, Penna.) 1976.

Murphy, L. B., & Ladd, H. *Emotional factors in learning.* New York: Columbia University Press, 1944.

Murphy, L. B., & Moriarty, A. E. *Vulnerability, coping, and growth: From infancy to adolescence.* New Haven, Conn.: Yale University Press, 1976.

Neisser, U. *Cognitive psychology.* New York: Appleton–Century–Crofts, 1967.

Rapaport, D., Gill, M. M., & Schafer, R. *Diagnostic psychological testing* (Rev. ed.). (Edited by R. R. Holt.) New York: International Universities Press, 1976. (Originally published, 1945.)

Sarason, S. B., Hill, K. T., & Zimbardo, P. G. A longitudinal study of the relation of test anxiety to performance on intelligence and achievement tests. *Monographs of the Society for Research in Child Development,* 1964, *29* (Serial No. 98).

Schachtel, E. G. *Metamosphosis: On the development of affect, perception, attention, and memory.* New York: Basic Books, 1959.

Shantz, C. U. The development of social cognition. In E. M. Hetherington (Ed.), *Review of child development research* (Vol. 5). Chicago: The University of Chicago Press, 1975.

Sherif, M. A study of some social factors in perception. *Archives of Psychology,* 1935, *27* (187).

Smith, M. B. Research strategies toward a conception of positive mental health. *American Psychologist,* 1959, *19* (11).

Taylor, J. A., & Spence, K. W. The relationship of anxiety level to performance in serial learning. *Journal of Experimental Psychology,* 1952, *44,* 61–64.

Werner, H. *Comparative psychology of mental development* (Rev. ed.). Chicago: Follet, 1948.

Werner, H., & Wapner, S. Toward a general theory of perception. *Psychological Review,* 1952, *59,* 324–338.

White, R. W. Motivation reconsidered: The concept of competence. *Psychological Review,* 1959, *66,* 297–333.

Witkin, H. A., Dyk, R. B., Faterson, H. F., Goodenough, D. R., & Karp, S. A. *Psychological differentiation: Studies of development.* New York: Wiley, 1962.

Witkin, H. A., Lewis, H. B., Hertzman, M., Machover, K., Meissner, P. B., & Wapner, S. *Personality through perception.* New York: Harper, 1953.

Youniss, J. Another perspective on social cognition. In A. D. Pick (Ed.), *Minnesota Symposia on Child Psychology* (Vol. 9). Minneapolis: The University of Minnesota Press, 1975.

Zimiles, H. An analysis of methodological barriers to cognitive assessment of preschool children. In F. J. Monks, W. W. Hartup, & J. de Wit (Eds.), *Determinants of behavioral development.* New York & London: Academic Press, 1972.

Zimiles, H., & Konstadt, N. Orthography and authority: A study of cognitive–affective interaction. *Psychological Reports,* 1962, *10,* 623–626.

Perspectives on Theory: Another Look at the Developmental-Interaction Point of View

Margery B. Franklin
Sarah Lawrence College

In this chapter, the developmental–interaction point of view provides a focus for exploring some ideas about theory in psychology. These ideas concern, first, concepts of world hypotheses, root metaphors, and family relations that provide a way of talking about thematic content in psychology; second, concepts of dominant foci pertaining to ways of delineating the "object" of study in psychology; third, concepts of widening and deepening as directions of theory development that can be realized through several means.

The developmental–interaction point of view had its origins within the child development movement and its evolution reflects the dynamic interplay of psychological theorizing, concerns about education and societal change, and considerations of practice that permeated the movement as a whole (Senn, 1975; Biber, this volume). Those near the center of the movement tended to ally themselves with certain psychological perspectives and to reject more widely accepted doctrine emanating from the academic establishment.[1] However, relatively little attention was given to articulating a systematic psychological theory base for child care practice and education. As the developmental–interaction point of view crystallized, this formidable task was taken on by Biber and colleagues (Biber, 1967, 1977; Shapiro & Biber, 1972). Developmental-interactionism thus includes a cohesive psychological theory base constructed in

---

[1]i.e., Watsonian behaviorism. Preference for psychodynamic and early developmental stage theory that was not considered sufficiently "scientific" made for considerable distance between child developmentalists and most of the psychological establishment. There appears to be considerably greater rapprochment on the current scene (Franklin & Biber, 1977).

accord with basic ideas about human nature and the educational process (Franklin & Biber, 1977).

The theory base of the developmental–interaction point of view draws on two major streams of psychological theorizing: psychodynamic theory (in particular, ego psychology) and developmental-stage theory (Piaget and Werner). In ways to be discussed later, the theory base is held to be integrative rather than eclectic. It evolved as a way of representing a conceptualization of the "whole child"—a being who is at once thinking and feeling, knowing, sentient, emotional (Biber, 1972).

World Hypotheses, Root Metaphors, and Family Relations

Not too long ago, it was widely held that psychology as an empirical science could solve its disputes by resort to the world of fact. Great emphasis was placed on the development of precise, "scientific" investigatory techniques that included modes of gathering and analyzing data designed in line with uncritical belief in the wonders of quantification. Furthermore, explications of scientific theory—where it comes from, what it is, and what it is meant to do—were largely if not entirely the province of philosophers of science (and their psychologist acolytes) deeply committed to an empiricistic view of knowledge and a restricted conception of the nature of science. Now, fortunately, the field has reached a stage of development in which this conception of the nature of psychological inquiry, and of "psychology as a science," is being strongly questioned and in many corners overruled, while at the same time there is growing interest in how to conceptualize theories—including scientific theories—as constructions of reality inherently tied to metaphysical presuppositions or "world views" (Black, 1960/1962; Kuhn, 1970).

This general orientation reflects a theory of theories—in particular, the view that theories, like personal beliefs and belief systems, are constructions of reality—more formal and systematic, subject to criteria not necessarily applicable to common sense, but similarly motivated by the human impulse to create order, and similarly to be recognized as *interpretations* (Cassirer, 1923/1953; Goodman, 1978).

Pepper (1942/1957) and Black (1960/1962) propose that a great deal of theory construction rests on model building or a more wide-ranging kind of metaphorizing. Elucidating how models and metaphors enter into theory construction and application, Black distinguishes different senses of "model," beginning with the most concrete (construction of miniatures) and proceeding to the most abstract (theoretical models, involving description but not actual building of imaginary structure). He then draws an important distinction between theoretical models of a manifest nature (constructed in the light of day, within a given disciplinary framework) and more embracing, sometimes hidden, schemata termed "conceptual archetypes.'' The latter are very closely related to what Pepper terms ''root metaphors''—the analogical forms that lie at the base of world hypotheses. Pepper (1942/1957) describes the ''root-metaphor method'' as follows:

> A man desiring to understand the world looks about for a clue to its comprehension. He pitches upon some area of commonsense fact and tries [to see] if he cannot understand other areas in terms of this one. This original idea becomes then his basic analogy or root metaphor. He describes as best he can the characteristics of this area, or, if you will, discriminates its structure. A list of its structural characteristics becomes his basic concept of explanation and description. We call them a set of categories. In terms of these categories he proceeds to study all other areas of fact whether uncriticized or previously criticized [i.e., common sense or previously theoretized]. He undertakes to interpret all facts in terms of these categories. As a result of the impact of these other facts upon his categories, he may qualify and readjust the categories, so that a set of categories commonly changes and develops . . . . Some root metaphors prove more fertile than others, have greater powers of expansion and of adjustment. These survive in comparison with the others and generate the relatively adequate world theories [p. 91–92].

In addition to putting forth a general theory of theories (namely, the theory of world hypotheses), Pepper delineates four major root metaphors: formism, mechanism, contextualism, and organicism. He shows that world hypotheses based on these differing root metaphors not only have radically different themes but accept different kinds of evidence or, in other words, have different truth criteria. For this reason, arguments about ''what is'' are virtually unresolvable.

Abrams (1953) is concerned not with scientific theory but with the emergence and development of the romantic critical tradition in the nineteenth century. He suggests that just as the examination of metaphors within works of art has proved fruitful, so critical theory may be illuminated by study of its metaphors— metaphors of creative activity inherently linked to concepts of mind. The shift in theories of art (from ''imitation'' to ''expression'') that marks the emergence of the romantic tradition in the nineteenth century can be understood as a shift from prevailing metaphors of the mind as mirror (a reflector of external events) to metaphors of the mind as lamp or fountain (a source, a projector that contributes to the actualization of the objects perceived). Abrams makes clear that these two embracing and fundamentally antithetical metaphors of mental functioning are deeply rooted in differing philosophical traditions and have significant exemplifications not only in critical theory but in other domains, including the scientific.

More than 20 years ago, Kaplan (n.d.) showed the relation between two of Pepper's root metaphors (mechanism and organicism) and Abrams' metaphors of mirror and lamp, and proposed that theories of psychology (in particular, theories of development) could be seen as embodying one or the other of two basically opposed views of human functioning. Further, it was suggested that theories sharing a common root metaphor could be regarded as constituting a "family." Thus, Kaplan's synthesis of Pepper and Abrams, interwoven with his explication of philosophical traditions, provided the basis for establishing two major "families" of developmental theories: the "mechanistic-passive organism view" and the "organismic-active organism view" (Kaplan, 1966, 1967; Langer, 1969; Overton & Reese, 1973; Reese & Overton, 1970).

Pepper and Kaplan argue that world hypotheses are autonomous—alternative constructions that are by their nature mutually exclusive. Although eclecticism exists as a matter of practice (and is advocated by some as a matter of principle), Pepper (1942/1957) believes that: "this method is mistaken in principle in that it adds no factual content and confuses the structures of fact that are clearly spread out in the pure root-metaphor theories; in two words, that it is almost invariably sterile and confusing [p. 106]." Alliances of theories sharing a root metaphor avoid the pitfalls of eclecticism and—by implication—have the possibility of being fruitful.

We can agree with Pepper's general theory and with his admonitions against eclecticism, and at the same recognize some problems. It follows from what Pepper has said that only if we can identify root metaphors of given theoretical formulations do we know when we are on safe ground in forming given alliances and when we are in danger of becoming eclectic. But it is not always easy to tell where a particular psychological theory falls in Pepper's schema. For example, Pepper mentions gestalt theory under mechanism; Reese and Overton suggest that it belongs under contextualism; I find that it does not quite fit in either category. Lack of "fit" could mean that the categories need some revision—or it could mean that psychological theories do not represent pure "types" as far as root metaphors are concerned. As Langer (1969) points out, it is not altogether clear where classic psychoanalytic theory stands with regard to the central tenets of mechanism and organicism (or, for that matter, passive organism versus active organism). Did Freud work with mixed metaphors and, if so, did this create problems? Would his theory have been even stronger and more elegant if he had been more consistent?

Clearly, we do not have to settle for a particular delineation of root metaphors, world views, or families to recognize that this general approach is extremely helpful on the level of theoretical analysis; it provides a theory of theories, a way of identifying commonalities that goes considerably beyond the usual dimensions employed for purposes of comparison and elucidation, and that displays the inherent links between psychological theories and more encompassing perspectives. Moreover, the kinds of root metaphors delineated by Pepper can be "translated downwards" and so serve as guidelines in another kind of endeavor: the identification of images that enter into the creative activity of theory construction (Gruber, 1978). On reflection, it seems likely that the kinds of themes delineated by Abrams in the context of literature and literary criticism have direct bearing on the study of images in specific creative endeavors, artistic and scientific; at the same time, as Kaplan has shown, Abrams' particular themes can be "translated upwards" to serve an illuminating function vis-à-vis psychological theory. The coalescence of these two streams is not fortuitous; metaphor is a peculiarly powerful form of conceptualization.

The notion of "family of theories" needs to be concretized and at the same time examined. A family is formed on the basis of shared assumptions or beliefs, but what level of shared assumptions or beliefs makes for "family" as opposed to acquaintances? For example, some American psychologists have assumed a deep commonality between Berlin gestalt theory and developmental theory as formulated by Piaget and Werner. Indeed, there are fundamental ideas that figure prominently in both. These can be briefly summarized as follows: opposition to elementaristic, associationist explanation; profound holism, involving consideration of part–whole relations and importance of context in determining any event; belief in inherent tendencies toward organization of action and thought; emphasis on organismic tendencies to establish and reestablish equilibrium, coupled with opposition to instinct–drive concepts; willingness to infer mental events; and preference for explanation in terms of underlying mental processes and/or structures. One might think that sharing belief in this set of assumptions would be sufficient to establish "family," but both Piaget (1950) and Werner (1978) emphasize their differences from Berlin gestalt theory—particularly on what Werner called the "genetic [developmental] point of view." In addition, although there is some Kantian heritage held in common, the thoroughgoing constructivism that underlies Piagetian and Wernerian theory is virtually invisible (and probably nonexistent) in orthodox gestalt theory. The high priority given to developmental-stage and constructivist precepts in Piagetian and Wernerian theory makes for close relations.

Psychoanalysis shares with these psychologies a profound developmentalism—development is conceptualized partly in terms of "stages," and there are assumed to be qualitatively different types of mental functioning that are ordered as "levels." These ideas provide natural points of contact with Piagetian and Wernerian conceptualizations. On the other hand, however much emphasis is now placed on ego development and ego functioning, psychoanalysis is a drive theory in a sense that is alien to Piaget and Werner as well as the gestaltists, and it is not primarily about processes of "knowing" in the sense that concerns core developmental theory.

Although Werner and Piaget are often grouped together—perhaps the closest relatives in the organismic–active organism family—there are important differences between them (Barten, 1980; Franklin & Barten, 1980). For example—and this is by no means an exhaustive listing—Werner, more than Piaget, emphasizes the importance of affect in the structuring of experience, not only in the early years but throughout life. This is linked to Werner's deep interest in subjectivity, and his belief that understanding the quality and vicissitudes of experience—however "irrational" such experience might seem from the ordinary point of view—should be a prime task of psychology. Second, and closely related to the foregoing, Werner was consistently concerned with what he called "primitive mental processes"—types of functioning in which there is relatively little self-world differentiation and experience is structured dynamically, physiognomically, with qualities of affect and movement playing a central role. Such modes of functioning are not eradicated by more advanced forms of thought but become integrated into higher modes of organization; clearly, Werner considered the more "primitive processes" a wellspring of creative activity. Piaget seems to conceptualize mental development in terms of progress in scientific-logical thinking, whereas Werner (1957/1978) makes clear his view that the more "mature" (developmentally advanced) individual is one "who has at his disposal a greater number of developmentally different operations [p. 123]."

We could go on adumbrating points of agreement and divergence between Piaget and Werner, or between Piaget and Werner on the one hand and Berlin gestaltists and/or psychoanalytic theorists on the other, or between all of these thinkers and mainstream American behaviorists. But the point is simple: Relative salience of commonalities and differences among theories shifts as a function of the particular comparisons being made, and these comparisons are formed not only by considerations of theoretical exegesis but—in a more pressing way—by ideological struggles within a discipline. Recognizing that there are shifts in salient commonalities and differences among theories, we are led to the conclusion that families may not be so stable as we once thought. Nonetheless, it seems both important and possible to make a distinction between familylike groupings and somewhat looser arrangements. To determine the closeness of intertheory relationships in given cases, we need to consider the number of shared assumptions, the position of these assumptions in each theory (central versus peripheral), and the nature of these assumptions (their depth and scope, in a root-metaphor sense).

Now to the case of developmental-interactionism. The formulations on ego functioning (including notions about self-concept, motivation, etc.) and many of the developmental conceptualizations are firmly grounded in the work of Erikson and other ego psychologists. The view of cognitive functioning embedded in developmental-interactionism developed gradually over a period of some years; it draws on Dewey's thinking as well as Werner and Piaget (particularly the earlier work). Kaplan (n.d.) and Reese and Overton (1970) include the ego psychologists, along with Werner and Piaget, as the central figures in the organism-active organism family. It is clear, then, that Biber and co-workers have developed a point of view that falls squarely within the organismic-active organism framework. The theory base of this point of view is *integrative* in the specific sense that it draws on concepts identified with different theories and belonging to the same general family (or, more conservatively, sharing certain high-level assumptions). The contrast is with theory combinations that are *eclec-*

tic (i.e., that amalgamate concepts from different theories belonging to different families). Interestingly, this integrative theory base did not emerge as a function of decisions explicitly based on concepts of root metaphors or families of theories but evolved quite naturally—and perhaps inevitably—from the guiding concept of the "whole child." Biber (1972) makes clear the theoretical aspect of this concept:

> the concept that the child, learning, is a "whole child" evolved as a rejection of psychological theories that fragmented psychological functioning. It was the foundation for rejecting traditionalism in education because of a serious error of commission—the stuff of learning was packaged in insulated subject-matter areas—and a major error of omission—the child was lost sight of except for the mastery of intellectual skills [p. 47].

It can be suggested that the "whole child" is not only a guiding concept in this approach but a powerful image, an almost concrete embodiment of ideas and sentiments that serves a central generative function in elaborating theory and thinking about practice in the context of a value system.

Dominant Foci: Psychologies of Mind, Organism, Person, and Situation

The contrast between mechanism and organicism, integrated with the distinction between a passive organism view and an active organism view, provides a way of thinking about psychological theory that has proved to be extremely illuminating. Such a classificatory scheme pertains directly to the deep thematic content of different psychologies. Psychologies also differ with regard to what they take as the "object" of study—whether they focus on entities or events. Here I am proposing a rather straightforward distinction among four prototypical forms of psychology—three that focus on entities (mind, organism, person) and one that takes events as the object of study. As will be seen, this classification in terms of dominant foci cuts across other ways of describing psychological theory; it is intended to provide a complementary perspective and thus could be used in coordination with other classifications.

Psychologies of mind seek to identify universals of human functioning and to explain these in terms of underlying processes and structures assumed common to the species. Such theories may be developmental or not; that is, they may or may not be concerned with the kind of changes that mark developmental sequences. Emphasis on general principles of mind does not involve commitment to a nativist position, but to the extent that processes or structures are assumed common to the species and/or that development is assumed to follow an invariant sequence of stages, the theory must include some innatist assumptions. Specific behaviors are viewed as "indicators" (i.e., as behavior samples providing information about the underlying structures and processes of mind that constitute the essence for these psychologies). Piaget's psychology is clearly a developmental psychology of mind; it may be exclusively so. To a greater extent than often realized, Freud's psychology is a psychology of mind. Freud also provides a *psychology of person* (see below) which for some has obscured the centrality of his psychology of mind.

Psychologies of the organism are like psychologies of mind in their emphasis on identifying basic principles of functioning and enduring properties of the organism, but differ importantly in that they are not focused on *human* mentality and do not necessarily involve assertions about the primacy of underlying structures and processes as contrasted with manifest behavior. Hull's (1943) behaviorism can be interpreted as largely a psychology of the organism—it specifies principles of functioning that apply across species and also contains constructs pertaining to enduring propensities and structures of the organism (e.g., habit strength, habit family hierarchy). By contrast, Skinner's (1938) behaviorism is not a psychology of the organism but primarily a *psychology of situations* (see the following).

A theory designed to account for both human and nonhuman functioning may be comparative or noncomparative in orientation. Schneirla's psychology (1960) provides an important example of a theoretical approach that—in contrast to that of Hull and other behaviorists—is comparative in the specific sense that it is based on concepts of qualitatively different levels of functioning (Novikoff, 1945; Schneirla, 1949/1972). Schneirla uses a hierarchically ordered explanatory apparatus that allows him to elucidate both similarities and differences in the functioning of animals at different phyletic levels. By the criteria set forth here, Hull and Schneirla are grouped together as having psychologies of organism. It should be clear that this does not connote a family relationship in the sense described earlier. Hull and Schneirla differ radically on basic conceptions of how organisms function, how to account for change, and how to conceptualize organism–environment interaction. But, as indicated, they are both concerned with the "organism" as the object of study, with infrahuman as well as human functioning.

Because psychologies of organism posit principles of functioning that apply across species and psychologies of mind center on human mentality and assume discontinuity or, more strongly, a distinctiveness to human functioning, there is an inherent conflict between these two prototypical forms. Nonetheless, it seems that some very important psychologies include both. Gestalt theory as formulated by Köhler, Koffka, and Wertheimer arose in the context of debate about the nature of mind and represents adherence to precepts that are shared by Werner (1957/78) and also Piaget (see the foregoing). Many of these pertain to mind per se. However, the theoretical formulations of Köhler and Werner—and to some extent the others—contain precepts that are assumed to apply not only to human functioning but to aspects of animal behavior and to some extent to nature itself.

For Köhler, such precepts have to do with invariant relations, part–whole relations, and the organization of form. For Werner, processes of differentiation and hierarchic integration are manifest in virtually all forms of life. Piaget regards processes of organization and adaptation (and, therefore, assimilation and accommodation) as manifest not only in human mental functioning but as universal in organic life; however, Piaget's emphasis is clearly centered on the explanation of human mental functioning.

If a theory centers on the consideration of human mentality—if it is concerned au fond with understanding the nature of human mental processes and functions—it should be classed as a psychology of mind. If a theory is not focused on the study of human mental functioning per se but seeks to establish modes of explanation that embrace infrahuman functioning as well, it should be classed as a psychology of the organism. It follows that gestalt psychology as formulated by Köhler, Koffka, and Wertheimer is appropriately viewed as a psychology of mind. Piaget's psychology appears to represent a relatively pure instance of psychology of mind, whereas Werner's psychology remains a somewhat problematic case. Werner's designation of his approach as "comparative-organismic" is not accidental; "comparative" refers not only to comparing differing levels of human mental functioning but to comparisons of human and infrahuman functioning. In this way, Werner's approach is close to Schneirla's. However, an examination of Werner's research and theoretical writings reveals a central focus on human mentality—a focus sharpened in collaborative work with Kaplan (Werner & Kaplan, 1963) and Wapner (Wapner & Werner, 1957, 1965).

This brief excursion is intended not only to clarify the proposed distinction between psychologies of mind and psychologies of organism but to show that work of a given theorist may contain aspects of both. It should be noted that psychologies of organism, like psychologies of mind, may be developmental or not; that is, they may or may not be centrally concerned with progressive change. This is also true of the next prototypical form to be considered: *the psychology of the person.*

Psychologies of the person focus on enduring aspects of human beings, conceptualized in terms of attributes or in terms of underlying structures and processes. In this way, they are like psychologies of mind but they differ crucially in their central concern: the identification of variation and individuality (see Shapiro & Wallace, this volume). Any theory concerned with variation takes for granted some base of universals and in this sense every psychology of the person rests on some psychology of mind (or, in the case of behavioristic theories of the person, a psychology of organism), but the latter may be virtually unarticulated. The attempt to describe and explain variation and/or individuality involves establishing a set of categories or dimensions to capture those characteristics of the individual viewed as most significant. Most psychologies of personality center around psychologies of the person although there is continuing debate about whether this is necessarily so (Mischel, 1979).

It has already been mentioned that Freud's psychology contains a psychology of the person as well as a developed psychology of mind. As a clinician, Freud was necessarily concerned with developing a highly differentiated system for talking about persons in a way that would provide a sense of their distinctive qualities. Clearly, it is the presence of a conceptual system—embodied in dimensions or categories—that makes possible the comparisons ultimately resulting in a picture of an individual. Allport's (1937, 1955) theory represents another psychology of the person. Here, the conceptual apparatus centers around—though it is not limited to—the notion of traits, which provides a way of characterizing the individuals and talking about individuality.

Many cognitively oriented theories contain what might be called a "theory of types" and thus some form of a psychology of the person. For example, Witkin's work (1962) is rooted in a psychology of mind but has at its center a psychology of the person that features concepts concerning person–environment relations (namely, field-dependence versus field-independence). Other cognitive-style theorists characterize individuals in terms of dimensions such as impulsive versus reflective, analytic versus synthetic, concrete versus abstract, and so forth. Some of these dimensions were originally articulated to characterize fundamental modes of thought or ways of functioning. In that role, they figure prominently in some psychologies of mind. This contrasts with the use of these same dimensions in psychologies of the person; as indicated, in the latter context the dimensions are used for differentiating among individuals, for characterizing "types."

As already indicated, some psychologies contain both a psychology of mind and a psychology of the person. For example, Werner's approach is primarily a psychology of mind but contains a partial psychology of the person. In fact, this was a recurrent theme in Werner's work—beginning with early writings on the artistic personality, undoubtedly fostered through close contact with William Stern during the Hamburg years (Hardesty, 1976; Werner, 1938), and appearing clearly in a later period (Werner, 1949; 1940/1957). A similar pattern may be discerned in the work of Kurt Goldstein (1938, 1940). The contrast with Piaget is striking.

The final prototypical form to be discussed[2] is *psychology of situations*. A psychology of situations takes the event or situation as the appropriate unit for

---

[2]The four discussed here seem to be most fundamental, but other forms exist and will be articulated as this scheme is further developed. For example, some contemporary approaches show focal concern with group characteristics and differences. In cross-cultural psychology, a fundamental debate continues: Should between-group differences be construed as variations on a common theme (as Piaget maintains) or as having prime significance? In a similar vein, approaches devoted to delineating a "psychology of women" usually emphasize notions of fundamental difference between male and female in our society (whether such differences are held to be biologically or culturally based). Clearly, these psychologists assume commonalities in the species and so, like *psychologies of the person, psychologies of the group* must have a *psychology of mind* hovering in the background. But in their central concern with the distinctive characteristics of given groups and contrasts among groups, these psychologies represent a fifth prototypical form: *psychology of groups*.

psychological study and seeks to account for the actions of persons (or other organisms) through analysis of components and their interrelations. The term "action" must be broadly construed—it is by no means limited to overt action. Equally important, psychologies of situation range from the highly elementaristic (Skinner) to the holistic (Lewin). What is it, then, that makes for a psychology of situations? As indicated, it is the focus on event or situation rather than mind, organism, or person as "entity"; the assumption that action is a joint function of organism characteristics and other situation variables; the conviction that the ongoing is as significant as the enduring in considering what psychology is (or should be) about. On this last point, it is worth emphasizing that psychologies of mind, organism, and person generally regard behaviors at a given moment simply as indicators of enduring propensities or abilities; otherwise, behaviors of the moment are not significant. In classical approaches to Rorshach interpretation, for example, it is assumed that the person's responses are reliable indicators of more or less stable feelings and attitudes. Clearly, psychoanalysis does not contain a psychology of situations.

Skinner's approach centers on a psychology of situations in which the organism's enduring characteristics have significance only in their contribution to the prediction of behavior in the current setting; no recourse is made to underlying processes or structures in the organism or to interactions of factors in the situation. The situation or event is elementaristically conceptualized as comprised of parts having no intrinsic relation to each other and "affecting" each other only in the sense that change in one part or element reliably predicts change in another (as intended by Skinner's use of the term "contingency" to describe such relations). The contrast with Hull makes clear that there is no inherent link between this prototypical form and a behavioristic-learning theory orientation. On our reading, Hull's behaviorism is more centrally a psychology of organism than of situation.

Clearly, Lewin's approach (1936) rests on a psychology of mind closely related to that of the Berlin gestalters with whom he studied and worked until his emigration to the United States. But at the center of Lewin's theory of motivation (and, by extension, his theory of personality) lies a highly elaborated psychology of situations. In fact, Lewin is distinguished from his contemporaries not by his resort to mathematization and concepts of field forces imported from physics (however important he considered these unique formalizations) but by his view that psychology should be concerned with conceptualizing and studying the actions of persons in situations. Further, Lewin (1943) developed a systematic way of talking about such events, giving credence not only to the organism's history (as manifested in the present) but to the psychological structuring of reality as an important determinant of action. Throughout, Lewin emphasized the complex nature of organism-environment relations.

On the contemporary scene, Wapner, Kaplan, and colleagues (Kaplan, Wapner, & Cohen, 1976; Wapner, 1980; Wapner, Kaplan, & Cohen, 1973) are developing an approach that joins a systems-oriented psychology of situations to

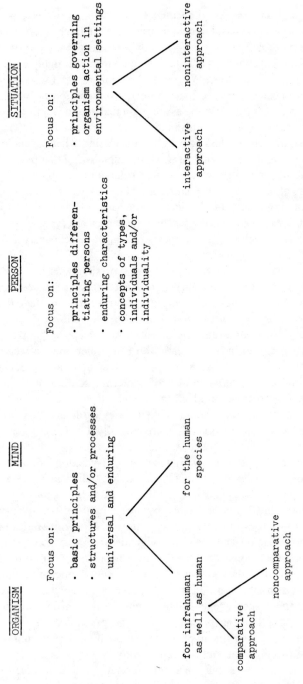

FIG. 4.1. prototypical forms of psychological theory: Commonalities and differentia.

ORGANISM

MIND

Focus on:

- basic principles
- structures and/or processes
- universal and enduring

for the human
species

for infrahuman
as well as human

comparative
approach

noncomparative
approach

PERSON

Focus on:

- principles differen-
  tiating persons
- enduring characteristics
- concepts of types,
  individuals and/or
  individuality

SITUATION

Focus on:

- principles governing
  organism action in
  environmental settings

interactive
approach

noninteractive
approach

a developmental psychology of mind basically identified with Werner's organismic theory. This psychology of situations takes the organism–environment unit as basic and emphasizes the profound reciprocity of organism–environment relations. Components of the situation (designated as agent, environment, ends, instrumentalities, and action) are delineated in a way that takes cognizance of their participation in a system and at the same time allows rigorous empirical investigation of transactional phenomena. The holism and phenomenological orientation evident in Lewin's conceptualizations are very much in evidence here—not stemming from Lewin's work but rooted in a shared intellectual tradition. Kaplan and Wapner take the situation as a paradigm for conceptualizing human action (alluding here to Burke's (1945) dramatistic theory) but this is not intended as a psychology of the "here and now"—it is wedded to a profound developmentalism. (Here, note the paradigm for symbolization developed by Kaplan in collaboration with Werner; see Werner & Kaplan, 1963.)

Let us consider developmental interactionism in this context. As stated earlier, the theory base of this viewpoint consists of the integration of precepts from psychodynamic theory and developmental stage theory. Many of these precepts concern universal properties of mind; the developmental–interaction viewpoint has a psychology of mind (or, more accurately, parts of several psychologies of mind) as part of its background. However, when developmental interactionism is put into use as a framework for research and educational practice, it is a psychology of the person—formed from several sources—that figures most prominently. The image of the "whole child" contains within it not only the aspect of wholeness (thinking and feeling) but of uniqueness or, more accurately, individuality (see Shapiro & Wallace, this volume). This is evident in early as well as more recent research (Biber, Murphy, Woodcock, & Black, 1942; Minuchin, Biber, Shapiro, & Zimiles, 1969). Furthermore, Biber's interpretations of children's classroom behavior and some other work in this tradition make clear that the developmental–interaction approach includes a partial (unelaborated) psychology of situations, which in some contexts of application becomes central. Understanding children's behavior at any given time involves a highly differentiated view of factors in the situation. Because the viewpoint is crucially concerned with aspects of social development and interpersonal behavior, it is not surprising that other persons are given a prominent role among factors to be considered; nonetheless other aspects of the environment (including physical features) are not ignored. This aspect of developmental interactionism may be related directly or indirectly to the work of Lewin (1936, 1946), which was very influential in the formative years of developmental interactionism; it may also be rooted in some of Dewey's thinking on organism–environment relations.

If the delineation of prototypical forms presented here (Fig. 4.1) has validity, it follows that amalgamation of forms is not only possible but desirable in order to develop a "whole" psychology. We have seen that a number of the great systems in fact contain more than one prototypical form of psychology. This is the principle of complementarity. In some cases, one form is primary and the other provides background or takes a secondary position—but this need not be the case; two forms can be of equal importance in the theoretical structure. Because psychologies of mind and psychologies of organism focus on the same point in the field and provide somewhat different views of this point, these two prototypical forms may come into conflict if located in the same theoretical structure. The conflict can be resolved through hierarchical arrangement in which the psychology of organism is given superordinate position and psychology of mind is articulated as a psychology of the human species as a species. This arrangement works only if the particular psychology of organism is a comparative psychology allowing a distinctive position to human functioning. Such an arrangement may be implicit in Werner's comparative-organismic psychology.

To avoid possible misunderstanding, it must be reiterated that a given approach can draw on more than one psychology of a given prototype category. Thus, one can presumably integrate aspects of Erikson's psychology of mind and Piaget's. In order for amalgamation of prototypical forms to meet criteria of compatability, the particular psychologies in question must be grounded in some shared assumptions or common world hypotheses. If a Piagetian psychology of mind were amalgamated with a behavioristic psychology of situations, the totality would—by definition—exemplify complementarity but not compatability, and would be—in our view—incoherent. The particular combination that provides the theory base for developmental interactionism appears to meet criteria for both complementarity and compatability.[3]

Development

Theoretical frameworks are born, they grow and change; some develop, many die, and others evolve into new forms. Differing analyses indicate that changes in theoretical perspective—for the individual and, on another level, for a scientific community—arise from some complex interaction of internal and external forces, where there is a felt inadequacy in the current way of conceptualizing things and a sense of possible solution that implicitly or explicitly embodies an idea of progress.[4] The *Zeitgeist* or, more precisely, occurrences in the matrix comprising a given discipline, will promote some theoretical developments and discourage others.

---

[3]As mentioned, current work of Wapner and Kaplan at Clark University conjoins a developmental *psychology of mind* and a newly developed *psychology of situations;* it also includes a partial *psychology of the person.* Here, again, the particular prototypical forms entering into combination are rooted in a shared world view—in this case, very consciously so—and the integrated theory thus meets criteria for compatability as well as complementarity.

[4]cf. Gruber and Barrett (1974) on Darwin's work and Kuhn (1970) on paradigm shifts in science.

In theory development in the social sciences, and perhaps more generally, two opposing and in some sense complementary tendencies can be readily identified. One is *widening:* the attempt to develop greater scope for a theory, to account for a wide range of phenomena. The other is *deepening:* the attempt to develop several levels of interpretation *and/or* complementary perspectives pertaining to some circumscribed set of phenomena—to develop a more differentiated, integrated, fuller account for this set of phenomena. To clarify this further: *Deepening* refers to both: (1) developing explanations where a set of principles accounting for manifest behavior, for example, is supplemented by principles accounting for the "underneath" and perhaps by principles accounting for the relation between the two planes—i.e., multileveled explanation; and (2) establishing different perspectives on a set of phenomena, where the perspectives (or "explanations") are conceptualized as distinct and complementary, but are not conceptualized in terms of degrees of depth.

Clearly, *widening* is a prevalent tendency in theory development. It is closely linked to the idea of a comprehensive theory—that is, a theory that accounts for a wide range of phenomena, often in terms of a few general principles. By contrast, a specialized theory takes a circumscribed area or problem and attempts to develop as elegant and precise a description or explanation as possible. Chomsky (1978) has drawn a related (but not identical) distinction based on different theories' assumptions about "the way facts are going to turn out." Talking about theory in linguistics, psychology, and artificial intelligence, he suggested that the "modular" approach is characterized by a view of the organism as a system of separate systems and organs, distinct domains, each governed by specific principles, whereas the "uniform" approach seeks general principles of human functioning that transcend particular systems or organs and, in Chomsky's terms, lack "domain specificity." He sees his own theoretical work (Chomsky, 1980) as embodying a modular approach and both Piaget's and Skinner's, for example, as representing the "uniform" approach.

Deepening is an equally important path of theory development and in our time may be the more significant and widespread, at least within developmental psychology. The tendency toward deepening often arises as a reaction against interpretations felt to be simplistic, reductionistic, or unidimensional.

How are widening and deepening achieved? Either can be accomplished by two means: *internal development* or *theory combination.* Widening (but not deepening) can also be accomplished through *extension* (see Fig. 4.2). *Internal development* refers to the elaboration of already existent principles of the theory, or the development of offshoots that are seen as direct extensions of already formulated principles. *Theory combination* involves the conjoining of precepts of two or more theories or, less dramatically, the annexing by a theory of precepts from another theory. *Extension* refers to applying existent principles of the theory to new phenomena—that is, to phenomena not originally regarded as cases for this theory—and may involve some *minor* modification of the princi-

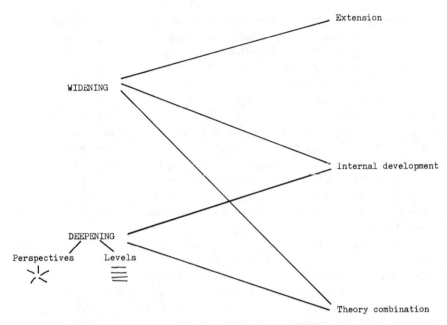

FIG. 4.2.   General schema of theory development.

ples. If the modification is more than minor, we have a case of internal development. Whether a particular theory of development represents internal development or theory combination may also be problematic and is partly a matter of how the change is perceived by its maker. The development of ego psychology within psychodynamic theory constitutes an important case for examination: To what extent are the new formulations direct developments of Freud's concepts and to what extent, or in what ways, do they represent dramatic departures? (See Drucker, this volume, for discussion of this and related issues).

In the case of developmental interactionism, we have an evolution that represents deepening achieved through theory combination. Biber and others working in this tradition have asserted unequivocally that neither psychoanalytic theory nor the developmental perspectives of Piaget and Werner provide a fully adequate account of the child's mental life and interpersonal functioning. Psychodynamic theory—in its ego psychology manifestations—allows description of cognitive functioning, but does not provide a sufficiently differentiated view and is both too specialized (in its selection of phenomena for fine-grained treatment, e.g., dreaming) and too general (in what it has to say about intellect and conceptualization). The more cognitively oriented approaches of Piaget and Werner fail to provide sufficiently textured, in-depth views of motivation and its vicissitudes, the complex of feelings about the self, and—more generally—the intricacies of interpersonal relations. Clearly, the objection to exclusive use of one framework is intimately tied to the image of the ''whole child'' that stands at the center of the developmental–interaction point of view and constitutes the embodiment of pretheoretical assumptions about human functioning. Drawing on concepts from both psychodynamic and developmental-stage theory, Biber and colleagues sought to develop a theoretical framework that would do justice to the complexity and three-dimensionality of the real child—and avoid the over-simplification and loss of understanding that results from a uniperspectival view.

As mentioned previously, the evolution of developmental interactionism represents theory combination employed in the service of deepening. Other arrangements also occur. As noted, deepening can be achieved through internal development. Hartmann's formulations (1939/1958) concerning the autonomy of the ego, undertaken within the frame of psychoanalytic theory, provide an important instance. Osgood (1953) worked to extend the purview of behavioristic learning theory with the aim of developing more adequate accounts of complex, specifically human, behavior. This is an instance of widening through internal development; it primarily involved developing the notion of mediating response as an elaboration of concepts of response already established within learning theory. By contrast, Dollard and Miller's (1950) combining of concepts from stimulus–response learning theory and psychodynamic theory represents an attempt at widening through theory combination.[5]

Theories and their less formal counterparts (frameworks, viewpoints) arise in certain contexts and are designed for specific ends. They may be more or less adequate to the ends for which they were designed and they change accordingly. We must also understand that as the disciplinary field or larger environment changes, there will be shifts in concepts of appropriate ends and changes in what is apprehended as adequate.

Concluding Comment

Taking the developmental interaction point of view as a focus for discussion, this chapter has explored some ideas about the nature of psychological theory and theory development. Several general ideas lie in the background of the present

---

[5]This work by Dollard and Miller seems to represent a particular type of theory combination—one in which aspects of one theory are translated into the terms of another. Such translation sometimes amounts to total incorporation. Even where it does not, serious distortion may result. If theories are whole structures, linked to encompassing world views, it follows that piecemeal matching (or translation), part to part, can only produce conceptual confusion. The interpretation of Vygotsky (1962) as a mediation theorist represents a prime example (Wozniak, 1972). It is argued here that *widening* through *theory combination* can be achieved without distorting either theory, *where there are significant shared assumptions*. For example, Wolff (1967) suggests integrating aspects of Piaget and Werner and Kaplan (1963) with psychoanalytic theory to develop a more complete view of early language acquisition. Drucker (1975) draws on both cognitive and psychoanalytic theory to develop an integrated multifunctional view of toddler play. These are "specialized" theories—of early language and play, respectively; they represent deepening rather than widening.

inquiry. First, and most general, the belief that progress in social science depends on establishing metatheoretical frameworks to provide means for understanding, comparing and evaluating the deep level assumptions and "ways of working" that characterize different theories within a given field. Recent writings by Bernstein (1978) and Giddens (1976), among many others, represent the prevalence of this concern. It seems to me that metatheorizing should move toward multiperspectival schemata: The kind of focus afforded by Pepper's theory of world hypotheses needs to be supplemented by other ways of considering theory, such as that proposed here in the concept of dominant foci. Second, we are only at the beginning of thinking about what makes for fruitful theory combination—what constitutes an "integrated" as compared with an "eclectic" position, a "whole" as compared with a "partial" psychology. Third, and closely related to the preceding, we need to develop ways of conceptualizing how psychological theories change or develop—to focus on the forms of change as well as the specification of conditions under which change occurs.

REFERENCES

Abrams, M. *The mirror and the lamp.* New York: W. W. Norton, 1953.

Allport, G. W. *Personality: A psychological interpretation.* New York: Holt, 1937.

Allport, G. W. *Becoming: Basic considerations for a psychology of personality.* New Haven, Conn.: Yale University Press, 1955.

Barten, S. How does the child know: Origins of the symbol in the theories of Piaget and Werner. *Journal of the American Academy of Psychoanalysis.* 1980, *9,* 77–92.

Bernstein, R. J. The restructuring of social and political theory. Philadelphia: The University of Pennsylvania Press, 1978.

Biber, B. A learning-teaching paradigm integrating intellectual and affective processes. In E. M. Bower & W. G. Hollister (Eds.), *Behavior science frontiers in education.* New York: Wiley, 1967.

Biber, B. The "whole child," individuality and values in education. In J. E. Squire (Ed.), *A new look at progressive education.* Washington, D.C.: Association for Supervision and Curriculum Development, 1972.

Biber, B. A developmental-interaction approach: Bank Street College of Education. In M. C. Day & R. K. Parker (Eds.), *The preschool in action.* Boston: Allyn & Bacon, 1977.

Biber, B., Murphy, L., Woodcock, L., & Black, I. S. *Child life in school.* New York: Dutton, 1942.

Black, M. Models and archetypes. In M. Black, *Models and metaphors.* Ithaca, N.Y.: Cornell University Press, 1962. (Originally published, 1960.)

Burke, K. *A grammar of motives.* New York: Prentice Hall, 1945.

Cassirer, E. *Substance and function.* Boston: Dover, 1953. (Originally published, 1923.)

Chomsky, N. From a paper on theory and research strategies, presented at meetings of the Society for Philosophy and Psychology, Boston, 1978.

Chomsky, N. *Rules and representations.* New York: Columbia University Press, 1980.

Dollard, J., & Miller, N. E. *Personality and psychotherapy.* New York: McGraw-Hill, 1950.

Drucker, J. Toddler play: Some comments on its functions in the developmental process. *Psychoanalysis and Contemporary Science,* 1975, *4.*

Franklin, M. B., & Barten, S. *Heinz Werner's contribution to a psychology of experience.* Paper presented at meetings of the Eastern Psychological Association, Hartford, Conn., 1980.

Franklin, M. B., & Biber, B. Psychological perspectives on early childhood education: Some relations between theory and practice. In L. Katz (Ed.), *Current topics in early childhood education* (Vol. 1). Norwood, N.J.: Ablex, 1977.

Giddens, A. *New rules of sociological method.* New York: Basic Books, 1976.

Goldstein, K. *The organism.* New York: American Book, 1938.

Goldstein, K. *Human nature in the light of psychopathology.* Cambridge, Mass.: Harvard University Press, 1940.

Goodman, N. *Ways of worldmaking.* Indianapolis, Ind.: Hackett Publishing, 1978.

Gruber, H. E., & Barrett, P. H. *Darwin on man: A psychological study of creativity.* New York: Dutton, 1974.

Gruber, H. E. Darwin's "Tree of Nature" and other images of wide scope. In J. Wechsler (Ed.), *On aesthetics in science.* Cambridge, Mass.: MIT Press, 1978.

Hartmann, H. *Ego psychology and the problem of adaptation.* New York: International Universities Press, 1958. (Originally published, 1939.)

Hardesty, F. P. Louis William Stern: A new view of the Hamburg years. In *Psychology in Progress, Annals of the New York Academy of Sciences,* 1976, *270,* 31–44.

Hull, C. L. *Principles of behavior: An introduction to behavior theory.* New York: Appleton-Century-Crofts, 1943.

Kaplan, B. *Lectures on developmental psychology.* Unpublished manuscript. Clark University, Worcester, Mass. No date.

Kaplan, B. The study of language in psychiatry: The comparative-developmental approach and its application to symbolization and language in psychopathology. In S. Arieti (Ed.), *American handbook of psychiatry* (Vol. 3). New York: Basic Books, 1966.

Kaplan, B. Meditations on genesis. *Human Development,* 1967, *10,* 65–87.

Kaplan, B., Wapner, S., & Cohen, S. (Eds.). *Experiencing the environment.* New York: Plenum, 1976.

Kuhn, T. S. *The structure of scientific revolutions, 2nd ed.* Chicago: University of Chicago Press, 1970.

Langer, J. *Theories of development.* New York: Wiley, 1969.

Lewin, K. *Principles of topological psychology.* New York: McGraw-Hill, 1936.

Lewin, K. Defining the field at a given time. *Psychological Review,* 1943, *50,* 292–310.

Lewin, K. Behavior and development as a function of the total situation. In L. Carmichael (Ed.), *Manual of child psychology.* New York: Wiley, 1946.

Minuchin, P., Biber, B., Shapiro, E., & Zimiles, H. *The psychological impact of school experience.* New York: Basic Books, 1969.

Mischel, W. On the interface of cognition and personality: Beyond the person-situation debate. *American Psychologist,* 1979, *34,* 740–753.

Novikoff, A. B. The concept of integrative levels and biology. *Science,* 1945, *101,* 209–215.

Osgood, C. E. *Method and theory in experimental psychology.* New York: Oxford University Press, 1953.

Overton, W. F., & Reese, H. W. Models of development: Methodological implications. In J. R. Nesselroade & H. W. Reese (Eds.), *Life-span developmental psychology: Methodological issues.* New York: Academic Press, 1973.

Pepper, S. *World hypotheses.* Berkeley, Calif.: University of California Press, 1942.

Piaget, J. *The psychology of intelligence.* New York: Harcourt, Brace & Co., 1950.

Reese, H. W., & Overton, W. F. Models of development and theories of development. In L. R. Goulet and P. B. Baltes, Eds. *Life-span developmental psychology: Theory and research.* New York: Academic Press, 1970.

Schneirla, T. C. Instinctive behavior, maturation—experience and development. In B. Kaplan & S.

Wapner (Eds.), *Perspectives in psychological theory: Essays in honor of Heinz Werner.* New York: International Universities Press, 1960.

Schneirla, T. C. Levels in the psychological capacities of animals. In L. R. Aronson, E. Tobach, J. S. Rosenblatt, & D. S. Lehrman (Eds.), *The selected writings of T. C. Schneirla.* San Francisco: W. H. Freeman and Co., 1972. (Originally published, 1949.)

Senn, M. J. E. Insights on the child development movement in the United States. *Monographs of the Society for Research in Child Development,* 1975, *40* (No. 161).

Shapiro, E., & Biber, B. The education of young children: A developmental–interaction approach. *Teachers College Record,* September, 1972, *74*(1).

Skinner, B. F. *The behavior of organisms: An experimental analysis.* New York: Appleton-Century-Crofts, 1938.

Vygotsky, L. *Thought and language.* Cambridge, Mass.: MIT Press, 1962.

Wapner, S. *Transitions of persons-in-environments: Some critical transitions.* Presidential address, Eastern Psychological Association meetings, Hartford, Conn. 1980.

Wapner, S., Kaplan, B., & Cohen, S. An organismic–developmental perspective for understanding transactions of men-in-environments. *Environment and Behavior,* 1973, *5,* 255–289.

Wapner, S., & Werner, H. *Perceptual development.* Worcester, Mass.: Clark University Press, 1957.

Wapner, S., & Werner, H. An experimental approach to body perception from the organismic-developmental point of view. In S. Wapner & H. Werner (Eds.), *The body percept.* New York: Random House, 1965.

Werner, H. William Stern's personalistics and psychology of personality. *Character and Personality,* 1938, *7,* 109–125.

Werner, H. *Comparative psychology of mental development.* New York: International Universities Press, 1957. (Originally published, 1940.)

Werner, H. Interrelationships between perception and personality: A symposium. Introductory remarks. *Journal of Personality,* 1949, *18,* 2–5.

Werner, H. The concept of development from a comparative and organismic point of view. In S. S. Barten & M. B. Franklin, (Eds.), *Developmental processes: Heinz Werner's selected writings* (Vol. 1). New York: International Universities Press, 1978. (Originally published, 1957.)

Werner, H. *Developmental processes: Heinz Werner's selected writings* (Vol. 1, 2). (S. S. Barten and M. B. Franklin, Eds.). New York: International Universities Press, 1978.

Werner, H., & Kaplan, B. *Symbol formation.* New York: Wiley, 1963.

Witken, H. A., Dyk, R. B., Faterson, H. F., Goodenough, D. R., and Karp, S. A. *Psychological differentiation: Studies of development.* New York: Wiley, 1962.

Wolff, P. Cognitive considerations for a psychoanalytic theory of language acquisition. In R. S. Holt (Ed.), Motives and thought. *Psychological Issues, 5,* 1967.

Wozniak, R. H. Verbal regulation of motor behavior—Soviet research and non-Soviet replications. *Human Development,* 1972, *15,* 13–57.

RECIPROCAL RELATIONS IN THE FIRST YEARS OF LIFE

It is perhaps in the first years of life that the interrelations of different aspects of psychological functioning are most apparent. Yet it is only in recent years that research devoted to demonstrating these interdependencies has been undertaken. The kinds of insights to be gained from opening research inquiry to multivariate questions are exemplified in the work of Sibylle Escalona and Leon Yarrow.

Escalona defines and illustrates reciprocal relationships in an ongoing longitudinal study of young children. She demonstrates the interrelation of social, emotional, and motor development and cognitive progressions during the toddler years and elucidates some early relations between developing control of impulses and concept formation.

Yarrow discusses the interdependence of different aspects of development in infancy; he describes studies of the relationship between infant characteristics and maternal behavior and presents case vignettes illustrating variation in maternal behavior toward infants of different temperaments. Relations between the infant and the environment are shown to be highly interactive; the characteristics of the infant play a significant role in determining maternal care giving responses.

The Reciprocal Role of Social and Emotional Developmental Advances and Cognitive Development During the Second and Third Years of Life

Sibylle K. Escalona
Yeshiva University

The term developmental–interaction can have a variety of meanings. It is of course the label that Dr. Biber and the Bank Street group have chosen to identify their conceptual approach to education. Yet in other contexts the term has come to refer to models of thought and/or to research methodologies that emphasize a multivariable approach, an approach that precludes simple cause and effect or antecedent–consequent relationships and seeks to identify clusters or constellations of forces and conditions that operate simultaneously. Lastly the term interactional places emphasis on part–whole relationships and therefore implies that any behavior or event must be viewed in context. As if that were not broad enough, sometimes the term is used to indicate that what is being studied are relationships not within a single system, such as perception, but among systems, such as the relationship between affective and cognitive behaviors. The label "interactional" could easily become something like a slogan, or also it may be reified as though it referred to a specific thing or belief.

I shall therefore begin with a definition of the term as it will be used in what is to follow. In my definition interaction is present whenever it can be demonstrated that a lawful relationship exists between or within systems, of such a kind that any change in *A* influences *B* and vice versa. In other words, a process is described as interactive when and only when there is genuine reciprocity. Thus, when one is able to show that a factor we call affective, for example, a notably high level of aggression, influences something in the cognitive domain, for example, mastery of orthography, I would label the phenomenon as interactive only if it could be demonstrated that what happens in the cognitive domain also exerts an influence on the level of aggression. Just to complete the pattern by way of an absurd example, if it turned out that both aggression and spelling were simultaneously controlled by a third factor, I would not think that we had shown interaction to be at work. Thus, interaction becomes but one of many possible and demonstrable kinds of systematic relationships that exist in nature.

It is true of course, as has been stressed by Biber and many others, that an overall ideology or point of view cannot wholly be divorced from even such a narrow definition. Our studies and observations imply a choice about the kind of relationship we are looking for. The classical experiment is designed to show primarily relationships of dependency, whereas a sequential microanalysis of mother–child or teacher–child behavior sequences is, by definition, a study of mutual regulation and interaction; it would fail to identify such dependent relationships as may be operating at the same time. The experimental analysis, on the other hand, would fail to identify such reciprocal relationships as may be operating at the same time. For the study of child development, as well as many other areas, I regard the contextual and interactive approach as uniquely rewarding and illuminating. Such a statement does not imply that noninteractional models are invalid. On the contrary, I think that many different questions must be asked of nature, that the question asked determines the appropriate methodology, and that the aggregate of results pertaining to a given issue can and should be synthesized so as to provide a maximum of understanding. It is true that I feel critical of generalizations that may be made on the basis of the less encompassing but more precise investigations. For instance, much that has been discovered from laboratory work in the areas of perception and of learning cannot, I think, be generalized to how people function in the classroom or in life situations generally. But then, the same criticism can be leveled against overgeneralizations based on multifaceted interactional studies.

Let me now turn to some ideas and observations, as well as some experimental data, that concern reciprocal relationships between what had perhaps best be called psychosocial aspects of development and cognitive progressions during the toddler years. This is not a formal report based on the results of research. The relevant data are still being collected and await analysis. Rather, some examples of what I believe to be truly interactive processes that occur during the first few years of life are presented, as examples of a model. Further, each of these issues has been selected for intensive study during the conduct of a research program currently under way.[1] The factual and observational material is drawn from the data already collected.

The first item has to do with reciprocal relationships between four seemingly separate developmental changes that take place between the ages of approximately 12 to 16 months in most children. Namely, the development of independent upright locomotion; change in the relationship to mother or whoever is a

[1] *Critical Issues in the Development of Infants at Biologic and Social Risk.* Supported jointly by a grant from the T.W. Grant Foundation, the National Foundation March of Dimes, and the Barbra Streisand Foundation.

primary caretaker; the cognitive advances in relation to the comprehension of spatial relationships; and finally the prelanguage learning of conventional gestures of communication.

There is no doubt that walking independently is a maturational event. Healthy children get up and go of their own accord, with or without encouragement or teaching from the environment. Our hypothesis concerns the impact of this newfound ability on other facets of development. Although children creep away from and toward things before they walk, they are basically subject to being picked up, moved somewhere else, and put down again. And even when they traverse spaces, and do in fact follow their mothers, the face-to-floor orientation gives little opportunity to gauge distances. I think it is no accident that systematic changes in the relationship to mother occur within the weeks and months following the acquisition of relatively effortless directed walking. Without specifying in detail it will suffice to say that these changes (extensively described by Mahler [Mahler, Pine, & Bergman, 1975] but also by others [Erikson, 1963]) refer to a growing awareness of separateness, of a kind of body self, and hence also lead to lessening and gradual disappearance of taken-for-granted symbiotic unity with mother. There begins to be a sense also of psychological distance, difference from, and degree of independence of the mother.

Consider the new situations that are encountered by someone who has just begun to walk alone. With young toddlers, most of the time, the starting point is somewhere close to mother. When they first walk, they mostly walk away from her. Then they turn, see the distance, and walk back to her vicinity. Much more frequently than before they have the experience of leaving and returning by their own efforts and under their own control and, significantly, they do this in what can be called a shared space. Like adults they are now scanning the surround from the upright position, which permits not only a perception of distances, but also of obstacles, paths around them, and detours. I believe that it is the oft repeated experience of going to, from, and around that reinforces both the cognitive mapping of spatial routes and the awareness of the distant–close dimension in terms of feelings about self and mother. This heightened sense of physical and psychological distance tends to activate simultaneously two conflicting impulses, namely, those toward independence, because roaming and climbing are joyous and eagerly sought out activities for healthy children. But the very exercise of these satisfying functions also brings the desire for unbroken contact and communication with the mother. And from this inevitable dilemma is born the need for conventional communication, which is soon to lead also to the first words. By conventional communication I mean signals that convey a specific message. Among the earliest are pointing at something to direct another's attention to it, the lateral headshake to designate negation, and holding things outward and upward in a showing gesture. Thus it is hypothesized that walking freely leads to changes in experience patterns that inevitably crystallize and make more vivid than before the very feelings of excitement, joy, and apprehension that move the mother–child relationship to more mature and less symbiotic levels. Further, these changes in the mother–child relationship lead to a readiness to participate in the conventionally structured network of adult communication by gesture and by word.

The last portion of the hypothesis, having to do with spatial comprehension at the level of stage V in Piaget's terms, does little more than to explicate what Piaget has said about the matter (Piaget, 1952). It is by walking about that children learn about spatial configurations of the "behind," "beneath," "above," "inside of," "connected," and "discontinuous" variety. Once this knowledge has been acquired on the sensorimotor level it can be applied to problem solving, as in the use of containers, tower building, and other cognitive achievements normally noted during the second year of life. Stage V of sensorimotor intelligence corresponds to this level of comprehension. I should add that it is not proposed that these various developmental changes occur during the same time interval. As best as we can determine from our studies, there is a period lasting weeks and perhaps months during which walking is exercised and spatial comprehension is acquired, but neither the sense of self nor the corresponding sense of unbroken unity with the mother person are any different from what they were before. This is the phase, often observed between 12 and 15 months, when you see mothers run after their mobile youngsters to retrieve them, especially in large areas such as waiting rooms, parks, and supermarkets. If and when their heedless wanderings are interrupted by an awareness that mother is not in sight, their behavior is quite the same as when, on other occasions, mother leaves them; they behave as if mother had abandoned them. It takes time and endless repetition for new experience patterns to induce changes in behavior organization.

What makes this notion of how things go together interactional is that all of the connections can be seen as two-way streets. If a child has very little opportunity to exercise his walking abilities, even indoors, this may well slow down the process of individuation/separation. But on the other hand, there are innumerable other pathways through which a growing sense of separateness from mother comes about, and as this intensifies so will the urge to walk and the interest in learning communication signals that span distances. Or also, we had children under study whose relationship with mother remained grossly immature for an unusual length of time. These children could walk but they showed little impetus to exercise this function, thus depriving themselves not only of more complex motor skills but also of a major way of learning about spatial relationships. My image is of a constant flux of changing comprehensions, changes in excecutive capabilities, changes in predominant feeling states, and more, all of which together constitute a labile system of mutual regulation. The human organism, especially when young and still relatively undifferentiated, is so constituted that a change or transformation in any one sphere has of necessity, a shaping influence on other spheres. Thus cognitive level plays a vital role in determining how the child interprets his experience and hence codetermines which affective patterns can arise. But equally, dominant needs, paramount tensions, or major styles of deriving gratification play a role in shaping cognitive activity into some channels and not others. They can act as stimulants or inhibitants to curiosity and affect the rate of learning, and so on.

The second example of the kind of interactional relationships that I believe characterize developmental processes in general refers to an important transition or change in both functioning and structure that takes place during the third year of life. In the cognitive domain this is the time when simple concepts and categories crystallize and mature sufficiently so that children can not only label objects as to color and type (I mean chairs as distinct from tables or red as distinct from blue), but can actively employ these concepts by matching and sorting. Sometime during the second half of the third year one typically sees children spontaneously identify "a car," "another car," "same thing"—they tend to scrutinize the environment for categories of interest to them and to take satisfaction in labeling them as such. And in spontaneous play one sees them group objects, as in bringing together all the toy cars, separating them from the dolls, the airplanes, or the toy dishes. Most developmental theories understand this newfound cognitive capacity for abstraction as the result of a decrease in egocentricity, that is, as based upon the circumstance that children are now able to recognize and appraise objects and their properties as distinct and separate from the immediate context of goals and feeling states. Piaget, Heinz Werner (Werner & Kaplan, 1963), and psychoanalytic ego psychology alike have described the direction of this change from sensorimotor unity between the acting subject and the acted-upon object to a separation between subject and object as "distancing." It is only after there is a felt and known gap between "me" and "it" that the diverse properties that objects have in common, such as shape, color, or function, can be recognized as attributes of the thing and thus can constitute genuine classes or concepts based on abstraction. Psychoanalytic theory postulates that this capacity for distancing becomes possible as another ego function begins to operate, which is termed "capacity for delay," or impulse control. Chronologically speaking, it is true that prior to and during the first half of the third year and before the emergence of concept formation at the level I described, a degree of impulse control is observed and expected. Descriptively this refers to the fact that anger, fatigue, distress, and other states of excitation are no longer expressed without restraint. Thus, youngsters begin to make a real effort to suppress crying; they begin to modulate movement impulse and can obey the command "sit still" at least for a little while. They begin to subdue temper tantrums, and the adult request "just wait a minute" is no longer responded to as equivalent to a straight "no."

What are some of the ways in which impulse control—the necessary precondition for concept formation—is acquired? Our notion is that it first arises in the context of affect-laden social interchanges that necessarily occur late in the second and throughout the third year of life. It is at this time that children are gradually compelled to internalize and understand social demands for conformity and control. This is the time when children "get into everything" and must be taught not to touch dangerous objects such as the stove knobs and electric outlets. The enterprises that appeal to a 2-year-old are bound to lead to conflict as they endanger household objects and themselves. They are not supposed to play in the toilet bowl, nor to empty each and every drawer, nor to bite people or pull their hair, nor to upend soup bowls, etc. As these initially entirely innocent endeavors are met with physical restraint, with scolding, and with punishment, youngsters learn to recognize their wishes, angers, and impulses as internal to themselves and thus begin to accept some responsibility for their misdeeds. Because uncontrolled behavior meets with disapproval, because also they learn to anticipate and recognize which action patterns are forbidden, and because the approval and affection of important adults is necessary for a sense of well-being, children are motivated and enabled to impose controls on their own behavior. As we all know, 2-year-olds develop a keen sense of good and bad, both in relation to themselves and to everything in their environment. Our observations of many toddlers indicate to us that once at least partial control of impulses has emerged in such highly charged situations, it is generalized and becomes a part of functioning in affectively neutral situations also. In other words, we think that the stormy encounters between toddlers and their caretakers generate delay capacity, which in turn allows cognitive distancing, sharper separation between acting self and the acted-upon object, and hence, early concept formation.

In order to specify how these connections are anything but straight linear progressive steps, but rather a cluster of interdependent and overlapping events, I need to mention some of the empirical support for this hypothesis. In the longitudinal study referred to earlier the hypothesis just described is one of the areas selected for fairly systematic study of especially important developmental transitions. Impulse control and its absence are readily observed, and the degree to which classification and simple concept formation are understood and actively employed in problem solving is tapped by standard developmental tests. In both areas we added special standard procedures designed to elicit and assess the presence and degree of both these competencies in a variety of situations and in a quantitative fashion. We see a sample of over 100 children at 28 months and again at 34 and 40 months (they have been seen regularly since they were neonates). The special procedures at the 28-months visit include a whole set of situations in which children have to wait, for a brief moment must not touch, are slightly frustrated as desired objects are removed, and the like. Also, each instance when the mother or the examiner uses persuasion, coercion, or prohibition in any context are scored and tallied. The same is done for all spontaneously arising occasions when these children encounter obstacles in executing self-chosen activities, such as climbing or trying to move a piece of furniture (2-year-olds are great furniture movers!).

Typically, at 28 months, impulse control is a central issue. Examples of total failure, when the youngster cannot wait at all or screams his displeasure and acts it out, occur for most, as do valiant efforts to modulate excitement that are of very short duration, as well as instances where—with visible effort—the child is patient and contained. Because so many relevant occasions occur during a 2- or 3-hour observation period, a clear-cut pattern usually emerges, descriptive of how much headway the child has made on this difficult road. At this age, simple classifications are often understood, both in word and deed. But active matching or sorting is rarely seen in our sample, and indeed the placement of such items on intelligence tests shows that such things as sorting buttons by color are not normative until well into the third year. By 34 months, the growth of impulse control is striking in every one of our normal children, that is, by comparison to what they were like at 28 months. The active use of simple concepts is seen in some and not in others. All the data are not in, but so far it has been true that only those who showed at least a moderate level of impulse control at 28 months can engage in active matching by 34 months. Those who do show reasonable levels of control at 34 months, but had little or none at 28 months, are the ones who cannot yet actively apply concepts in relation to manipulative tasks. It is necessary to remember that, although there is a relationship between matching and overall intelligence, overall cognitive status does not account for the variation in this particular cognitive ability of matching.

This is an especially good example for interactive processes because the socialization process takes such different forms in different families. In some, a nice balance between allowing scope for toddlerlike activities and well-chosen areas where demands are made and enforced (plus a host of far more complex aspects of family atmosphere and mother–child relationships) facilitates the emergence of impulse control. In some the taboos are very many and rigidly enforced, yet at the same time affection and closeness between child and parents is intense, and the result can be a child who is overcontrolled and so eager to be "good" that spontaneity suffers. In our sample it is precisely children from such a background who are outstanding for precocious ability to abstract.

Another of the many constellations that is often seen is a combination of harsh discipline with respect to the many taboos and extraordinary indulgence amounting to infantilization in other areas, so that, developmentally speaking, both too much and too little is expected of the child. This appears to be one of the situations that makes impulse control very hard to come by. These are the youngsters who act like little tyrants, who storm against restrictions that remain externally imposed, and to whom the term "spoiled" can be applied with real meaning. These same children can be sophisticated social manipulators and bright in a lot of ways—but abstraction and its cognitive precursors show a developmental lag. On the other hand, there are also individual temperamental differences related to activity level and to the urgency or intensity of impulses, which make self-control easier or harder to come by—on a basis other than interpersonal relationships and child rearing practices. For some children, the socialization process is less tumultous than is usual, impulse control and abstraction capacity can then be acquired more readily—barring extremely unfavorable environmental circumstances. And interaction is seen most clearly in the degree to which partial acquisition of distancing and of concept formation, once they begin to operate, smooth the way for the later phases in the establishment of impulse control. A child clearly aware of the fact that eating utensils, ashtrays, balls, and toy trucks are separate classes of objects has a much easier time accommodating to the fact that the identical activity of throwing or rolling objects is appropriate and permitted with some of them, and not with others. He can apply a degree of abstraction to his understanding of the social complexities of his life. Thus impulse control improves and, on that basis, so does the cognitive advance.

As you will recognize, in order to state these relationships as we see them, it has been necessary to lift them from their context—in other words, to abstract some features of behavior from the total behavior stream. All the functions mentioned, from walking effortlessly to learning to talk, to the developmental level of the mother—child relationship, and the rest, are influenced by innumerable other variables, both within the child and impinging from without. Some of you may be familiar with a prototypic model of behavior and development that I have formulated elsewhere (Escalona, 1968). Space does not permit an elaboration here of the manner in which the notion of experience patterns, as distinct from the many forces and conditions that determine them, can help detect regularities and order amidst the confusing multiplicity of component elements. Here it will have to suffice to say that if a physical disability should hinder walking independently, or if a particularly distant or otherwise deviant mother personality should do the same for the individuation/separation process, we think that spatial comprehension, communication, and cognitive learning will thereby be altered in a fashion consistent with these hypotheses. Note that I said altered, not done away with. Children who cannot walk at all also learn about space, achieve separateness from the mother, and learn to abstract. But the implication is that they will do so with some delay and also will get there by alternate routes, at least in part. In fact, given a normal CNS, and barring continous and extreme deprivation or trauma in life circumstances, all children go through these developmental phases; they get there somehow. On the other hand, if you think of school-age children or of adults, you realize that the impulse control issue remains an active one throughout life and that, although no normal person lacks it altogether, some of us have more trouble in that area than others. I chose this example because educators know what research has also shown, namely, that greater levels of impulsivity are generally antithetical to the cultivation of the higher levels of abstraction. In short, I think that for each older child and adult, the vulnerabilities and cognitive as well as behavioral characteristics that define an individual personality bear a systematic relationship to the earlier experience patterns that made us what we are.

REFERENCES

Erikson, E. H. *Childhood and society* (2nd ed.). New York: Norton, 1963.

Escalona, S. K. *The roots of individuality: Normal patterns of development in infancy.* Chicago: Aldine, 1968.

Mahler, M. S., Pine, F., & Bergman, A. *The psychological birth of the infant.* New York: Basic Books, 1975.

Piaget, J. *The origins of intelligence in children.* New York: International Universities Press, 1952.

Werner, H., and Kaplan, B. *Symbol Formation.* New York: Wiley, 1963.

6 Perspectives on Interactional Research

Leon J. Yarrow
National Institute of Child Health and Human Development

INTRODUCTION

The interactional view represents a significant shift in psychology from a simple, unidirectional, cause–effect orientation to a much more complex bidirectional orientation. For a long time, psychologists have placed inordinate value on reduction of complex phenomena to simple elements of behavior that could be studied in isolated situations. Paradoxically, the overevaluation of reductionism probably stems from recognition of the subjectivity and tremendous complexity of most psychological data. To avoid being overwhelmed by complexity and to guard against subjectivity, we have made valiant sometimes extreme efforts to objectify and simplify data.

The gradual shift to an interactional orientation over the past decade reflects a growing recognition of the limitations of the reductionist model. Reductionism and analysis of single variable relationships have contributed to simple understandings of some simple behaviors. Although this model may be useful in the early stages of defining problems and in investigating relationships, it has obvious limitations for dealing with the complex multivariate questions with which psychology must ultimately be concerned. It is questionable whether research on this level will continue to make a significant contribution to the advancement of theory or will yield knowledge useful in dealing with practical problems.

In this chapter I shall discuss two kinds of interdependencies; the interrelationships among cognitive, emotional, social, and motivational development, and the reciprocal interactions between characteristics of the child and the parent's behavior with the child. (See Escalona in this volume for discussion of similar issues.)

INTERDEPENDENCE OF MOTOR, COGNITIVE, SOCIAL, AND EMOTIONAL DEVELOPMENT IN INFANCY

During infancy, motor, cognitive, emotional, and social development are delicately intertwined. The development of gross and fine motor skills influence cognitive, social, and emotional development, and these developments in turn influence motor skills. The acquisition of fine motor skills enables the infant to explore objects and to learn about their properties and functions. The refinement of fine motor skills ultimately leads to feelings of object mastery. By producing effects, securing feedback from objects, managing to obtain objects by reaching around barriers, the infant acquires a sense of control. These activities are likely to be rewarding; the positive feelings associated with such activities in turn encourage the infant to practice and improve fine motor coordination.

There are similar relations between the development of gross motor skills and cognitive development. Through locomotion the child learns about spatial relations concretely, and in time is able to translate this concrete knowledge into concepts of above and below, behind, near and far.

These examples illustrate interdependencies of skills in which one builds upon another. Another kind of interdependency is illustrated by the association between growth in gross motor abilities and the development of language. When the child is able to move away from the caregiver, communication by gesture becomes unsatisfactory, the infant must learn to communicate with him or her when he or she is out of view and at a distance; thus there is incentive to use language. Most infants learn very early that crying is likely to bring someone to them, but this undifferentiated form of communication may not lead to behavior appropriate to satisfy them. More specific communication is required. The infant learns that through sounds he or she can influence the behavior of others and through words can gain more precise control. This control may be associated with a sense of social mastery. The child's verbal communication is likely to stimulate the verbal communication of others and thus, through this reciprocal interaction, language comprehension and vocabulary are enlarged.

Similarly, as the infant develops gross and fine motor skills and through practice perfects them, he or she becomes increasingly independent of caregivers. The ability to engage in independent exploration of the world helps in consolidating awareness of the boundaries of his or her body and in distinguishing self and environment. This development contributes to the awareness and consolidation of object permanence, and also enhances feelings of autonomy.

At first when the infant leaves the mother or the mother goes out of his or her field of vision, the baby may assume that the mother is gone, that she has been lost forever, and if the infant is unable to walk independently, he or she cannot find her. With the development of the capacity to crawl or walk toward the mother, the infant can find her and also realizes that he or she has the capacity to regulate distance from the mother, to leave her, and to return to her on his or her own volition. This is a striking example of the reciprocal relationship between the infant's motor and cognitive development and the development of feelings about the mother or other caregivers and feelings about self (see Escalona, this volume).

The infant's experiences with responsive people and objects contribute to an awareness that he or she can have effects. When the infant vocalizes, parents may come. When the infant shakes a rattle it makes a sound. Awareness of a relationship between these actions and these events may at first be transitory. In time and with the development of memory, the relationship between the infant's own actions and consequent events becomes consolidated. The infant develops a contingency awareness (Watson, 1966), a generalized expectancy (Lewis & Goldberg, 1969), that he or she can have an impact on the environment. These feelings of mastery may in time become associated with positive feelings about the self, with a positive self-evaluation.

For a long time we have been aware that emotions influence the processing of stimulus events. We know that feelings in adults influence performance on cognitive tasks, but the relationships are not simple. Some emotions, under certain circumstances, enhance alertness, they serve to focus attention and increase persistence on difficult tasks; other emotions may lead to disorganization of behavior and an incapacity for clear thinking and may also decrease alertness and inhibit or slow down responses. Emotions may also seriously bias perception of stimuli; how a child sees a stimulus–event is certainly influenced by immediate feeling states. Feelings may facilitate or they may interfere with learning; they may enhance attention to stimuli or they may bias perception and distort interpretation of events. The particular aspects of a stimulus or situation of which the child is aware and his or her interpretation of the situation will differ when the child is in a state of anger and when he or she is joyful.

Although the influence of emotions on the child's perception of events and on learning has long been accepted, the reciprocal interactions between cognitive, social, and emotional development have not been given explicit attention until recently. Basically, the experience of emotions, whether it be fear of strangers, a loud noise, or a new situation, involves cognition to some extent. The infant must first be able to discriminate gross differences in stimuli, then he or she is aware of subtle variations; similarities are also perceived on several levels. The perception of similarities in overt characteristics is the simplest level, the level on which the young infant functions. The young child is able to discriminate familiar and strange people and familiar and novel objects. Thus, the infant's wary response to strangers, as well as his or her excitement and pleasureable response when the familiar caregiver reappears after a brief absence, show the interdependence of emotion, perceptual discrimination, and person permanence. On another level, the capacity to be aware of similarities on a symbolic level, or to relate familiar and strange stimuli to past experiences and to integrate remote and recent events, requires memory, object and person permanence, as well as the ability to generalize beyond an immediate context. It is evident that the links between cognition and emotion become increasingly complex as the child grows older (Yarrow, 1979).

Most emotions are directly or indirectly associated with people. For the infant to be able to invest emotionally in the outside world, he or she must have developed the capacity to differentiate self from the physical and human environment. The differentiation of self from the environment is dependent on other more basic cognitive processes. Some maintain that this capacity is dependent on the development of object permanence, a capacity about which some controversy still exists regarding the age at which it appears. Piaget (1952) suggests that object permanence does not occur until around 10 months, whereas studies by Bower (1971) and Gardner (1971) indicate that 5- to 7-month-old infants search for missing objects and anticipate their reappearance. It is difficult to reconcile the view that object permanence does not occur until after 6 months with our firm belief that the infant is sensitive to the caregiver's behavior and feelings and establishes a rudimentary relationship with him or her even in the first days of life. Simple logic would lead one to assume that for the infant to be able to develop an intense, loving relationship with a given person, he or she must have the capacity to remember that person in his or her absence. (One might contend that this early rudimentary relationship may be simply a recognition of and adaptation to a frequently encountered stimulus–configuration, but the latter is an explanation tailored to fit a hypothesis rather than to fit research findings.)

In the first months of life, crying is primarily a response to physical discomfort; as the infant matures, physical instigators of affect become less significant and psychological instigators become increasingly important. Emde and Harmon (1972) contend that the shift from a smile primarily induced by internal states to the social smile, in response to another person, is an important milestone, indicating that the infant is able to express pleasure voluntarily. It may also indicate that the infant has begun to differentiate self from the environment. This differentiation of self and environment in turn is necessary for the child to be able to monitor his or her own behavior and feelings and to exercise control over the expression of emotions (Spitz, 1965).

In examining the impact of emotional and social developmental changes on cognitive development and the effects of cognitive attainments on emotional and social development, these reciprocal interdependencies become evident. These relationships are not one-way cause-and-effect relationships; they are bidirectional interactions. The ability to walk permits the toddler to move on his or her own, and being able to do so heightens the child's sense of control over self and environment. These feelings in turn motivate the infant to perfect locomotor skills that increase control over larger segments of the environment. The acquisition of locomotor skills also enables the infant to move away from the mother; the fact that the child takes the initiative in leaving the mother rather than the mother leaving the child places separation in an entirely different perspective. The ability to walk increases feelings of autonomy, it allows the toddler to come close to the mother or to leave her and pursue his or her own interests. Thus we see an interactive process in which the early development of skills leads to satisfying consequences that in turn motivate the infant to perfect these skills. There are similar reciprocal interactions between affect, exploratory behavior, and mastery. To the extent that positive feelings enhance the child's attention to an object, he or she may engage in more visual and tactile exploration of objects and thus arrive at increased understanding of their properties and functions. This knowledge in turn contributes to the ability to obtain feedback from objects or to solve problems, which may then enhance feelings of mastery and positive self-evaluation.

In considering the interdependencies among affective, cognitive, social, and motivational functions, many complex research issues have been highlighted. In addition, there are developmental issues. For example, one might ask whether the degree of interdependency is greater during infancy than it is later in life. As the child becomes more differentiated, might there be greater independence between areas of functioning?

INTERACTIONS BETWEEN INFANT CHARACTERISTICS AND THE PHYSICAL AND SOCIAL ENVIRONMENTS

Another aspect of interdependency that has only recently been given explicit recognition is the interaction between the infant and the environment. For a long time in developmental psychology we have looked at the effect of stimuli in the inanimate environment and parental behavior on the infant. We have thought of the infant as a simple recipient of stimulation and largely ignored the infant's influence on the environment; only recently have we come to recognize that these influences are bidirectional.

The revived interest in temperamental characteristics present at birth (Escalona, 1968; Thomas, Chess, Birch, Hertzig, & Korn, 1968) has sensitized us to the fact that the infant's characteristics influence interactions with the environment. Infants differ in general alertness, in sensitivity to auditory, visual, and tactile stimuli, in how easily they are upset and how readily they can be soothed, in their capacity to buffer stress. Parents also show a great range of variation in their sensitivity to the infant's characteristics and likes and dislikes; they also differ in their feelings about the dependency demands of the infant. Other variations in personal–social characteristics of parents such as activity level, ease of being upset, tolerance for frustration and the "fit" between parents and infants in these characteristics may also affect their interactions.

Two types of interactions between infant and parental characteristics can be distinguished, defensive and eliciting. In defensive interactions the infant responds selectively to stimuli through his or her special sensitivities. These sensitivities may screen or modulate the impact of the environment on the infant. If the young infant is especially sensitive to auditory or visual stimuli, he or she may effectively shut out loud sounds or bright lights, or the ambulatory infant may move away from the vicinity of the noise or light. The young child may also elicit certain kinds of behavior from others. The caregiver's behavior toward the infant is at least partly a response to the cues the infant gives about likes or dislikes; it is also a response to his or her subjective perception of the infant's characteristics. One infant may actively invite vigorous play; another infant who is seen as delicate or sensitive may induce inhibited, careful, or tense handling.

There are several ways in which the interaction between the infant's characteristics and the environment can be studied. One can assess temperament very early, preferably in the neonatal period, and investigate relationships between defined temperamental characteristics and concurrent parental behavior or behavior later in infancy. Another design is to study the concurrent behavior of a caregiver to two infants, preferably infants who differ distinctly in salient characteristics. One limitation of the first approach is that neonatal characteristics tend to be unstable; in general, high relationships have not been found between characteristics of the neonate and the 4-week-old infant. The second design is difficult to implement. It is extremely difficult to find caregivers who are simultaneously caring for two infants of similar age with distinctly different characteristics. Except for nonidentical twins, who are likely to be similar in many ways, such a situation exists only in group care or in foster care. We present some findings from studies using both of these designs, one in which relationships between neonatal measures of infant temperament and mother–infant interaction at 4 weeks and at 6 months were examined, the other in which foster mothers' behaviors towards different infants were studied.

Relationships Between Infant Characteristics and Maternal Behavior

In an investigation of the interaction between neonatal temperamental characteristics and maternal caretaking patterns, 46 parents and their firstborn infants, 24 boys and 22 girls, were studied (Yarrow, Soule, Standley, Duchowny, & Copans, 1974). Infant characteristics were assessed at 3 days, using the Brazelton Neonatal Assessment procedures (Brazelton, 1973). Observations were made of mother–infant interaction in the home at 4 weeks and at 6 months. A number of relationships were found between neonatal characteristics and maternal behavior at 4 weeks. Alertness in boy infants was significantly related to several aspects of maternal care; the amount of stimulation the mother gave the infant ($r = .41*$), her sensitivity to the infant's expression of needs ($r = .42*$), the rapidity with which she responded to his signals of distress ($r = .44*$), the degree of physical closeness she showed in holding him ($r = .53**$), as well as to more

---

$*p < .05$
$**p < .01$

specific behaviors such as the amount of smiling to the infant ($r = .44*$). Maternal behavior was similarly influenced by the social orientation of male infants, as indicated by a measure of the infant's attentiveness to auditory and visual stimulation by people. This variable, social orientation, was significantly related to mothers' positive emotional expression towards male infants ($r = .57**$), to the total amount of positive stimulation she gave ($r = .40*$), to the degree of physical closeness she showed in holding him ($r = .59**$), as well as to the amount of smiling to boy infants ($r = .44**$). Consolability, a measure of the ease with which the infant responded to attempts to soothe him, was significantly related to the mother's sensitivity and responsiveness to male infants ($r = .43*$) and to her adaptation to the infant's needs and rhythms ($r = .45*$). The relationship to temperamental characteristics of female infants was quite different; only two characteristics of female infants were significantly related to maternal behavior. Irritability of infant girls was related to the amount of mutual regard between mother and infant, ($r = .46*$), consolability was positively related to the amount of positive stimulation mothers gave female infants ($r = .51*$).

Some significant long-term relationships were also found, relationships between neonatal characteristics and maternal caregiving at 6 months. For the group as a whole, the neonate's visual and auditory orientation to people was related to the mother's expression of positive affect ($r = .48*$), the amount of time she actively played with the infant ($r = .55**$) and the variety of inanimate stimulation she provided ($r = .40*$). Separate analyses by sex indicated that the relationships were much stronger for boys than for girls. Male infants' visual and auditory orientation was significantly correlated with mother's positive affect ($r = .66**$), with play ($r = .70**$), with variety of social stimulation ($r = .62**$), and with the variety of inanimate stimulation she provided ($r = .55**$), whereas there were no significant relationships between female infants' social orientation and maternal behavior. At this age, we found negative relationships between irritability in girls and both the mother's positive affect ($r = -.65**$) and the amount of time she played with the girl infant ($r = -.57**$), whereas there were essentially no relations between the irritability of boys and mother's behavior. These long-term relationships might be considered truly reciprocal. The neonate who is positively oriented to the mother receives more positive stimulation, which in turn reinforces the infant's positive responsiveness.

These findings seem to indicate that the mother's positive behaviors are significantly influenced by positive characteristics of male infants, whereas negative behaviors are elicited by negative characteristics of female infants. Alertness and social orientation both seem to be valued characteristics in male infants; moreover, the infant's social orientation might be seen by the mother as an expression of the male infant's responsiveness to her. Negative emotional expressiveness in female infants is associated with negative affect in the mother, whereas female infants who are easily consoled tend to receive positive stimulation from the mother.

It is difficult to understand the bases for the findings of significant relationship between characteristics of male infants in the first days of life and maternal behavior 4 weeks or 6 months later, especially in view of the instability of neonatal behavior. One explanation may be that the mother's perception of the infant becomes "set" very early and tends to persist in spite of changes in the infant. Patterns of parental behavior that are initiated during the first weeks of life may persist, despite changes in behavioral characteristics of the infant.

In a previous study, many more significant relationships were found between maternal behavior and the developmental status of female infants at 6 months than for male infants (Yarrow, Rubenstein, & Pedersen, 1975). At that time, we assumed that the infant's functioning on the Bayley scales and on measures of exploratory behavior were *outcome* variables, a consequence of early patterns of maternal behavior; however, the direction of the relationship is not clear. The possibility exists that female infants' developmental status and exploratory behavior might equally well have influenced maternal handling. From these two sets of data, one might conjecture that mothers may be more responsive to the *developmental functioning* of female infants, that is, to their cognitive characteristics, whereas they are more responsive to the personal–social characteristics of male infants. Obviously this is a purely speculative interpretation of two sets of findings. It is offered only to stimulate thinking and research on the interactions between sex of infant, infant characteristics, and maternal behavior.

Differences in Concurrent Maternal Behavior Toward Infants Differing in Temperament

A study of children in foster homes awaiting adoptive placement alerted us to the differences in a foster mother's behavior toward two infants who differed markedly in temperamental characteristics. The case materials to be presented are simply examples of these differences; they are not crucial tests of specific hypotheses or definitive findings regarding the interaction between infant temperament and maternal behaviors. The differential impact of two infants on the same mother was most dramatically evidenced by a foster mother who was caring for two infants of the same age and sex at the same time. These two male infants differed markedly on the broad dimension of activity–passivity, in vigor of expressing needs, in initiating social interactions and in level of responsiveness to people and objects. One infant, Arthur, was vigorous, active, and highly responsive to people; the other, Potter, was a very quiet and passive infant who showed limited interest in people, his responses to social approaches were consistently restrained. Potter made few demands, he cried infrequently and then usually managed only a weak whimper.

Arthur, from very early infancy, showed a high degree of alertness and vigor and a high level of awake motor activity. These characteristics were expressed in many ways—in vigorous sucking on the bottle, in forcefulness in expressing his needs, and in persistence in demands until he was satisfied. In contrast to Potter's lack of interest in people, Arthur was highly responsive to people and very early began to initiate social interaction. During the 6 months these infants were in this foster home, the initial differences in behavior characteristics and responsiveness became accentuated, and in turn the foster mother's behavior toward them became more divergent.

For both infants, feeding was on a demand basis. Although the foster mother was strongly committed to demand feeding, it became clear that within this pattern there were marked differences in the feeding experiences of the two infants. Arthur's greater forcefulness in making his needs known resulted in more immediate response; his hunger needs were consistently gratified with little delay. It was evident that the gratifications within the feeding process were also very different. Arthur was described by the mother as a cuddly baby. He responded positively to handling. In turn, the foster mother and members of the family enjoyed holding him. Observations of the feeding process indicated that it was a mutually gratifying experience for Arthur and the foster mother. Potter, on the other hand, was tense, restless, and apparently uncomfortable in being held. Consequently, his bottle was sometimes propped. Even when he was held, the foster mother's low physical involvement and the quality of tactile contact together with his high level of tension suggested that there was little gratification associated with feeding. (This observation points up the inadequacy of using gross categories such as demand or scheduled feeding as antecedent variables to be related to later behavior.) After a few months, Potter was allowed to lie in his crib much of the time and was essentially ignored.

The temperamental variations between these infants on the activity–passivity dimension and in reactions to tactile contact elicited different patterns of handling and evoked very different maternal feelings. Whereas the foster mother was extremely positive and accepting of all of Arthur's characteristics (his demandingness was valued as a sign of "spunk"), her evaluations of Potter were consistently negative. In contrast to the many projections made spontaneously about Arthur's future development, she never spoke about Potter's future. The pattern of isolation, deprivation, and basically negative evaluation of this infant was evident very early. The dissimilar patterns of care and the differences in feelings toward the two infants that were apparent before they were 3 months old became accentuated with time.

All mothers do not respond in the same way to given infant characteristics. The mother's reactions to the infant's level of activity and level of social responsiveness seem to be determined in part by her own motivational systems. Other foster mothers in our sample showed very different patterns of response toward quiet babies and active, expressive infants, reflecting the interaction between their values and preferences and the infants' characteristics. In one home, the foster mother initially was very effusive in expressing pleasure in both male infants for whom she was caring. In this home, Martin was a "perfect baby" from the beginning. He slept soundly, took his food well, rarely cried, almost never made any strong demands on the foster mother, and accepted contentedly everything that was given him. He enjoyed being held, but did not object when he was put down after being held. Elbert came into this home 11 days after Martin. He was developmentally advanced, showed a high waking activity level, and expressed his needs very forcefully and persistently. The foster mother very early characterized him as being demanding and irritable. He apparently was very sensitive to tactile contact, became unhappy when he was bathed or dressed or even when he was held. After repeated episodes of this kind of behavior, the foster mother concluded that Elbert did not like to be handled.

The amount and quality of physical contact, although initially comparable for the two infants, gradually diverged, so that by the end of the second month, the patterns of handling had become very different. The foster mother responded to Elbert's irritable demandingness with increased avoidance. Most striking was the difference in affective response to the two infants; her negative evaluation of Elbert became more pronounced with time. By the time these infants left this foster home, before they were 3 months old, they had elicited very different attitudes and patterns of behavior from the same mother figure.

These vignettes are prototypes of other cases that suggest that differences in activity level in infants may be associated with differences in such aspects of maternal care as immediacy of gratification, and amount of social and object stimulation. Disparities in level of muscular tension are likely to affect the amount and character of physical contact. Finally, these combinations of infant characteristics may influence very markedly the affective tone of the relationship between caregiver and child.

These case examples illustrate the interaction between patterns of infant behavior and maternal temperament and preferences. The characteristics of the infant elicit certain patterns of maternal behavior; the infant's responses to these behaviors in turn are likely to reinforce the maternal behavior. These cases also point up the difficulty in drawing simple conclusions about the effects of infant characteristics per se on maternal behavior. In one instance, the caregiver preferred a high-activity level baby; in the other, a low-activity baby who enjoyed tactile contact was preferred to a high-activity forceful baby who disliked tactile contact. The foster mother in the latter case was slow-moving and felt imposed upon by the quick, active child. These case vignettes emphasize that relationships between single temperamental variables and single variables of maternal behavior give only limited understanding of reciprocal interactions.

CONCLUSIONS

The interactional perspective introduces considerable complexity in our view of development. Our resistances to recognizing complexity are undoubtedly grounded in our early professional training. If psychologists are to begin to deal with the multidimensional interdependent realities of behavior in complex environments, it is imperative that we give up ancient models that are no longer useful, that we not cling to values inculcated in the impressionable period of our professional youth.

The shift to an interactional view has many implications. It has relevance to the formulation of the problems we study, the behaviors on which we focus, the contexts in which we obtain our primary data, the methods we use in collecting data, and our basic research designs. Obviously we must deal with larger units of behaviors that are by necessity more difficult to define, objectify, and measure. We do not yet have adequate research designs nor appropriate methods for studying cognitive, emotional, social, and motivational interdependencies. We are also in need of imaginative designs for investigating the reciprocal interactions between characteristics of the infant and characteristics of the environment (Bell & Harper, 1977). New observational and analytic techniques (Cairns, 1979; Sackett, 1977, 1978) enable us to study sequences of behavior more adequately than we have done in the past, but at the present time they deal only with small units of behavior and do not adequately capture the interactional process. There are many methodological problems as well. For example, in studying chains of events, it is difficult to set criteria for identifying the beginning and the end of a sequence (Yarrow & Anderson, 1979). We have made some progress in conceptualizing reciprocal interrelationships among infant characteristics and in conceptualizing reciprocal interactions between infant temperament and parental behavior. However, we still have far to go before we have an adequate theoretical framework or designs to begin to do justice to multidimensional interactive complexities.

REFERENCES

Bell, R. Q., & Harper, L. V. *Child effects on adults*. Hillsdale, N.J.: Lawrence Erlbaum Associates, 1977.
Bower, T. G. R. The object in the world of the infant. *Scientific American*, 1971, *11*, 182–193.
Brazelton, T. B. Neonatal Behavioral Assessment Scales. Phila: J. B. Lippincott, 1973.
Cairns, R. B. (Ed.). *The analysis of social interactions*. Hillsdale, N.J.: Lawrence Erlbaum Associates, 1979.
Emde, R., & Harmon, R. Endogenous and exogenous smiling systems in early infancy. *Journal of the American Academy of Child Psychiatry*, 1972, *11*, 177–200.
Escalona, S. *The roots of individuality*. Chicago: Aldine, 1968.
Gardner, J. *The development of object identity in the first six months of infancy*. Paper presented at the Biennial Meeting of the Society for Research in Child Development, Minneapolis, 1971.
Lewis, M., & Goldberg, S. Perceptual–cognitive development in infancy, a generalized expectancy model as a function of the mother–infant interaction. *Merrill–Palmer Quarterly*, 1969, *15*, 81–100.
Piaget, J. *The origins of intelligence in children*. New York: International Universities Press, 1952.
Sackett, G. P. (Ed.). *Observing behavior* (Vols. 1 and 2). Baltimore, Md.: University Park Press, 1977, 1978.
Spitz, R. A. *The first year of life*. New York: International Universities Press, 1965.

Thomas, A., Chess, S., Birch, H. G., Hertzig, M. D., & Korn, S. *Behavioral individuality in early childhood.* New York: University Press, 1968.

Watson, J. S. Development and generalization of "contingency awareness" in early infancy: Some hypotheses. *Merrill-Palmer Quarterly,* 1966, *2,* 123-126.

Yarrow, L. J. Emotional development. *American Psychologist,* 1979, *34*(10), 951-957.

Yarrow, L. J., & Anderson, B. J. Procedures for studying parent–infant interaction: A critique. In E. B. Thoman (Ed.), *Origins of the infant's social responsiveness.* Hillsdale, N.J.: Lawrence Erlbaum Associates, 1979.

Yarrow, L. J., Rubenstein, J. L., & Pedersen, F. A. *Infant and environment: Early cognitive and motivational development.* New York: Halsted, 1975.

Yarrow, L. J., Soule, B., Standley, K., Duchowny, M., & Copans, S. *Parents and infants: An interactive network.* Papers presented on Symposium at the annual convention of the American Psychological Association, New Orleans, 1974.

IV QUESTIONING THE ROLE OF DEVELOPMENTAL STAGE THEORY

Analysis of the developmental sequence in terms of stages has been central to much of theory and research in developmental psychology, especially in the past two decades. The developmental–interaction approach is grounded in a conception of stages drawn from the work of Werner, Piaget, and the ego psychologists, especially Erikson. The two chapters in this section raise questions about the usefulness of stage theory and suggest that, despite its undeniable appeal and conceptual power, its limitations need to be examined.

Edna Shapiro and Doris Wallace discuss the ways in which developmental stage theory does and does not illuminate thinking about the individual. They point to certain problems inherent in current stage formulations, touching also on uses and misuses of stage theory, especially Piagetian theory, in applications to educational practice.

Evelyn Weber traces the alliance between those interested in studying children and those who develop curricula for children to the beginning of this century, the days of G. Stanley Hall. The desire to base curricula for young children on the facts of development has eroded, however, in recent years. Weber raises questions about developmental assumptions as they influence psychological and curriculum theory, and notes that psychologists and educators face similar perplexities about underlying values.

7

Developmental Stage Theory and the Individual Reconsidered

Edna K. Shapiro, Doris B. Wallace
Bank Street College of Education

Although psychological theories are built from discoveries made on the basis of individuals or on close observation and experiments with single cases, once the theory is constructed the individual is lost. Indeed, it is precisely a function of any theory that it be *generally* applicable. The preferred way of verification—through the experimental method, using large numbers of subjects and analysis of central tendencies—further obscures the very thing that the theory may have taken as its starting point: the behavior of a single individual. The individual in such instances begins as the figure but ends as the ground for the theory. Once the theory becomes the figure, the individual sinks rapidly from consideration.

Detailed observation and analysis of single cases has significantly shaped modern concepts of psychological processes and human development. Itard studied and lived with Victor, the so-called wild boy of Aveyron; George Stratton observed his own responses to the inverted retinal image; Watson conditioned and deconditioned Albert's reactions to a white rabbit; Ebbinghaus memorized—and forgot—his nonsense syllables; some of Freud's central constructs were based on and exemplified by individual cases like Anna O, Little Hans, and Freud himself; and Piaget largely developed his theory of the sensorimotor stage from observing his own three babies in natural and contrived situations.

The distance between the purity of theory and the manifest clutter of individual behavior is taken for granted as inevitable and often remains unacknowledged. But there are inherent tensions in the relationship between the theory and the individual that deserve examination. Mental life, as William James said, is uniquely and individually presented in nature, and the organization of its particular and private qualities may be the primary experience of daily life. Much of these subjective data escape the nomothetic interests and objective methods of the psychologist who is intent, above all, on discovering general laws and regular sequences (this is also seen as a problem in anthropology, see Schludermann & Schludermann, 1976). Practitioners, on the other hand, deal with individuals— not with Piaget's epistemic subject, Erikson's eight ages, or Kohlberg's six levels. Even the skilled practitioner may find the abstract theory insufficient for understanding and dealing with the specific behavior of an individual. When that happens, the theory has not merely lost the individual but has become counterindividual. Tensions between constructs in developmental stage theory and individual behavior are the subject of this chapter. We focus on certain core concepts in developmental theory and research—universality, discontinuity, organism-environment interaction—to point up some of the ways in which current formulations obscure thinking about individual behavior, in the abstract and in everyday contexts. Our attempt to confront the practitioner's dilemma yields more questions than answers, but we believe that identifying these questions is an important and necessary step.

How the Theory Leaves the Individual Behind

There are several ways in which theory and individual behavior diverge. In general, as the theory is elaborated, certain aspects of the behavior of the individual become critical and others are no longer considered relevant. What is critical depends on the focus of the theory, because any theory, by its nature, pares and discards in order that only theory-relevant behavior will remain in view. The range and variety of individual behavior itself becomes irrelevant to the theory, which takes as a criterion for what is critical, the assumed generalizability of the behavior. It is at this point that all the behaviors that distinguish one individual from another—that is, those that define individuality—are sacrificed.

Obviously not all generalizable behavior is encompassed by the theory. Of the myriad behaviors of the individual that are not considered pertinent to the theory, some may be just as generalizable as those that are considered relevant. Indeed, these other behaviors may have lawful relations with the theory-relevant behaviors. They may be explained in terms of another competing or parallel theory of behavior. (As yet there is no general developmental theory that subsumes the range and complexity of human development.)

Second, the psychological dimensions of the theory may be formulated in idealized, friction-free terms, which take no account of contextual variables or individual differences. The study of individual differences is itself a subarea in psychology, but in developmental theory it is often dismissed as an irritant (some are faster, some are slower). Individual differences have sometimes been referred to as individuality. What we mean by individuality is a third way in which individuals are blurred by theory.

Individuality—the configurations that describe the uniqueness of any individual, the idiosyncratic mix of endowment and experience that makes each of us a special instance—has no place in general theory. The singularity of the person as a whole is most often considered to be the province of poets and clinicians; it is outside the realm of science.

A fourth way in which theory and the individual diverge follows from the fact that theory is a condensation and abstraction of behaviors seen from above and outside. Theories of human behavior are about beings who are themselves capable of constructing theories about their own and others' behavior; persons who are capable of verifying, refuting, qualifying theoretical statements. What points of connection are there between the theoretical construction and the person's own construction of his or her experience, between the theoretical and the phenomenological? What the theorist knows about the child is different from what the child knows about himself or herself. The theorist knows his or her own thoughts, which include the thoughts about the theory and some of the child's thoughts. The child knows nothing of the theory. Thus, the objects of knowledge for the theorist are quite different from those of the child. The points of interaction between the theorist's construction of the child's experience and the child's experience itself are themselves only theoretical, embedded as they are in the subjective experience of each—which is precisely what no theory can encapsulate. This reminds us that although the theorist's knowledge of the theory may be quite complete, his knowledge of the child is quite incomplete. This is partly because the theory itself is incomplete; that is, it includes only a portion of the child's psychological functioning. In addition, the theory is an adult construction about the child, which by definition is beyond the child's grasp.

Basic Assumptions and Dilemmas in Developmental Stage Theory

Neither Freud nor Piaget, who have given us the grand designs of developmental psychology, accepts the concept of an individual who is merely acted upon by the environment nor one who is outfitted with preset ideas and motives. Freud and Piaget both place the functioning human being into an environment whose components are essential to the theory although conceived quite differently in each. In Freudian theory the objective world consists primarily of people (significant others) or their symbolic representations. In Piaget's theory, the external world is primarily a world of material objects.[1] Development for both is concerned with internal–external interactions, with trying to understand the child's conception of

---

[1]This is not strictly accurate because Piaget, especially in his earlier work, was also concerned with children's concepts of the nonmaterial, for instance, the development of ideas about social rules (Piaget, 1932/1965) and of the symbolic function (Piaget 1945/1962).

reality, and, above all, as Jahoda (1977) has pointed out, with a child-centered point of view: "in tacit recognition," as she says, "that the nature of the construction put on reality is always a function of the abilities of the construer [p. 83]." Both Freud and Piaget see each developmental stage as putting constraints upon how the world can be constructed. Each has discovered a set of facts and created a theory that is meant to apply to all human beings. Each has taken a developmental approach requiring not only conceptualization of the desired end state—the mature, well-functioning person, the person capable of logical deductive thinking—but also delineation of the steps en route, the structures in transition; that is, the stages of development.

Stage theory is currently a dominant mode of thinking among many developmentalists. It has also been attractive to people who work with children, especially teachers. Perhaps one reason is that, in our age-graded schools, teachers are already attuned to thinking of children in terms of age markers. In this they have followed the early child psychologists and diarists for whom age was the touchstone for their careful and extensive documentation of aspects of development. Conceptualizing development in terms of stages or levels provides an organizing framework that is clearly a more powerful way of describing changes in psychological functioning than is chronological age.

Thinking about development in terms of stages rather than chronological age (or any single critical variable) has become so attractive that stage concepts are being used to characterize and demark the life span. As applied to the study of adulthood, however, stages are used in what seems to be a metaphoric or what Kessen (1962) calls a literary-evocative way. They describe modal patterns, adjustments, crises, and resolutions that are characteristic of Western society in the current era; they deal with social and role relationships and events and their emotional concomitants, in which cognitive processes are accessory and not a central concern as such. Differences in life patterns and cultural conventions necessarily erode the claim to universality and the stages remain descriptive, less compelling, and not inevitable (Neugarten, 1977).

Piaget, whose stage analyses are the most elaborately worked out, sees stages primarily as an "instrument for the analysis of formative processes," not as "an aim in their own right" (Piaget, 1955, in Gruber & Vonèche, 1977, p. 817). He goes on to say that they are like zoological classifications in biology, where classification precedes analysis. From this perspective, stages are typologies, an approach also taken by Loevinger (1976). Stages are considered to represent fundamentally different ways of processing information and of responding to it. They define different ways of construing reality; they are not just different lists of competencies.

Theories that organize development into stages have a number of generally agreed-upon characteristics, which, like aspects of development itself, are intimately related to each other.

Universality. First, by and large, developmental theories claim universality for the stages they postulate. This is certainly so for Freud and Piaget; because both assume biological substrates for the stages, the stages must apply to all people regardless of cultural variation. There have been many arguments and counterarguments about the universality of such psychoanalytic concepts as the Oedipal conflict, or the idea that heterosexuality and genital sexuality are the desirable, "healthy," and mature outcomes of psychosexual development. Discussion of these issues seems to us less germane to our central concerns than the more recent efforts to assay the universal applicability of the developmental sequence posited by Piaget, and we therefore focus on the latter.

Many researchers, both anthropologists and psychologists, have assumed the universality of human cognitive competence, but have assumed also that such competences are demonstrated in different ways in different cultural contexts (Cole, Gay, Glick, & Sharp, 1971). Others, especially psychologists, have taken Piagetian tasks to nontechnological societies and found a delay in emergence of certain cognitive structures (see Dasen, 1972, and Ashton, 1975, for reviews of many of these studies). A number of studies have found that many adults in both Western and non-Western societies do not show formal operational thinking on the Inhelder and Piaget tasks. Such findings have been attributed to the starkness of the tasks and their lack of familiarity or relevance to ordinary problems, or to the fact that attainment of formal operations is not universal.

By far the greatest number of cross-cultural studies have focused on the period of concrete operations. Both Piagetian and psychodynamic theory point to a dramatic shift in the child's functioning in the 5- to 7-year-old period. Especially in recent years, considerable research has been devoted to demonstrating that a shift (from preoperational to operational thinking) does occur, and toward demonstrating its universality. White, for example, has brought together both experimental findings and cultural practices to strengthen the case for a stage shift at this time (Rogoff, Sellers, Pirotta, Fox, & White, 1975; White, 1965). Because Piaget's theory is explicitly concerned with external and universal concepts like number, substance, and space, many of the tasks, especially those in conservation and seriation, have apparent built-in transportability and have seemed eminently suited to almost any culture and geographic location. These tasks have therefore been taken as an ideal medium for verifying the universality of this stage shift. But this has turned out to be a specious transportability. As Sylvia Scribner (1976) has put it: "The idea that an experiment consists of a fixed set of materials and operations that can be taken abroad like a piece of luggage has been replaced by an emphasis on the need to adapt features of the experiment to the culture in which the research is being carried out [p. 312]."

The universality of stages has not been unequivocally accepted, if research activity is any sign. Universality poses a fundamental paradox for any theory that takes the concept of organism–environment interaction as central (Greenfield,

1976). Piaget, as has often been noted, does not specify the nature of these interactive processes. Considering the wealth of variation in physical, material, and interpersonal environments and the variations in the nature of individuals' transactions with these environments around the globe (no less within any given culture), the assertion of universality implies that these variations are of negligible consequence. It is the ultimate nomothetic statement.

Piaget (1972) has indicated that there may be more diversification of development with age, that is, different kinds of experiences may provide contexts for the development of more "advanced" thinking. Thus competences, or structures, may be universal, but the contexts for using them cannot be. It seems likely that more sophisticated research will lead to a refinement of what is meant by the idea of universality, as well as to refinement of developmental theory. But the evidence is still being gathered and the issues are far from resolved.

Invariant Sequence.   Second, stage theory offers a sequential analysis of development. Development is progression forward—from simple to more complex, from few to many, early to late, primitive to advanced, global to differentiated—and the stages are a mechanism for ordering this progression. Most critical for the theory is the corollary assumption that the stage sequence is invariant.

This invariance of stage sequence is, indeed, the major "universal" in stage theory (for Freud and Piaget). But given the stages, it is logically impossible to conceive of a different sequence from the one given. In Piagetian theory, the qualitative changes in cognitive structures that characterize the preoperational stage could not conceivably occur without the sensorimotor stage having occurred first, and so on. It is not plausible that operational thought could precede preoperational thought. A crucial, *built-in* aspect of the theory as a whole is the successive growth and elaboration of ever more complex and interrelated cognitive structures, making a logical impossibility of any succession other than that hypothesized. Both Dasen (1972) and Ashton (1975), in reviewing Piagetian cross-cultural research, gloss over this intrinsic problem. They mention that the invariance of stage sequence is postulated by Piaget as a universal and then go on to state that this hypothesis can only be put to the test by longitudinal research, which to date has not been undertaken. By definition, however, no research could supply evidence that the four hierarchic stages described by Piaget occur in a different sequence from that put forward.

The sequence of development *within* stages is also postulated as invariant. The concept of décalage carries a heavy burden, for what is at issue is the manifestation of a presumed underlying structure—which brings us back to the context of and materials for assessing cognitive structure, and the role of experience. There is a dilemma here. If thought (cognitive structures) grows through action, what kinds of action and what kind of thought enable a person to conserve number and liquid, quantity and weight, but not volume? If it is also true that the kind of action that can be undertaken is a function of the level of thought achieved, how can it be that some individuals who have ''achieved'' the stage of formal operations are incapable of conserving volume? Perhaps the concept of conservation has classified into a single category quite different domains of logic or thought.

Discontinuity Versus Continuity.   A third assumption in stage theory is that each stage is fundamentally different from the preceding (and following) stages. In this way, the stages offer convenient markers, milestones along the developmental terrain, separating one class of functioning from another. Yet, paradoxically, each stage also incorporates and builds upon the preceding stage. Similarly, movement from stage to stage is hypothesized to be highly regular and consistent. But we know from commonsense observation, as well as from the laboratory, classroom, and clinic that behavior is often erratic and inconsistent.

Any account of development has to provide for both continuity and change. Stage theories by definition oppose a quantitative additive concept of change and posit progressive and dramatic reorganizations in the structure and meaning of experience. The child who, for example, says that the longer line of checkers has more checkers is looking at and ordering the world in a manner that differs radically from that of the child who can deal with invariance and transformation. From the point of view of the child, when she understands that both rows contain the same number of checkers, the old ways are gone. The transformation in cognitive organization is so radical that for some the very idea of considering the longer row as containing more is laughable. When faced with her previous nonconserving responses, the conserving child of 9 is incredulous. She is telling us that she is no longer capable of thinking in the same way as before; further, she cannot now conceive of being in her former state.

The discontinuities apparent here suggest a problem for any adult working with children (and indeed for older children communicating with younger children). The adult and the child are already far apart from each other chronologically. As we have described, the structural reorganizations involved in development make for changes of such scope as to create successively different views of the world. What were two different wholes (the two rows of checkers) at one stage, become two parts of a new whole at the next. This transformation can occur as a stable state only when the governing law is grasped. Once this has occurred, there is no going back. The irreversible nature of changes of this kind is vividly apparent in parallel processes in biology (Novikoff, 1945). The discontinuities entailed in such shifts make it necessary for the adult not only to look down a long corridor to see the child, but to see around corners.

The idea of major discontinuities in development, of transformations so dramatic as to preclude (for the most part) continuity of perceived experience, is not restricted to concepts involving physical objects. The development of social thought also is seen to involve conceptual reorganizations that represent discontinuous changes (e.g., Damon, 1979; Selman, this volume; Turiel, 1978). In another domain, Schachtel (1959), offering an analysis of the amnesia for the experiences of early childhood, suggests that: "the categories (or schemata) of adult memory are not suitable receptacles for early childhood experiences and therefore not fit to preserve these experiences and enable their recall [p. 284]." It seems likely that this hypothesis can be applied not only to the break between experiences at the preverbal and verbal levels and the gradual acquisition of conventional concepts, but also to that between any radical cognitive or affective reorganization and prior experience. The successive discontinuities of these transformations make it especially difficult for the adult to take the perspective of the child.

That continuity and change must both be accommodated in developmental-stage theory is a problem that cannot be resolved by opting for one or the other. Continuity and discontinuity are both apparent to the developing individual as well as to those in long-term contact with that person.

In theory, continuity is accounted for by postulating that each stage incorporates and builds upon the preceding stage. But, as Pinard and Laurendeau (1969) remarked some years ago: the "initial absence of conservation does not become an integral part of operational conservation [p. 129]." Indeed, the idea that the absence of conservation could be part of conservation is logically absurd—the very point that Pinard and Laurendeau wished to bring home. The notion that what has gone before is integrated into a new, more differentiated schema does not mean that prior modes of adaptation and functioning are totally effaced by new modes, nor that they take their place in the new schema uninfluenced by their position in what is now a different system. Prior modes are not lost or eradicated; the dominant mode changes. But this statement describes change more than it does continuity. It tells us that even though earlier behavior or ways of thought continue to exist, they have changed as a result of their new position in a new organization. They continue, but in a changed way. Nevertheless, continuity, at least in its purest sense, is the enduring and unbroken presence of something *un*changed.

When we specify the dominant mode of any stage, this in turn affects our way of looking at behavior. The characterization of early development, for instance, as sensorimotor serves to make us focus on certain aspects of learning, growth, and adaptation. When the child moves into the preoperational stage, however, what do we have to say about sensorimotor development? It is no longer the dominant mode, but it is obvious that sensory and motor development continue: The kinds of discriminations the child is capable of making and the kind of control of motor responses increases tremendously during the preoperational and operational stages. We tend then to subsume at least some of this development under the cognitive rubric. But it takes a back seat in our considerations because it is not at the center of theoretical concern, and the task of delineating the development of what *is* considered dominant is massive enough.

Theoretical descriptions and explanation of developmental change are more advanced and systematized than are ideas of continuity. At least this is so in stage theory. Change in developmental stages is often bold and arresting, partly because it *is* a transformation—a special and dramatic instance of change. But continuity in such a context turns out to be a different kind of change—more ephemeral and harder to pin down for inspection and analysis than a transformational change.[2]

There are interlocking problems here. One is a problem of definition. What do we mean by continuity? In attempting to answer this question, we find that it depends on the vantage point being taken. One can say, for example, that in development, change is continuous. (Taken to an extreme, this stress on the ubiquity of change in development deemphasizes equilibrium, see Riegel, 1976.) Or, as Piaget does, one can emphasize that adaptation and organization are invariant. These are statements or metastatements about the continuity of governing processes. When we turn to the operations or behaviors that these processes can mobilize, we are at another level—the level of behavior. Has the child changed who has just mastered the conservation of liquid? Yes and no. He has changed radically because he has grasped a new law and a new logic. He has remained unchanged because he cannot yet master the conservation of weight and volume—a direct continuity of a former state. Furthermore, unless the child is made aware of the transformation in his thinking, he knows nothing of it. Not being aware of it, he did not know that he did not know it, and is similarly unaware of his new capacity as new. There is a difference between growth one is aware of and growth that occurs without awareness. Experiments in conservation are not everyday events in the lives of children and only a few have witnessed and reflected on their own changing capacities in such tasks, when the researcher or some other chance event has caught them on the wing. (Practitioners often try to make explicit the child's new accomplishments on the assumption that pointing it out helps to crystallize and value the new knowledge. Becoming aware of change is another kind of change and may trigger further reorganization.)

Because the behaviors governed by transformational change are often conspicuous, some have acquired meaning as a "Ding an sich." This is entangled with the fallacy of seeing the stages simply as containers for the presence or absence of discrete behaviors, as a series of uneven milestone achievements (for example, object permanence, or level 4 on a moral judgment scale). That one child can be labeled a nonconserver and another a conserver demonstrates this way of thinking, in which the behavior is taken as the stage. It is as if making this

---

[2]Like one's sensations when meeting a person, known well, after a gap of many years. The face has changed radically, but there is instant recognition. It is easy to describe the changes; the unchanged features may be harder to define—the cast of the eye, the contour of a cheekbone, a smile—because they now exist, elusively, in an altered context.

diagnosis, that is, labeling the stage by the behavior, is an explanation and, therefore, an endpoint.

Developmental theory, with its sequential analysis of developmental processes, sets up a forward progression of development, and the stages order this progression. Adults who are in daily contact with children, such as parents, teachers, and clinicians, also tend to look to goal points, to be oriented to the future. This may be especially prevalent in our culture, where achievement and speed of attainment are so highly valued, and where adults tend to see children in progress (not process). Even accepting the fact that at any time the individual functions on a range of levels, the forward-looking character of the hierarchical sequence in stage theory seems to invite descriptions of stage-characteristic behaviors that are laid out in terms of what is absent, or what the child lacks. It is a way of anticipating the next stage, but at the expense of the present. To say that the child cannot yet conserve quantity, or that the baby has no idea of a permanent object ''out there,'' no notions of space and time, and therefore of causality, that is, to describe someone in terms of what he or she cannot do is counterindividual. It is a kind of ''description by prevision,'' in teleological anticipation of what is in store ahead.

Unevenness.   A fourth assumption, or recognition, in developmental stage theory is that development is uneven or inconsistent, both in the collective and individual sense. Each stage has a different duration because developmental changes are temporally as well as qualitatively unequal. It is uneven also because within stages, not all accomplishments occur in one short burst or at the same rate. Moreover, these asymmetries imply intraindividual differences, as well as variation between individuals in the pacing and regularity of development. Another way in which the theory implies an uneven path is through the characterization of each stage as fundamentally different from preceding and following stages. Indeed, this characterization is a built-in requirement and an intention in stage theory: Another stage is another state of the system as a whole.

Finally, there is unevenness because more primitive and more advanced operations can coexist at any level. As Werner (1940/1948) has pointed out, this means that the more mature person has a greater number of developmentally different operations available. In terms of psychodynamic theory, it also means that certain modes or patterns of relating may color our behavior throughout our lives. Although the content or means of expression may take different forms at different periods of life, the underlying issue may be the same (consider, for example, the vicissitudes of orality, or the premise that unresolved conflicts continue to influence our perceptions and actions). The coexistence of earlier and current cognitive and affective organizations and the pervasiveness of inconsistency suggest that stage definitions require further clarification. In addition, as Damon (1979) has noted, consistency is not an absolute notion but is relative to what the investigator is looking for. Thus, the single construct of unevenness has many meanings depending on the theory, the variable being described, the period of life, and the point of view being taken.

The Child, the Environment, and Reciprocity

Issues of continuity and discontinuity, regularity and irregularity, as well as of universality must be seen in the context of a fundamental tenet of developmental theory, that is, the assumption of organism–environment interaction. One of the sources of difficulty in describing individuals, in relating individuals to general principles, derives from our lack of clarity about the implications—for research and theory—of this reciprocal interaction. We have already noted this in discussing the issue of universality. It is not only that the nature of the interaction remains unspecified, but that the significant dimensions of the environment have not been adequately characterized. This is especially so with respect to the social and cultural environment in Piagetian theory, possibly because the theory has been concerned primarily with the child's construction of the physical world. Psychoanalytic writers particularly emphasize and carefully specify details of the social environment. Erikson (1950), for instance, in describing early developmental crises, pays as much attention to what the mother does as to the child's response. In the Piagetian frame, recent work has turned to a developmental analysis of social knowledge, that is, the child's construction and interpretation of social relations, of morality, and of social conventions. Here, too, levels and sequences have been identified, and the child's construction of the social world is seen to be more complex and more differentiated than had been thought.

The social world is different from the physical world. People are not objects. People's actions are less predictable, and regularities of behavior are more difficult to apprehend, certainly for the child. Further, social interaction is reciprocal: People act, whereas objects are more likely to be acted upon. Thus, the meaning of interaction of person and environment is different depending on whether one is referring to the physical or the interpersonal environment.

It seems that the implications of placing the individual in a posture of active engagement with the environment are only beginning to be spelled out. Are the structures that underlie cognition about social phenomena identical to, comparable with, or variants of those that underlie cognition about the physical world? There is no single "environment" to be constructed but rather interrelated sets of environments. Furthermore, reciprocal interaction takes place among (at least) three sets of factors: the characteristics of the social, psychological, and physical environments, the dispositions and characteristics of the individual, and the person's level of cognitive organization.

Describing the characteristics of environments seems to be in rather a primitive state in psychology. The environment has to be characterized as a psychological field, as it is perceived by and responded to by the individual. In order to begin to know how a particular individual construes the environment, we need, first, to view it from that person's perspective. Escalona, for example, has developed a method for defining stable "patterns of experience" (Escalona, 1968; Escalona & Corman, 1971). In observing the behavior of very young children, it is the baby's behavioral response rather than the adult's intention that is the base for judging the quality of the encounter between child and adult. Taking the point of view of the baby, the subject, allows the researcher to begin to define the effective environment of people and objects. It is a means toward describing the phenomenal rather than the geographic (or photographic) environment. This gives us, as adults, a tool for a kind of perspective taking that few have been able to achieve. We often ask the child to take the perspective of another child or adult; but, as researchers, we have only occasionally been able to do it ourselves.

The evidence supports the view that environmental variables can mitigate or amplify early difficulties in development, but for the most part those studied have been distal (e.g., social class), and the processes of influence are not clear (Sameroff & Chandler, 1975). By contrast, a number of studies (Escalona, 1968; Escalona & Heider, 1959; Thomas, Chess, Birch, Hertzig, & Korn, 1968) point to the way the characteristics of the child influence parent–child interaction. It is sometimes difficult to believe that it was not until 1968 that Bell's paper brought the concept of the bidirectionality of effects forcefully into the literature; it is now accepted that children influence parents, as well as that parents influence children. The idea that the child participates in shaping the environment has, for the most part, informed thinking and research on very young children and has not been systematically tied in with developmental concepts (see Yarrow, this volume, for provocative work in this direction).

At another level, it is necessary to get at the dimensions of difference among individuals that interact with developmental level and are associated with different ways of construing environments. The study of personality, of stable sources of variation in the ways that individuals interpret and respond to phenomena seems still to be out of favor these days, but the way individuals cope and interact with their environments must be influenced, if not determined, by personal characteristics and history. Surely an active, coping, self-initiating person interacts with the environment differently from one who is passive and more likely to be acted upon. The attraction to novelty, to risk taking, a positive attitude toward change must shape the way one approaches and assimilates environmental stimuli, even, possibly, what stimuli are attended to. With all the arguments over the continuity or discontinuity of stable patterns of adaptation, one generalization seems to be generally accepted—that those patterns that are supported by the social milieu are likely to endure (Kagan & Moss, 1962). At the same time, by definition, both the organism and the environment are changing. Further, the individual functions in an expanding set of environments and as children grow in our society they are expected to function in an increasing number of environments. Thus the meaning of organism–environment interaction requires a set of multiple interlocking specifications.

Theory into Practice

What meaning and relevance does knowledge of developmental theory have for those who are actively engaged with children in practical everyday situations? If we accept the proposition that behavior is motivated by implicit as well as explicit hypotheses about causal linkages, we must assume that the way a teacher, clinician, or parent interacts with children in the classroom, the clinic, or at home derives from that person's framework of ideas about what has led, or might lead, to what. Such a framework may be more or less articulate, coherent, or naive. It may be held as an ideological position, or it may be a set of utilitarian techniques, or it may be largely intuitive. Those who have been interested in education, and certainly those who have been committed to a developmental-interaction point of view (see Biber, this volume; Shapiro & Biber, 1972) have argued that teachers must be informed about psychological theory and developmental processes, believing that such knowledge can provide an essential base for action and decision making in teaching.[3] Yet both psychological theory and lay wisdom tell us that knowledge is not enough; there are no easy rules for what to do with it. Further, we have argued that between theory and practice there are differences in perspective intrinsic to the nature of each. To the extent that theory and practice are complementary enterprises, and they do share a fundamental concern for children's development, facing the issues may be illuminating for each.

Theoretical concepts can serve many functions. They give stature to impressions, hunches, or half-formed ideas: Ah yes, I always knew that, but didn't realize it was worth knowing. Concepts and their vocabulary broaden the scope of behavior that one can fathom and that one pays attention to, and labeling offers a simple intellectual pleasure: Someone's slip of the tongue brings knowing smiles around the room; a 3-year-old paints a "typical" 3-year-old painting. Theoretical constructs can offer relief: If one does not expect development to march on in an irrevocably linear way, one is not so distressed by apparently regressive behavior; suddenly one realizes that one is asking a child to take an alternative perspective in a way that is beyond his capability. Theory can change one's view of the meaning of behavior and consequently of action to be taken: Concepts of

---

[3]We take teaching as a paradigm, although a number of the issues considered are relevant also to relationships between therapists or parents and children. Each type of relationship is predicated on concepts of development and assumptions about the course of change and growth. Examining the application of theory to educational practice is especially pertinent, however, because there are a number of programs designed to make such applications.

attachment change caregivers' expectations for and interpretation of the way young children separate from their mothers; awareness of preschool children's confusion of the real and the imagined changes our response to a patently improbable assertion; concepts of language as rule-governed change the interpretation—although not necessarily the correction—of children's often incorrect though logical approaches to pluralization or past tense; concepts of interaction as reciprocal and mutually regulated can lead the adult to think about her contribution to a difficult situation.

But theories are not meant to be guides for action, nor are they phrased so as to provide such guides. The way the theorist thinks about theory is different from the way the practitioner thinks about it. What the theory can offer are guides for *understanding and interpreting* behavior, a way of conceptualizing the meaning of behavior that has or may have implications for action. One source of the power of stage theory is its ability to accommodate diverse behaviors within a single frame.

As we have said, theories deal with the general and abstract. The practitioner has to deal with the particular and the concrete. This perspective is accentuated in the developmental-interaction approach because it explicitly calls for the teacher to view and respond to each child as an individual, to take into account the manifold intricacy of this child's intellectual, social, motivational, and physical functioning. The classroom situation is at once circumscribed and variegated. Even in a highly controlled conventional classroom, hundreds of different events and behaviors occur each day; the range is considerably broader in a class where the teacher accepts child initiative and diversifies the program. It is the variety and individuality of behavior that is most compelling to the teacher.

Some children may sit quietly and listen to the teacher; others resist or ignore her; they talk to each other, play, write, draw, fill out worksheets, conduct experiments, ask questions—relevant and irrelevant to what is going on. Some may struggle trying to understand a problem, others may think they understand although they are actually confused, another may be triumphant because he has grasped it. One child may appear listless and subdued because of some sadness that has nothing to do with school; another may be irritable and recalcitrant because of something another child has said to him or her, and so on. Many things happen simultaneously, and there is no moment when nothing is happening; many if not most of the children's actions are not talked about in developmental theory.

The teacher is drawn to notice differences among the children also because, by and large, children in any one classroom are likely to be in the same developmental stage.[4] The concept of stage as an organizing frame, attractive and potent as it is, is of little practical help. Insofar as stages represent major reorganizations

---

[4]First-grade children are the exception here. They are in a period of transition and their teacher is likely to be dealing with quite a broad developmental span.

of psychic processes and modes of relating to experience, they cover broad sweeps of time. The bulk of the elementary school period is covered by the stage of concrete operations (or latency, or the conflict between industry and inferiority). In order to make differentiations within these large spans the teacher must be familiar with intrastage markers, sequences, and progressions. This, in turn, requires more than a superficial acquaintance with the theory and its experimental and speculative differentia. The teacher has a closeup view of a segment of the developmental continuum, or rather, of segments of an array of developmental continua. She is continually confronted by the differences among children, at the same time that their stage sameness assures that they share certain abilities and concerns, a sameness that makes it possible to devise curricula "appropriate to the children's developmental level."

Responding to the individual child does not mean that the teacher creates a different curriculum for each child. Eleanor Duckworth (1979) has remarked that the notion that the teacher should attempt to "diagnose children's intellectual level and tailor individual instruction accordingly" is a misapplication of Piagetian theory. The amount of time it would take to assess each child on a representative number of tasks and to check on progress during the year, would be extremely impractical, and beside the point: "The only diagnosis necessary," she says, "is to observe what the children in fact do during their learning [p. 310]."[5]

Even if one would want to and could assess each child on a dozen Piagetian concepts, one still would not know enough about each child. The teacher's approach to individualization is more likely to be in helping the child to pursue interests and ideas, remembering and making connections to individual preferences, temperament, and circumstances, accepting idiosyncracies, responding to personal associations, as well as in adapting levels of difficulty. Adults cannot turn themselves into children, but at least they have the advantage of greater and future knowledge. Their knowledge of what the child can and cannot do should in principle enable them to make contact with the child on the child's terms. (For example, a skilled practitioner does not assume that because differentiated meaning is not expressed, differentiated thought is therefore not present.)

No single theory is comprehensive enough to provide the necessary range of insights and there is certainly none to give directives for what to do and how to do it in naturalistic contexts. (Nor have the theorists intended to create blueprints for

---

[5]Taking too narrow a view of theory-relevant behavior can lead to another kind of misapplication. In a different context, the anthropologist, Washburn (1978) has noted a distorted application of evolutionary theory. Archeologists had ordered stone tools used by Neanderthals into a sequence from "simple" to "complex," thus demonstrating evolutionary stages. But when the tools were dated by independent means, differently categorized tools were found to be contemporaneous. The archeologists had ignored a readily available index—the order in which the tools had been found in the ground. The desire to demonstrate evolutionary stages overcame empirical common sense.

action.) It is for this reason that a skilled and knowledgeable teacher can make eclecticism an advantage in interpreting behavior that, in the theory building, would be viewed with suspicion.

Between the practitioner and the theory there are intermediaries, notably the researcher and the curriculum developer. The researcher (who is often also the theorist) takes an essentially nomothetic stance. The researcher concretizes theoretical statements by creating microcosms or analogues that represent critical features of theoretical constructs, or that focus on ambiguities in the theory. Sometimes the researcher will take up the task of translation and specify ways in which theory and "new findings" relate to practice (cf. the journal *Theory into Practice*). A great deal then depends on how much the researcher knows about the kinds of transactions that take place in classrooms, because in the classroom, variables are inevitably confounded and the abstract formulations of theory (as well as some of the concrete ways of demonstrating them) are often irretrievably distant from everyday life.

The educator or curriculum developer, on the other hand, is assumed to be conversant with the intricacies of both theory and practice. This dual perspective should serve, one hopes, to clarify issues in both domains. But what often seems to happen is that the translation is literal rather than idiomatic. We see this, most clearly, in some applications of Piagetian theory where the very tasks used to appraise development have been taken as teaching devices, where the artifacts of theory have become curriculum.

Deanna Kuhn (1979) has argued that the difficulties encountered in applying Piagetian theory to education point to ambiguities within the theory itself. She deals with such issues as the lack of clarity of the processes underlying developmental transition from one stage to another, the meaning of "self-directed activity," and the narrow definition and means of assessing formal reasoning. Her approach, like ours, assumes that a critical examination of the efforts to use developmental theory in educational practice, and of the efforts to refine developmental theory, can be mutually instructive. But we add one further caveat, bringing us back to the dilemma or paradox with which we began: The way individuals function has to be considered as potentially illuminating for developmental theory, rather than as an irritant.

The issue is hardly a new one for psychology (or any science). As Kurt Lewin (1942/1951) posed the problem 40 years ago:

psychology is in a dilemma when it tries to develop "general" concepts and laws. If one "abstracts from individual differences" there is no logical way back from these generalities to the individual case. Such a generalization leads from individual children to children of a certain age or certain economic level and from there to children of all ages and all economic levels. . . . What is the value of general concepts if they do not permit predictions for the individual case? Certainly, such a procedure is of little avail for the teacher or the psychotherapist [p. 60].

Neither exhortation nor denial will make the issue disappear. What we need is to create interconnected sets of models of development that can span the gap between the constructs of theory and behavior in everyday contexts.

Conclusions

The problem of finding a place for the individual in developmental stage theory has seemed intractable. We noted at the beginning that many psychological theories are generated from the close observation and analysis of individual cases, and that it is in the nature of theory building to move from the particular and concrete to the general and abstract. Perhaps because of this, whenever we express relations in abstract terms, whenever we deal with what is not manifest, we feel triumphant; we have gotten to the truth. On the other hand, it is important, if theory is to inform action, to be able to separate what, in individual behavior, the theory can and cannot account for.

In the past few years there have been a number of critical reexaminations of the generality of developmental principles and the adequacy of current research paradigms (McCall, 1977; Sameroff & Chandler, 1975; Wohlwill, 1973). An extreme version of the generality question is posed by Weisz (1978), who asks: "Can we expect the psychological study of human development to yield durable principles, valid across changes in time, culture and cohort? [p. 1]." Such principles would have what Weisz calls "transcontextual validity." They would be the most remote from the individual, but would encompass more individuals, in the effort to arrive at a world view of human development. We have examined the assumptions and constraints of developmental theory in relation to individual behavior from the point of view of the theorist and the practitioner—both of whom have a stake in this issue.

There is a tradition, going back at least to Kurt Lewin, in which the individual is the main topic of study.[6] This tradition is not antitheoretical but is part of an effort to understand human behavior while retaining the complexity of individuality. Lewin's concept of life space is a way of connecting a highly flexible theory to manifold aspects of concrete individual behavior at a given time, in a particular situation, and his analysis of the contrast between Aristotelian and Galileian modes of thought remains critical and relevant (Lewin, 1935).

---

[6]We are not dealing here with either the clinical or the psychometric tradition of working with or analyzing individuals. In the clinical approach, the individual is seen as a concrete instance of the operation of preexisting theoretical constructs, and the case study is used to demonstrate, illustrate, and refine theory. The psychometric tradition identifies variables that differentiate individuals and orders individuals on these variables. The number of variables along which individuals can be ordered is so vast, however, and the behavior measured is often so remote from behavior in vivo that the individual is, it seems to us, obscured once again. Significantly, the study of individual variation in cognitive processes has not been conducted within the framework of developmental theory (Kagan & Kogan, 1970).

Currently, there are others who, like Lewin, are taking the behavior of individuals as a central focus. For example, Gruber's (1980) investigation of the growth of Charles Darwin's evolutionary theory uses detailed analysis of Darwin's own records to illuminate and reconstruct the process and development of his thought. Gruber's work with individuals is part of a larger undertaking—to understand creative processes. Feldman's (1980) study of individual prodigies tackles some of the problems inherent in the concept of universality in developmental theory. Arguing that not all of development has to do with universals, he proposes a continuum of development from the universal to the unique.

These different efforts to bring individuals into the realm of scientific discourse signal a new approach to theory building in which the struggle is to retain rather than to efface the individual.

If we cannot find the individual in the theory, do we have to reconstruct the theory?

ACKNOWLEDGMENT

We thank Howard E. Gruber for constructive comments on an earlier version of this paper.

REFERENCES

Ashton, P. T. Cross-cultural Piagetian research: An experimental perspective. *Harvard Educational Review,* 1975, *45,* 475–506.

Bell, R. Q. A reinterpretation of the direction of effects in studies of socialization. *Psychological Review,* 1968, *75,* 81–95.

Cole, M., Gay, J., Glick, J., & Sharp, D. W. *The cultural context of learning and thinking.* New York: Basic Books, 1971.

Damon, W. *The nature of social–cognitive change in the developing child.* Paper presented at meetings of the Jean Piaget Society, Philadelphia, Penna., 1979.

Dasen, P. R. Cross-cultural Piagetian research: A summary. *Journal of Cross-Cultural Psychology,* 1972, *3,* 23–39.

Duckworth, E. Either we're too early and they can't learn it or we're too late and they know it already: The dilemma of "applying Piaget." *Harvard Educational Review,* 1979, *49,* 297–312.

Erikson, E. H. *Childhood and society.* New York: Norton, 1950.

Escalona, S. K. *The roots of individuality: Normal patterns of development in infancy.* Chicago: Aldine, 1968.

Escalona, S. K., & Corman, H. H. The impact of mother's presence upon behavior the first year. *Human Development,* 1971, *14,* 2–15.

Escalona, S. K., & Heider, G. M. *Prediction and outcome.* New York: Basic Books, 1959.

Feldman, D. H. *Beyond universals in cognitive development.* Norwood, N.J.: Ablex, 1980.

Greenfield, P. Cross-cultural research and Piagetian theory: Paradox and progress. In K. F. Riegel & J. A. Meacham (Eds.), *The developing individual in a changing world* (Vol. 1). Chicago: Aldine, 1976.

Gruber, H. E. *Darwin on man: A psychological study of creativity.* Chicago: University of Chicago Press, 2nd ed., 1981.

Gruber, H. E., & Vonèche, J. J. (Eds.), *The essential Piaget.* New York: Basic Books, 1977.

Jahoda, M. *Freud and the dilemmas of psychology.* New York: Basic Books, 1977.

Kagan, J., & Kogan, N. Individual variation in cognitive processes. In P. Mussen (Ed.), *Carmichael's manual of child psychology* (3rd ed., Vol. 1). New York: Wiley, 1970.

Kagan, J., & Moss, H. A. *Birth to maturity: A study in psychological development.* New York: Wiley, 1962.

Kessen, W. "Stage" and "structure" in the study of children. In W. Kessen & C. Kuhlman (Eds.), Thought in the young child. *Monographs of the Society for Research in Child Development,* 1962, *27,* 65–82.

Kuhn, D. The application of Piaget's theory of cognitive development in education. *Harvard Educational Review,* 1979, *49,* 340–360.

Lewin, K. *A dynamic theory of personality.* New York: McGraw-Hill, 1935.

Lewin, K. *Field theory in social science* (D. Cartwright, Ed.). New York: Harper & Bros., 1951. (Originally published, 1942.)

Loevinger, J. *Ego development: Conception and theories.* San Francisco: Jossey-Bass, 1976.

McCall, R. Challenges to a science of developmental psychology. *Child Development,* 1977, *48,* 333–344.

Neugarten, B. L. Personality and aging. In J. E. Birren & K. W. Schaie (Eds.), *Handbook on the psychology of aging.* New York: Van Nostrand Reinhold, 1977.

Novikoff, A. B. The concept of integrative levels and biology. *Science,* 1945, *101,* 209–215.

Piaget, J. *Play, dreams and imitation in childhood.* New York: Norton, 1962. (Originally published, 1945.)

Piaget, J. *The moral judgment of the child.* New York: Free Press, 1965. (Originally published, 1932.)

Piaget, J. Intellectual evolution from adolescence to adulthood. *Human Development,* 1972, *15,* 1–12.

Piaget, J. The stages of intellectual development in childhood and adolescence. (1955) In H. E. Gruber & J. J. Vonèche (Eds.), *The essential Piaget.* New York: Basic Books, 1977.

Pinard, A., & Laurendeau, M. "Stage" in Piaget's cognitive developmental theory: Exegesis of a concept. In D. Elkind & J. H. Flavell (Eds.), *Studies in cognitive development.* New York: Oxford University Press, 1969.

Riegel, K. F. From traits and equilibrium towards developmental dialectics. In W. J. Arnold (Ed.), *Nebraska Symposium on Motivation* (Vol. 23). Lincoln: Univeristy of Nebraska Press, 1976.

Rogoff, B., Sellers, M. J., Pirotta, S., Fox, N., & White, S. H. Age of assignment of roles and responsibilities to children. A cross cultural survey. *Human Development,* 1975, *18,* 353–369.

Sameroff, A., & Chandler, M. Reproductive risk and the continuum of caretaking casualty. In F. D. Horowitz, E. M. Hetherington, S. Scarr-Salapatek, & G. M. Siegel (Eds.), *Review of child development research* (Vol. 4). Chicago: University of Chicago Press, 1975.

Schachtel, E. *Metamorphosis.* New York: Basic Books, 1959.

Schludermann, S., & Schludermann, E. H. A conceptual model for the study of individual development in different cultures. In K. F. Riegel & J. A. Meacham (Eds.), *The developing individual in a changing world* (Vol. 1). Chicago: Aldine, 1976.

Scribner, S. Situating the experiment in cross-cultural research. In K. F. Riegel & I. A. Meacham (Eds.), *The developing individual in a changing world* (Vol. 1). Chicago: Aldine, 1976.

Shapiro, E., & Biber, B. The education of young children: A developmental interaction approach. *Teachers College Record,* 1972, *74,* 55–79.

Thomas, A., Chess, S., Birch, H. G., Hertzig, M. D., & Korn, S. *Behavioral individuality in early childhood.* New York: University Press, 1968.

Turiel, E. Social regulations and domains of social concepts. In W. Damon (Ed.), *New directions for child development. I: Social cognition.* San Francisco: Jossey-Bass, 1978.

Washburn, S. L. The evolution of man. *Scientific American,* 1978, *239,* 194–208.

Weisz, J. R. Transcontextual validity in developmental research. *Child Development,* 1978, *49,* 1–12.

Werner, H. *Comparative psychology of mental development.* New York: Follett, 1948. (Originally published, 1940.)

White, S. H. Evidence for a hierarchical arrangement of learning processes. In L. Lipsitt & C. Spiker (Eds.), *Advances in child development and behavior* (Vol. 2). New York: Academic Press, 1965.

Wohlwill, J. *The study of behavioral development.* New York: Academic Press, 1973.

8

Stage Theory and Curriculum Development

Evelyn Weber
Wheelock College

The alliance between child study and early childhood education was forged in strong links from the very inception of empirical investigation of the child. Some of the first child study conferences, instituted by G. Stanley Hall at Clark University in the 1890s, attracted forceful leaders constructing curricula for young children. Patty Smith Hill, Anna Bryan, Alice Putnam, and Jennie B. Merrill were among those attending summer seminars and thus exposed to Hall's strong stand concerning developmental stages grounded, both biologically and behaviorally, in an acceptance of evolutionary development. Each stage needed to be lived through completely for healthy development, according to Hall. Furthermore, Hall (1901) proposed that the characteristics of each stage of development supplied the ideal base for determining the curriculum. He was convinced that any real advance in educational theory and practice would stem from an: "ever clearer realization that in the nature of childhood itself and its different stages of development must be found the norm for all the method and the matter of teaching [Hall, 1924, p. 500]." Early childhood leaders at the turn of the century, seeking new bases for curriculum development, seriously considered the implications of Hall's statements.

When Arnold Gesell, a student of Hall, presented detailed norms of growth, this delineation seemed to form clear directives for curriculum recommendations. Gesell assisted researchers in the collection of a vast new literature of descriptive data about specific items of human development. Undergirding Gesell's work was his acceptance of Hall's evolutionary hypothesis, a concept of inherent genetic predetermination. Investigation of "the innate processes of growth called maturation" revealed to Gesell and Ilg (1943) the: "progressive morphogenesis of patterns of behavior [p. 41]." These patterns, as Gesell presented them, became

131

known as "ages and stages" of development. This considerable body of data, added to all spheres of growth—physical, intellectual, emotional, and social—as it applied to the genetic period under investigation, was a segmented and compartmentalized approach. Furthermore, data were collected from only one segment of society, essentially children of students and faculty in the college community, but the results were immediately generalized. From the normative data categorized by age, the presumed characteristics, interest, and abilities of children at each level were derived.

Engaged in curriculum revision, replacing the Froebelian curriculum with newer conceptions, leaders in early childhood education seized upon the normative revelations as an important basis for planning the details of the experiences and activities to be provided children. The literature concerning programs for young children rapidly reflected the dissemination of normative data. For example, one influential book on the kindergarten opened with a chapter describing the characteristics of the 5-year-old child (Foster & Headley, 1936, Chapter 1). The authors, members of the Institute of Child Welfare at the University of Minnesota as well as recognized leaders in kindergarten education, established a format followed in early childhood literature through the 1950s. Statements about 5-year-olds depicted their physical growth, language ability, play interests, competence in routines, and similar traits revealed by observational data. As developmental characteristics were thoughtfully considered, it was implied that a program could be planned appropriate to the child's stage of development that would be satisfying to the child and fruitful for subsequent learning. A picture of the "average" or "normal" child was presented to the teacher as the essential for curriculum planning. This method of utilizing normative data became standard practice in the literature of early childhood. Curriculum builders thus pursued a basic direction laid down by Arthur Jersild (1946) as part of his definition of the child development point of view: "The child development approach to curriculum means an effort to apply to the education of children the lessons learned from the study of children themselves [p. 1]." They were, thus, advancing the use of generalized stage characteristics as opposed to individual proclivities. What a graphic example of the dilemma of maintaining an individual view of growth within the context of stage theory—yet this remained unrecognized for some time.

Early childhood educators, maintaining a developmental view in the decades of the thirties, forties, and fifties, were aligning themselves with the prevailing assumptions of their times. Beliefs concerning predetermined development and fixed intelligence supported faith in maturation and its correlary conception of readiness as fundamental premises for curriculum building. These assured "an attitude of respect for children at all stages of their growth," another element basic to Jersild's definition of the child development point of view; they also encouraged a "hands off" attitude concerning growth, an emphasis on allowing children's genetically determined natures to unfold. The resultant curriculum was conceived as supporting the child's own pace of learning and as guiding him or her loosely toward more mature functioning. A supportive educational setting could include the Deweyan emphasis on interaction and the reconstruction of experience even though key premises differed. It could also include a gradually accepted belief that early environments did effect emotional response and personality development, then considered more mutable than intelligence. The inclusion of the psychoanalytic emphasis was facilitated by its embracing stages of growth.

The invariant, qualitatively different developmental stages integral to Piaget's theory of cognitive functioning have been the ones under consideration most recently. Teachers seem to need pegs on which to organize their observations and study of children with whom they are working. Stage theory provides such a series of pegs to help teachers uncover elements of growth and to view them with some sense of continuity. One teacher (Smart, 1968), informed about Piaget's work, wrote: ''Now that I have experimented in my classroom with some of Piaget's intellectual tasks, never again will I look at children in quite the same way—and the change is for the better [p. 294].'' The ensuing discussion reveals her reliance on analysis of the qualitatively different levels of operational thinking to understand a child's intellectual growth and for designing classroom experiences.

Another direct application of Piagetian stage theory to curriculum is illustrated by a teacher of college science (Sanders, 1978), who offers the Piagetian paradigm as a basis for curriculum reform. This recommendation to extend stage theory to embrace curriculum for older students stems from Sanders' belief that the typical class of college students consists of two subgroups, one which has obtained formal operations and one which has not. That the members of each group employ different problem-solving techniques should cause, in Sanders' view, all teachers to reevaluate what they are doing in the classroom. If teachers use knowledge of students' thinking to inform their guidance of learning, individuals may benefit; if this knowledge is used to set up dichotomous curricula a false polarization will result. The significant problem ignored in Sanders' proposal is that of supporting growth from stage to stage. If some students have not developed the flexibility, the ''combinatorial'' abilities, the concern for possibility, and the capability for abstract thought that characterize formal operations, what support can they be given to move in this direction? Not surprisingly, this huge task is not confronted; neither has it been probed in the development of stage theory itself.

Although Kamii and DeVries (1977) were attracted to Piagetian theory first by the insights it offered into the nature of thought and the stages of development, they now repudiate such a simplistic, direct application of this stage theory to curriculum planning. They found that extracting only limited aspects of the theory opened it to misapplications. To insure against false adoption of the theory and overreliance on stage aspects, Kamii and DeVries have come to believe that educators must understand Piaget's epistomological orientation, his constructivism. This active organism position represents a big shift in fundamental assumptions from the reliance on orderly unfolding to a belief in the learner's construction of his own knowledge. The influence of maturation is now placed in the context of the role of experiences in growth. Active interactions with the world are essential for the growth of intellectual structures as well as for other areas of growth.

The nature of interaction becomes, then, central to psychological study, and the recognition of its centrality has been gaining credence with psychologists under the rubric of ecological psychology. In the early sixties, Benjamin Bloom's (1964) analysis of data on human characteristics revealed stabilities that he believed to be an artifact of the lack of focus on varying environmental conditions. The recognition that behavior and environment are inextricably continuous in time, that they are relentlessly interdependent and interactive, moves psychology toward ecological problems and methods, entailing a view of interaction as reciprocal rather than linear. Most developmental research has tended to be unidirectional, thus failing to recognize that in most social situations the person is part of the stimulus of events. The importance of reciprocity as a defining property would make the research model a two-way system. Bronfenbrenner (1973) proposes an ecological research model to replace the scientific model of the past, based on the physical and biological sciences. Research limited to a two-person system—an experimenter and a child— has tended to make the child the object of study, the recipient of stimuli. Ecologically valid research would view the child as an instigator of behavior in others and as a socializing agent as well as a responder to the behavior of others. Studies of socialization systems such as parent and child, teacher and child, the child in a group, bringing out the importance of reciprocity, could provide information crucial for the determination of adequate curricular practices. In a study of early childhood intervention programs, Irving Sigel (1972) concludes that: "it is very important to conceptualize not only the growth of the child but also the system within which he is functioning, e.g., to be aware of and to identify the ecological systemic variables, ranging from school room equipment to the child's relationship to his own mother [p. 372]." Thus, the variables to be studied need to be more than distal ones, to be those of immediate interaction. Concluding from extensive observational study, Roger Barker (1978) claims ecological approaches to be neither incomplete nor defective but able to be differentiated with precision.

Arguing for the relativity of human development, Kenneth Keniston (1971) warns against ready acceptance of apparent uniformities in human development derived from studies carried out in Western culture. This would seem to repudiate a set of stages as now institutionalized, for: "what we now know consistently supports the hypothesis that human development from infancy onward is contingent upon the environmental matrix [p. 431].'' It will take decades, Keniston believes, to develop data to fill significant environmental matrices.

At this particular time, obviously a watershed period in the study of human development, it would seem that the new fundamental assumptions would prevail, especially the active-organism position. Yet a colloquy (Wapner, Cohen, & Kaplan, 1976) held to explore theory, problem formation, and methodology as they are evolving in the embryonic field of environmental psychology revealed how dependent the construal of complex phenomena are on the values and needs of the perceivers. The image of man (considered generically) underlying the different perspectives revealed how strong is the cleavage between: "the tacit conception of human beings as reagents and respondents to environmental stimuli" and "the view of human beings as active striving agents, capable of construing their worlds in various ways [p. 235]." Thus, the study of man-in-environment has not eliminated the necessity for probing underlying assumptions.

CRITIQUE OF APPLICATIONS OF STAGE THEORY

Let us turn now to an evaluation of the use of stage theory so attractive to the curriculum designer in early childhood education, for it has presented serious problems in its implementation. Overzealous utilization of stage theory in planning programs for young children has sometimes led to rigidity. One example would be the widely accepted practice that no child should learn to read in kindergarten, but that all children should learn as 6-year-olds. The human need for certainty has led often to inflexible, unyielding employment of theoretical stage constructs in an antidevelopmental manner. In spite of protests from child development specialists, the rigid application may well have gone against the grain of an individual child's growth.

Even more questionable may be the procedure of gearing instruction to perceived developmental lacks. Curriculum then focuses on the child's inadequacies rather than his or her strengths. Shapiro and Wallace (this volume) have pointed out the incongruence between a phenomenologically based curriculum and developmental theory construed as existing deficits at a particular stage. It is antiindividual and negates much that psychology has revealed about motivation and the impact of expectations in learning.

Less readily recognized but equally problematic is the use of descriptive data for prescription. Developmental metaphors, valid within the context in which they were established, lose some of that validity when they are extrapolated and projected into instructional settings. Quite some time ago Ausubel (1959) argued that although readiness is crucially important in learning, in practice it is so confused with maturation that it only muddies the educational waters. He contends that the specificity of any particular readiness is such that it cannot be derived from logical extrapolation but requires meticulous research in a school setting.

Most vocal right now, however, are those who reject stage theory because of its means-end relationship. The positing of a set of stages implies a mature end stage, necessarily defined, consciously or not, by a set of values. Someone must guide the process of growth into the mature state, with the very enunciation of maturity equal to exalting certain modes of behavior. Because most developmental research has been carried out in Western cultures, Third World critics attack the elitist connotation of the developmental metaphor. Development, to them, is interpreted as becoming like Western society, with differing values ignored.

It is, however, the opacity of stage theory with regard to the place of the individual that explains the rejection of the developmental point of view by a number of contemporary curriculum theorists. This refers not to those leaning on behaviorist psychology, which has failed consistently to recognize stages of growth, but to those phenomenologists grounded in concern for personal development. The existential emphasis on the self and the growth of personal meaning and relatedness leads curriculum theorists, whose values elevate these concerns, to move away from constructs not congruent with their personal values. Statements by writers in the curriculum field confirm this emerging position.

The essence of the existential rejection of stage theory is linked to the use of individuals as objects of study. "The term *individual,*" writes James Macdonald (1966): "is for the most part a psychological metaphor [p. 39]." What one person shares with all other persons is simply the human condition, according to this view. It is not the commonalities of growth, nor even the assessment of individual traits or characteristics that Macdonald selects as a keystone for curriculum building, but a view of each person as possessing his or her own unique unity. The psychological sense of individuals becomes meaningless in such a discussion of *persons* in the curriculum, in which each person strives to create meaning out of human existence in the world and to maximize his or her potential for expression in deep personal commitment. In this sense the person-oriented curriculum allows choice and freedom in the struggle for personal meaning. Choice and freedom—not permissiveness—characterize this conception of curriculum. In Macdonald's (1966) words, it is: "the unimpeded process of building patterns of personal knowledge systems out of the knowledge 'stuff' of our world [p. 43]."

"Inherent in our view of the person," write Louise Berman and Jessie Roderick (1977) as they extend the phenomenological view: "is the concept that man is a dynamic organism capable of deciding, becoming involved, and interrelating with his fellows in humane ways [p. 25]." They elevate the persistent interplay between the person and his or her world, each having a bearing on the other. These authors view that interaction in a positive sense when they state:

"Because persons want and need the conditions for growth, expansion and constant remaking, they tend to interact with persons, ideas and institutions so that the self can be enhanced [p. 71]." Attention then is focused on an environment with great vitality eventuating in a heightened existence for the person. In consideration of man's temporality, Dwayne Huebner (1966) also considers the curriculum designer's task to fabricate an educational environment that: "takes care of students, keeps them alive and makes them grow [p. 109]."

These statements reveal curriculum specialists abandoning the "abstract purity of stage theory," to use the Shapiro-Wallace phrase, as well as discarding "the manifest clutter of individual behavior" as psychologically revealed. For these contributors to the curriculum field would move from a conception of the individual in the psychological sense of an object for study to a conception of the person—to the idiosyncratic nature of persons, each possessing his or her own unity and identity. It is a conviction "that man's spirit is much more complicated than we have ever been willing to believe [Huebner, 1966, p. 98]."

The search for meaning in its existential significance has been traced to the distress with meaninglessness in our society, with self-deception, with depersonalized mass culture, with the impersonality and objectifying of the I-It relationship, as revealed by Paul Tillich, Jean Paul Sartre, Karl Jaspers, and Martin Buber (Phenix, 1964, pp. 43-44). It leads directly to concern for meaning in selfhood and in human relationships, to authenticity in existence, to a loving I-Thou affirmation. Curriculum specialists following this point of view are moving toward a reconceptualization supported less by psychological and more by philosophical premises. Interest, then, focuses on the learner's interaction within the social complex in the search for meaning and selfhood.

The existential moment-by-moment environmental interaction supercedes an interest in—even a recognition of—developmental factors for these curriculum specialists. For them, education takes place in a contrived environment, one that necessarily is a form of influence over persons and is influenced by them. Influence does not need to be understood technologically, that is, as a means to an end. Rather, it is used to designate "under the influence," to describe a present relationship. Instruction is the interaction between persons, materials, ideas, performances, and objects in the contrived curriculum environment as they enhance the present struggle for personal meaning. Nor do these writers accept the concept inherent in stage theory that growth necessarily means attaining succeeding stages that have an invariant order and lead to a mature end state for this means that the end state must be known and predictable. To prescribe educational experiences by means of a designated end state raises the same moral issue for curriculum developers as for psychologists: How and by whom is the end state determined? From the phenomenological point of view, growth is personal, present oriented, with "I-Thou" defining the nature of interactions as reciprocal.

Those reconceptualizing curriculum theory in this direction are expressly rejecting the Tyler curriculum model (1950, 1977) so much in use for a quarter of a century, for they believe it is built on the general technological rationale dominating American life. This means–end model (specifying objectives, selecting activities, organizing learning experiences, and evaluating outcomes) partakes of the technological consciousness and leads to prizing optimum growth and maximum efficiency. Teaching then becomes unrelated to everyday life in the classroom or to the uniqueness of persons. The coming of modern technology has served only to reinforce the "design specification" view of the production model of curriculum. A new conceptualization is long overdue, but what will replace the means–end design? A number of curriculum theorists calling themselves reconceptualists are focusing on this task.

Certainly the discovery of the latent or hidden curriculum existent in classrooms has brought into question the rationality of the Tyler model. Unrecognized norms and values pervade classroom life. The ritualistic quality of much school experience, the unequal use of power, the basic evaluative nature of school living, the presence and pressure of many other students are all characteristics well documented by Jackson (1968). Focusing on early childhood, Goodlad and Klein (1974) found: "an excess of routine and vicarious rather than direct experience; a limited variety of ways of doing things [p. 99]." Interaction patterns tended to maximize those between teacher and child and to minimize those between and among children. Unquestioning acceptance of authority, uniformity of response, and conformity to strict routines were found in another study to be early learnings in kindergarten (King, 1976). Analyses of the social milieu in which children tacitly dwell are intended to bring to a conscious level the hidden ideological assumptions that structure the decisions made by teachers and the environments they design. "It is an ethical necessity," writes Apple (1975): "for educators to engage in searching analyses of the ways in which they allow values and commitments unconsciously to work through them [p. 121]."

The recognition of bureaucratic values permeating environments for learning has moved curriculum specialists with an existential orientation to place the person with all his or her continuously evolving uniqueness in the center of classroom interaction. Interaction then—interaction in a social setting—becomes critical to curriculum development from a phenomenological point of view, and it is a search for organism–environment transactions enhancing reciprocal relationships.

Curriculum literature is moving, if tentatively, toward the problem of accounting for quality in experience, for concern with the inward experience of students acting in their educational environments. This is not new; John Dewey, for one, maintained that education could be intelligently conducted only in light of a philosophy of experience. Yet, new is the increasing appreciation of experience and the search for experience with meaning. To construct meaningful patterns out of experience requires an active learner in "an environment supportive of exploratory thought that encourages children to entertain ideas in a spirit of tentativeness [Eisner, 1979, p. 271].'' The teacher's role is that of orchestrating an educational environment for creative intelligence at work.

THE DEVELOPMENTAL POSITION

With expanding attention to experiencing one may well ask what has happened to the developmental aspect of the dyad? A pure existential position, untempered by a developmental point of view, places a heavy responsibility on the teacher for great sensitivity to the feelings, abilities, concerns, and the nature of thinking of each person in the classroom. Particularly at that often baffling preoperational stage can developmental insights inform a great deal of the teacher's behavior.

Some observations of actual classroom experiences may help to illustrate this point. Children in a classroom of 6-year-olds were asked to write a story centered on two fish that had been acquired recently. The children were asked to put themselves in the place of the fish and answer the questions: "Why are these children here? What are they doing?" The teacher put words on the board to help; children used picture dictionaries, their own individual word cards, and they helped each other. Something was written, but it was reported that the stories were not as good as those the children usually created.

A teacher understanding the persisting egocentrism of young children would recognize how unsuitable the topic was. Some of the children in this classroom were probably thinking quite preoperationally; some may have attained concrete operations, at least in some areas of thought; others may have been making the transition and operating intuitively. Those in the preoperational stage would have difficulty taking the point of view of another. Even for those children whose egocentrism was waning, the ability to generalize underlying explanations of behavior would be at a primitive stage.

Let's consider an example on another level. A group of 15 4-year-olds were requested to begin their school day by learning to tie shoelaces strung through a paper plate. After completing this task, they were free to select their own activity. To those recognizing that girls come to school with different abilities than boys, including better fine-muscle coordination, it would not be surprising that most of the girls quickly finished the task and moved on to other activities. One girl achieved success on the day of the observation and, feeling the joy of accomplishment, she repeated the act over and over again, showing the bow to all who would observe it. But for the boys it was different. Most of them struggled valiantly, but one boy threw the plate and laces to the floor in desperation. His frustration continued throughout the morning, the only thing he pursued at length was throwing bean bags through a hole.

The developmentalist would consider that such painful classroom experiences could be avoided if more attention were given to the children's level of growth.

The teacher comprehending the nature of thought or of motor coordination of these children would eschew experiences not in tune with their abilities. Certainly, too, they would consider individual differences that would make indefensible such assignments for all children.

Curriculum designers turning to a phenomenological interpretation would address the problem differently. The developmental accomplishments of each child would not be violated because children would not be pressed into prescribed experiences. Rather, elements of choice, responsibility, and freedom pervasive in the educational setting would free the learner to pursue experiences naturally stemming from growth already attained. Learnings would be extensions into the phenomenal world guided toward increased mastery and understanding without sacrificing any of the perceptions or attainments of the person involved.

To turn again to a consideration of the problem on a theoretical level, Reese and Overton (1970) unite stage theory to an active-organism perspective; they find organizational changes an essential of growth. They write: "As organization changes to the extent that new system properties emerge (new structures and functions) and become operational, we speak of a new level of organization which exhibits a basic discontinuity with the previous level [p. 143]." A necessary relationship exists, they propose, between "level of organization" and theoretical "stage." Indeed, Reese and Overton find stage, thus defined, to be a central concept of the active-organism model that distinguishes it from a reactive model. These two different families of theories the authors find incompatible, for they reflect different ways of viewing the learner and the world.

On the other hand, Kessen (1975) reinforces the cultural embeddedness of all developmental study, for he sees research and theory "often in large measure, instrumentalities of other powers in American life." Whatever facts of growth stem from the clinical or laboratory mode, Kessen affirms: "come surrounded by veils, more or less transparent, of political and ideological bias [pp. 101–102]." Psychologists as well as educators have allowed values and commitments unconsciously to work through them. A healthy skepticism concerning certain designated uniformities of growth thus seems in order.

Early childhood educators following the recommendations of Hall and Jersild to ground program specifics in child study believed that curriculum would be based on scientifically obtained "facts." Not only is the "factual" nature of such data in question, but also the heavy reliance on it for "the method and matter" of teaching. In a revised relationship between education and child study, the educator would call on derived data only when it illuminated aspects of complex behavior. The researcher would not be perceived as leading the way for the educator but as providing one resource for the educator in dealing with the diversity and fluidity of young children's behavioral manifestations.

Curriculum specialists today recognize that sound prescriptions for educational practices cannot be supported solely on our understanding of the development of the human. Decisions concerning the content of learning in school inevitably reflect the intricate demands of a changing culture. The complexity of curriculum designing demands a multiperspective approach. Indeed, Goodlad's (1979) study of curriculum found that political, social, and transactional processes must be grappled with as well as the acts and the actors [pp. 3–4].

THE VALUE QUESTION

Obviously, at the level of theory, both psychologists and curriculum designers are confronting similar perplexing problems: the nature of environmental interactions, the means–end dilemma, the inescapable value orientation. Present day perspectives, stripping away blinders of the past, have propelled each discipline into corresponding directions. The importance of reciprocity in personal interactions and the ethical responsibility inherent in establishing desirable end states are being addressed by both. The underlying value orientation of each is being probed.

One value expressed by Jersild in the forties and increasingly acknowledged today was his insistence on utter respect for personal growth. This is framed by psychologists in terms of each person's construction of his or her own knowledge. Or on a holistic developmental level and drawing from an intensive longitudinal study, Murphy and Moriarity (1976) write:

> the child is an active, dynamic creature who quietly or noisily tries to select from the environment what satisfies his individual, vegetative, sensory, motor, cognitive and social needs. . . . Each child struggles to find solutions and out of these struggles and their solutions develops an implicit or explicit view of life as well as self [p. 13].

Illustrative of a growing number of studies planted in environmental interactions, it carefully takes account of personal growth and the circumstances that influence it.

For the curriculum designer wishing to select values, the concept of man in the literature of existentialism that emphasizes his or her aloneness, uniqueness, and potential for developing selfhood provides high personal regard. To actualize this philosophically conceived position, Berman (1968) sets the task of education as aiding: "the person in harnessing his energies in such a way that he is able continuously to bring his new insights into line with a view he is developing about himself [p. 2]." Process values are dominant here: communicating, loving, knowing, making decisions, creating, valuing.

Perhaps Millie Almy (1973) has captured the essence of both views when she writes:

> Guiding today's young children for tomorrow's world, lighting the lamps of their own intelligence is, of course, a matter of providing a physical and social environ-

ment in which they can act, interact, do, think, and *become*. But it is also a matter of providing time, space and atmosphere in which they can experience and be—a matter of lighting the spirit as well as the mind [p. 49].

REFERENCES

Almy, M. Guiding children for life in tomorrow's world. In R. H. Anderson (Ed.), *Education in anticipation of tomorrow*. Worthington, Ohio: Charles A. Jones, 1973.

Apple, M. W. Commonsense categories and curriculum thought. In J. B. MacDonald and E. Zaret (Eds.), *Schools in search of meaning*. Washington, D.C.: Association for Supervision and Curriculum Development, 1975.

Ausubel, D. Viewpoints from related disciplines: Human growth and development. *Teachers College Record*, 1959, 60, 245–254.

Barker, R. D. (Ed.). *Habitats, environments and human behavior*. San Francisco: Jossey-Bass, 1978.

Berman, L. M. *New priorities in the curriculum*. Columbus, Ohio: Merrill, 1968.

Berman, L. M., & Roderick, J. A. *Curriculum: Teaching the what, how and why of living*. Columbus, Ohio: Merrill, 1977.

Bloom, B. S. *Stability and change in human characteristics*. New York: Wiley, 1968.

Bronfenbrenner, U. A theoretical perspective for research on human development. In H. P. Dreitzel (Ed.), *Childhood and socialization*. New York: Macmillian, 1973.

Eisner, E. W. *The educational imagination*. New York: Macmillan, 1979.

Foster, J. C. & Headley, N. E. *Education in the kindergarten*. New York: American Book, 1936.

Gesell, A. & Ilg, F. L. *Infant and child in the culture of today*. New York: Harper, 1943.

Goodlad, J. I. (Ed.). *Curriculum inquiry*. New York: McGraw-Hill, 1979.

Goodlad, J. I. & Klein, M. F. *Looking behind the classroom door*. Worthington, Ohio: Charles A. Jones, 1974.

Hall, G. S. The ideal school as based on child study. *Journal of Proceedings and Addresses of the National Education Association*. 1901. 474–488.

Hall, G. S. *Life and confessions of a psychologist*. New York: D. Appleton, 1924.

Huebner, D. Curriculum as a field of study. In H. F. Robison (Ed.), *Precedents and promise in the curriculum field*. New York: Teachers College Press, 1966.

Jackson, P. W. *Life in classrooms*. New York: Holt, Rinehart and Winston, 1968.

Jersild, A. T. *Child development and the curriculum*. New York: Bureau of Publications, Teachers College, Columbia University, 1946.

Kamii, C. & DeVries, R. Piaget for early education. In M. C. Day & R. K. Parker (Eds.). *The preschool in action*. Boston: Allyn & Bacon, 1977.

Keniston, K. Psychology development and historical change. *The Journal of Interdisciplinary History*. 1971, II, 329–346.

Kessen, W. Commentary. In M. J. E. Senn (Ed.), *Insight on the child development movement in the United States*. Monograph of the Society for Research in Child Development. 1975. 161.

King, N. R. *The hidden curriculum and the socialization of kindergarten children*. Unpublished doctoral dissertation. University of Wisconsin, 1976.

Macdonald, J. B. The person in the curriculum. In H. F. Robison (Ed.), *Precedents and promise in the curriculum field*. New York: Teachers College Press, 1966.

Murphy, L. B. & Moriarty, A. E. *Vulnerability, coping, and growth from infancy to adolescence*. New Haven: Yale University Press, 1976.

Phenix, P. H. *Realms of meaning*. New York: McGraw-Hill, 1964.

Reese, H. W. & Overton, W. F. Models of development and theories of development. In L. R.

Goulet & P. B. Baltes (Eds.), *Life-span developmental psychology*. New York: Academic Press, 1970.

Sanders, S. The importance of Piaget learning theory for the college teacher. *Journal of College Science Teaching*. 1978, 7, 283–287.

Sigel, I. Developmental theory: Its place and relevance in early intervention programs. *Young Children*. 1972, 27, 364–372.

Smart, M. What Piaget suggests to classroom teachers. *Childhood Education*. 1968, 48, 294–300.

Tyler, R. W. The organization of learning, experiences. In V. E. Herrick & R. W. Tyler (Eds.), *Toward improved curriculum theory*. Chicago: University of Chicago Press, 1950.

Tyler, R. W. Desirable content for a curriculum development syllabus today. In A. Molnar & J. A. Zahorick (Eds.), *Curriculum theory*. Washington, D.C.: Association for Supervision and Curriculum Development, 1977.

Wapner, S., Cohen, S. B., & Kaplan, B. Introduction. In S. Wapner, S. B. Cohen & B. Kaplan (Eds.), *Experiencing the environment*. New York: Plenem, 1976.

V THE NATURE AND DEVELOPMENT OF GENDER DIFFERENCES

In our society the handling of gender differences in social, economic, and political arenas is a matter of serious debate. Jeanne Block and Dorothy Ullian probe underlying psychological factors responsible for boys' and girls' differing psychosexual premises and behavior. Although both Block and Ullian recognize developmental and interactive components in the formation of gender differences, they offer divergent explanations of the genesis of these differences. Differing values seem to adhere to each explanation.

Block, integrating a broad array of research data, places major emphasis on socialization experiences, which, in turn, are assumed to shape a child's cognitive structures. She provides a coherent organization for interpreting the gender differences that have been reliably identified. In linking gender differences to a conception of cognitive modes of processing new experience, she suggests that females appear to rely more on existing cognitive and personality structures, whereas males appear to excel in problems that involve restructuring earlier premises.

Ullian advances a constructivist hypothesis and explicates the developmental factors entailed. She proposes that the sex differences indicated in the literature are determined by sex-role concepts spontaneously generated by children as they actively seek to interpret the psychological significance of biological gender. Values, rather than reflecting predetermined categories, are examined within the framework generated by each gender as experiences are organized and interpreted.

9

Gender Differences in the Nature of Premises Developed About the World

Jeanne H. Block
University of California, Berkeley

In considering gender differences from the developmental–interaction perspective, I have elected to focus on parental socialization emphases and shaping behaviors and their influence on the cognitive heuristics and problem-solving strategies developed by males and females. However, before turning to that agenda, I enumerate briefly several problems characterizing the data base surrounding the question of gender differences and contributing to the difficulty of abstracting dependable generalizations. These deficiencies are cited because they have helped to shape the thoughts I am presenting.

The literature on gender differences is an agglomeration of inconsistent, often conflicting findings, based on research largely unguided by theory. Empirical assessments of psychological differences between males and females have been essentially undirected, and findings frequently have emerged *en passant* because the investigator's primary interest was focused on other questions. As Fairweather (1976) concluded after reviewing the evidence for sex differences in cognition:

> It must be stressed, finally, that the majority of studies reviewed here and elsewhere are both ill-thought and ill-performed. Whilst in other circumstances this may be regarded as the occupational hazard of the scientific enterprise, here such complacency is compounded by the social loadings placed upon these kinds of results. It is clearly very easy to include sex as a bonus factor in experiments which have little scientific merit. We cannot pretend that we are testing a theory of sex differences, since at present none can exist. *Legitimate studies of sex differences can only grow out of observations of clear individual differences in the investigation of salient psychological processes....* [italics added] [p. 267].

These "salient psychological" processes must be identified, embedded in a conceptual framework, and used to inform empiricism on sex-related differences.

A second, related problem contributing to the inconsistent findings surrounding research on gender differences is that the variables studied are often conceptualized and operationalized in different ways by different investigators. Consider, for example, the many ways used to operationalize the construct of suggestibility (e.g., the Asch group conformity experiment, yielding to group concensus in discussion situations, responses to questionnaires, observations of targeted behaviors following presentation of information designed to modify opinion) and the confusing, often inconsistent results eventuating from studies using these very different methods to investigate presumably the same psychological phenomenon. Also complicating the problem of achieving a more coherent literature surrounding specific constructs is that particular operational transformations may not be supportable as an indicator of the construct supposedly the focus of investigation. Consider the ways in which prosocial behaviors have been assessed, for example. The correlates of prosocial behavior when operationalized as the sharing of redeemable tokens with an unseen, anonymous, nonexistent peer are different from those found when prosocial behavior is assessed using observations of a child's actual "helping" behaviors in situations where providing help is appropriate. Also contributing to untidiness in the empirical realm is the tendency to define psychological variables in global, insufficiently articulated ways, a practice that tends to obscure relationships that might be discerned if more differentiated measures of the construct under consideration were used.

A third problem characterizing the data base on which our conclusions about gender differences depend is that in many areas this base is neither sufficiently comprehensive nor robust with regard to statistical power to support generalization. In research on sex-related differences, there is need for more focused studies that respect conventional methodological principles, utilize samples that are large, salient, and relatively free of selective bias, and employ instruments meeting conventional psychometric standards.

Fourth, the aggregated data pertaining to sex-related differences is biased in a number of ways. Young children are over-represented. In Maccoby and Jacklin (1974), conclusions about sex differences are based on studies conducted predominantly with children. Seventy-five percent of the researches included in their tables used subject samples 12 years of age and younger (Block, 1976a, 1976b). To the extent that gender differences increase with age (Block, 1976a, 1976b, 1979a; Terman & Tyler, 1954), this data base cannot be considered fully representative or pertinent. Another source of bias is the unfortunate tendency of psychologists to use "samples of convenience," samples selected for reasons of ready availability (e.g., university nursery school children, college students enrolled in introductory psychology courses). It is unlikely that such samples are representative of the population of preschoolers or of young adults. Bias in sampling strategies can affect the results of gender comparisons and, if present, must qualify conclusions.

In summary, operations used to evaluate particular constructs are often conceptually insensitive and are frequently lacking in reliability and/or construct validity. In view of these problems (and others uncited), it is suggested that we need to chart some new directions in gender-related research that are guided by explicit conceptual models and implemented with finely tuned instruments.

What follows is a still inchoate, tentative formulation that seeks to provide a coherent organizing structure for interpreting some of the gender differences that have been reliably identified. This conceptual interpretation of gender differences is then related to the cognitive processing proclivities of the two sexes, specifically to modes of processing new experiential inputs, both cognitive and affective. Finally, a link is forged between the differential socialization experiences of males and females and the development of personality structures. The formulation being offered does not derive from a set of critical experiments. Rather, it represents an aggregation and integration of a number of discrete, isolated, but implicative results obtained by other investigators in an attempt to provide links in the evidential chain being constructed.

Before embarking on this conjectural voyage, it is important to note that the emphasis on sex-differentiated socialization practices accorded here does not imply that gender differences are viewed solely as a function of sociocultural-psychological forces. Rather, gender differences are viewed as manifestations of genetic, biological, historical–cultural, and psychological factors complexly interacting in an open system in which particular factors assume differential salience at different developmental periods. It is assumed that a fundamental life task for individuals is that of mediating between coexisting internal biological impulses and external socializing forces (Block, 1973, 1979b). Manifestations of gender, then, represent a synthesis of biological and cultural factors and forces as these are mediated by the individual's cognitive and ego structures (Block, 1973).

A CONCEPTUAL ORGANIZATION OF SEX-RELATED PSYCHOLOGICAL DIFFERENCES

It is suggested here that the gender differences established with some degree of reliability can be organized and viewed as representing different ways of processing experience by males and by females. Based on the evaluation of research on sex differences offered by Maccoby and Jacklin (1974), the reinterpretation of their conclusions by Block (1976a, 1976b), and earlier assessments of sex differences by Maccoby (1966), Tyler (1965), and by Terman and Tyler (1954), females appear, on the average, to excel relative to males in areas of cognitive processing that involve verbal ability—memory for narrative and verbal fluency.

Females appear, on the average, to differ from males in the personality realm in manifesting lesser curiosity and exploratory behavior, greater timidity, greater influenceability, lesser confidence in performance, and in being more susceptible to anxiety. In their social behaviors, females also differ from males. Accordingly, females, when contrasted with males, are more empathic when empathy is defined as manifesting more vicarious, veridical responses to another's distress (M. L. Hoffman, 1977) and engage in more prosocial behaviors (Smith, Haan, & Block, 1970). They also maintain closer proximity to friends, demonstrate greater compliance to authority, and manifest greater concern about behaving in ways that are socially approved. Underlying this set of phenotypically dissimilar intellectual and personological characteristics is, I suggest, a common theme. In processing experiences that deviate from previously established expectations, females, more than males, appear to be more conserving and to rely more—and longer—on the utilization of existing cognitive and personality structures, responding to new experiences in ways that are consistent with prior understandings. Attempts are made to fit new, discrepant information or experience into existing structures and these structures or schemata are extended or revised only when required and then by a series of incremental steps, parsimoniously taken. This mode of processing experience—more frequently used by females than males as proposed here—may have important advantages for the species. Females' greater emphasis on the conservation of existing structures insures greater continuity across time and generations and may well serve a sociobiological function in preserving those cultural traditions and historical values having special survival utility.

Turning now to reliably identified characteristics distinguishing males, it is suggested that males differ from females in their characteristic modes of processing new experiences. With regard to cognitive processing, males appear to excel in problems that involve restructuring, breaking set, and developing new strategies for generating solutions. Males also score higher, on the average, on measures of spatial and quantitative abilities, measures that require extrapolation in the perceptual–spatial domain. Males differ from females, on the average, in personality characteristics that include exploratory behavior and curiosity, activity, and self-confidence in problem-solving situations. In their interpersonal relationships, males, relative to females, tend to be more aggressive, dominant, and competitive. A common thread underlying this phenotypically disparate set of behaviors is the greater tendency of males to deal with new experiences deviating from previous understandings in ways that involve active attempts to transform or to restructure earlier premises. Males more readily initiate efforts to construct new cognitive structures capable of encompassing the information that has stressed existing structures. This mode of processing information—more frequently used by males than by females as proposed here—also has advantages for the species. The greater tendency of males to respond to disequilibrating experiences by restructuring, by devising alternative premises, and by creating new psychological structures provides a source of innovation for society and may serve a sociobiological function in giving impetus to social and cultural change. (For a more extended discussion of these sex-differentiated modes of processing new informational inputs and the relationship of these modes to Piaget's concepts of assimilation–accommodation, see Block, 1979b and Block, 1980).[1]

There is a risk that the conceptualization being offered only provides yet another bipolar dimension for differentiating males and females. To be sure, there is some overlap with the conceptualizations of others: the agency–communion distinction of Bakan (1966), the allocentric–autocentric concepts of Guttman (1965), the instrumental–expressive orientation discussed by Parsons and Bales (1955), and the conservation–initiation dimension as elaborated by Gough (1968). This conceptualization would represent only a trivial rephrasing of the works of these theorists were it to stop at this point. However, the differences in ways of processing experience here postulated are implicative for the quality of psychological (and human) functioning and are importantly affected by differences in the early socialization of males and females, differences that help to create diverging environmental contexts in which the development of males and females occurs. If this conjecture proves to be correct, then we may be in a position to suggest modifications of a socialization process that derives perhaps more than is now required from a cultural past no longer relevant. Modes of socializing children and differentiating gender roles that were once useful may no longer have functional significance in contemporary technological societies and may serve to constrain the possibilities of both males and females as they attempt to forge identities, formulate life goals, and realize their potentials (Block, 1973; L. W. Hoffman, 1977).

Before going on to discuss early experiences influencing the ways in which individuals manage new experiential inputs, a few caveats and qualifications are required. For purposes of exposition, the distinction between two modes of processing experience is being emphasized. Of course, all individuals use both modes of processing experience at different times and under different circumstances. However, it may prove useful to consider the *preferred* or *dominant* mode characterizing a person. In reacting to new experiences that fail to conform to expectation, some persons, and females more than males, tend to be oriented more toward fitting new observational data into existing psychological structures; they tend to persist longer than males in efforts to fit (to assimilate, in Piagetian terms) new information before shifting their efforts to create new structures (to accommodate, in Piagetian terms). Processing of new experiential inputs by other persons, and males more than females, tends to be characterized by a

---

[1]My recognition that the use of the assimilative and accommodative modes of processing new experiences may be sex differentiated derived from discussions with my husband, Jack Block, who has discussed Piaget's concepts of assimilation and accommodation in the context of personality as well as cognitive functioning.

greater readiness to abandon psychological schemata not articulating readily with new experiences in favor of restructuring or transforming existing structures or formulating new schemata that will encompass refractory information. All persons use both modes of processing experience at different times, ideally invoking each in context-responsive ways. Overreliance on any one strategy for processing information may be dysfunctional. The use of procrustean methods to fit or mold new perceptions into existing schemata results in a selective, distorted, oversimplified view of the world (Perry, 1968), whereas premature jettisoning of established structures and zealously sought redefinition of premises may result in an ahistorical, overarticulated, compartmentalized view of the world.

SOCIALIZATION INFLUENCES ON
SEX-DIFFERENTIATED MODES OF PROCESSING
EXPERIENCE

Modes of processing experience and the psychological structures resulting therefrom are influenced by the child's very early experiences in interaction with primary caretakers. Caretakers affect in many ways—both implicit and explicit—the child's interests, play, opportunities for manipulation and exploration, and expectations that inform his or her constructions about the world. Parental choices of toys and play materials, channeling of play, encouragement of the child's "experiments in nature" (Piaget, 1952), tolerance for active exploration, and even assignment of household chores not only influence the child's developing conceptions of gender roles but help to determine, within the limits set by genetic inheritance, the course of psychological development as well.

In attempting to elucidate the development of sex-related differences from the psychological perspective that is the focus of this chapter, it is proposed that sex-differentiated parenting, socialization, and shaping behaviors influence boys and girls in ways that differentially affect their cognitive and affective development. Four principal areas of influence are discussed:

1. It is proposed that the child's cognitive constructions about the world, that is, the nature of the premise system developed by the child, will be affected by sex-differentiated parental behaviors.

2. It is proposed that the extent and quality of exploratory behavior manifested by the child will differ as a function of parental concepts of sex-appropriate behavior.

3. It is proposed that the frequency with which the child encounters conflict or disequilibrating experiences that challenge previously established understandings will be influenced by sex-differentiated parental socialization emphases.

4. It is proposed that the strategies developed by the child to deal with new experimental inputs—strategies that have just been described—will differ in boys and girls as a function of their differential experiences with parents, toys, and teachers.

The differences between the sexes alluded to earlier are now documented and discussed in some detail to show how the different experiences of boys and girls and the different environmental contexts in which they live, learn, and grow shape the nature and the development of both their cognitive and ego structures.

Influences on the Child's Developing Premise System

Although many experiences in early childhood influence the child's developing conceptions of the world, for purposes of discussion here, only those socialization experiences that are sex-differentiated are considered. Three such sex-differentiated parenting behaviors are discussed: (1) differential experience of boys and girls in receiving contingent responding; (2) differential opportunity accorded boys and girls for independent exploration; and (3) differential exposure of boys and girls to disequilibrating experiences. With regard to the nature of the premise system that the young child begins to establish very early in life, it is contended that the differential exposure of boys and girls to contingency relationships affects the nature of the premises about the world and about the self that are being evolved. Among the sources of this differential experience with contingency relationships are parental and teacher responses to the behaviors of the young child and the characteristics of toys made available to boys and to girls.

Contingent Responding of Caretakers.   Observations in the literature suggest that males experience more contingent responding from both mothers and fathers than do females. Murphy and Moriarity (1976), for example, note that mothers of males are more responsive in the feeding situation to the child's signals of wanting to stop feeding than are mothers of females. Walraven (1974) also observed mothers and infants during feeding and found that following a loud auditory stimulus, mothers were more attentive to their male infants' reactions than to those of their female infants. Both mothers and fathers have been observed to respond more frequently to vocalizations initiated by their sons while more frequently initiating vocalization with their daughters (Lewis & Freedle, 1973; Parke & Sawin, 1976; Yarrow, 1975.) Mothers have also been found to be more responsive to infant-initiated movement and playlike activites demonstrated by male infants than by female infants (Lewis, 1972).

Turning to data on somewhat older children, the results of studies of sex differences in positive and negative reinforcements given children are consistent over a broad age range and indicate that boys receive both more physical punishment and negative feedback from parents when they behave in ways that violate parental standards (Maccoby & Jacklin, 1974). In an elegant study specifically designed to assess differences in the contingent responding of mothers and fathers to their sons and daughters, using sequential analysis, Margolin and Patterson (1975) found that boys receive significantly more positive responses from both their mothers and fathers than do girls. Observing parental behaviors that immediately followed either deviant or prosocial behaviors, these investigators found that fathers responded positively to their sons almost *twice* as often as to their daughters. These results accord with data summarized by Maccoby and Jacklin (1974), who conclude that boys receive more negative contingent responding and that when sex differences in positive reinforcement are found, the results tend to favor boys. Thus, the data from numerous studies, using different methods and assessing parental behaviors with children of various ages, suggest that boys appear to experience more contingent responding from their parents than girls.

Contingent Responding of Teachers.   Not only does the literature yield evidence of more frequent contingent responding to the behaviors of the child by parents of males than of females, but this pattern of response is characteristic of teachers as well. Serbin, O'Leary, Kent, and Tonick (1973) investigated sex-differentiated contingent responding to specific child behaviors on the part of nursery school teachers. The rate of teacher response to disruptive behavior in boys was significantly higher than it was to girls. Their analyses controlled for difference in the frequencies of such behaviors by boys and girls. Teachers also showed higher rates of response to boys' solicitation behaviors than to girls' and, additionally, solicitation of attention on the part of boys evoked significantly more instructional behavior on the part of the teachers. Specifically, in response to boys' requests, teachers held more extended conversations, gave more brief instructions, and provided more extended directions than they did in response to solicitation behaviors from girls. Other studies of nursery school teachers' behaviors support the Serbin et al. findings, demonstrating that the behaviors of boys in the classroom are more likely to evoke attention and response, both positive and negative, than the behaviors of girls (Felsenthal, 1970; Meyer & Thompson, 1956).

Together, these several findings suggest greater adult contingent responding to the behaviors of boys than to girls. Because few studies have looked explicitly at sequential contingency behaviors of parents and teachers it is difficult to provide vigorous documentation for the assertion about sex differences in contingency experiences being proposed here. The available evidence is supporting and it is hoped that these conjectures might stimulate additional systematic research efforts in this area.

Differential Experience with Feedback from Toys

A second source of differential experience with contingency relationships on the part of boys and girls derives from the nature of the toys that are provided to and considered sex-appropriate for boys and girls. The literature on toy preference is replete with lists indicating the preferred toys of boys and girls (Fagot, 1977; Fein, Johnson, Kosson, Stork, & Wasserman, 1975; Goldberg & Lewis, 1969; Rheingold & Cook, 1975). However, it is necessary to go beyond simple cataloging of preferred toys and examine more deeply the characteristics of toys preferred by males and females with regard to their potential influence on the psychological development of children. Yarrow and his colleagues (Yarrow, Rubinstein, Pederson, & Jankowski, 1972) have demonstrated the incisive results that can be obtained when a conceptual approach is used to classify toys. These investigators categorized inanimate objects in the infant's environment according to their *responsiveness, complexity,* and *variety.* These three dimensions were then found to relate to a variety of infant behaviors in several domains, including motor development, exploratory behaviors, and goal-directed behaviors. Rheingold and Cook (1975) also developed "higher-order" categorizations of toys on the basis of "world orientations" and concluded, from their analysis of toys found in the rooms of girls and the rooms of boys, that: "boys were provided objects that encourage activities directed away from home . . . and girls (were provided) objects that encourage activities directed toward the home—keeping house and caring for children [p. 463]."

Reflecting on the aggregated data surrounding the nature of the toys provided to and preferred by boys and by girls suggests that the toys differ in six important ways:

1. Boys' toys, more than the toys of girls, provide more contingent feedback.
2. Boys' toys, more than the toys of girls, encourage active manipulation.
3. Boys' toys, more than the toys of girls, encourage engagement of the *physical* world.
4. Boys' toys, more than the toys of girls, afford inventive possibilities.
5. Girls' toys, more than the toys of boys, encourage imitative play.
6. Girls' toys, more than the toys of boys, encourage engagement of the *social* world.

These differences in the formal characteristics of toys, it is proposed, provide boys and girls with different experiences during their early formative years, experiences that affect the development of the premise systems that underlie their self—and world—orientations.

The nature of the preferred toys of boys (e.g., blocks, vehicles, tools) encourages manipulative play and provides more feedback. Yarrow et al. (1972) found that toy responsiveness (feedback potential) was related to the developmental level of the infant, exploratory behavior, goal orientation, reaching and grasping behaviors, and to secondary circular reactions that reflect: "the infant's repeated efforts to evoke feedback from objects [p. 27]." These results emphasize the importance of considering the higher-order effects of toys on the development of cognitive schemata in boys and in girls.

Girls' toys, in contrast to boys' toys, encourage imitative play, particularly in the context of household and nurturing activities (Rheingold & Cook, 1975). The toys made available to girls are less amenable to inventive changes (Rosenfeld, 1975) and their uses are more prescribed. The toys typically provided to girls encourage interaction in the social, in contrast to the physical world. The inherent characteristics of girls' toys provide less informative feedback than the toys of boys, which encourage play in the physical world. Inadequately balanced block constructions, for example, will topple; however, haphazard arrangements of doll furniture are unlikely to evoke *physical* consequences. Such arrangements are more apt, however, to elicit *social* consequences in the form of critical comments or corrective suggestions from mother, siblings, or peers. It is suggested that differences exist in the quality of feedback from the physical and social worlds. Feedback from the physical world is more likely to be immediate, consistent, and unambiguous. The clarity of this feedback benefits the eduction of principles about the workings of the physical world. Feedback from the physical world is also impersonal and, for these several reasons, is likely to encourage self-generated problem-solving attempts to test the nature of the physical reality and/or to rectify mistakes. Feedback from the social world, however, is less consistent, less clear, and often delayed. Given these conditions, the principles guiding social interactions are difficult to discern. Further, feedback from the social world is more often personal than impersonal and comments may imply criticism, criticism that may disrupt play and dishearten the child's feelings of efficacy and competence.

Importance of Contingent Responding

Contingent responding appears to have consequential implications for cognitive development. Contingent responding on the part of mothers has been found to relate to the early development of object relationships (Sander, 1976), the infant's general developmental level, social responsiveness, and goal-directed behaviors (Yarrow et al., 1972), the quality of attachment as shown by 1-year-olds' responses to a strange situation (Ainsworth & Bell, 1969), and later coping behaviors (Murphy & Moriarity, 1976).

Contingent responding to the baby's signals and behaviors facilitates the infant's developing awareness of his or her evocative role in eliciting responses and effects from both the social and the physical worlds, thereby influencing the premises the young child develops about the nature of his or her relationship with the larger world. These early experiences of efficacy are the precursors of later instrumental competence. The construction of a premise system that suggests "my actions can produce effects in the world" increases the child's motivation to explore, to experiment, and to master. These observations about contingent experiences and their influence on cognitive development and the acquisition of particular personological characteristics have been noted and emphasized by numerous investigators. Characteristics of the inanimate and/or the social environment have been related to infant motivation (Yarrow et al., 1972), to White's effectance motive (White, 1959), to Hunt's concept of "intrinsic motivation" (Hunt, 1965), to Lewis and Goldberg's "generalized expectancy model" (Lewis & Goldberg, 1969), to Watson's "contingency awareness" (Watson, 1966; Watson & Ramey, 1972), to Seligman's "learned helplessness" (Dweck, Davidson, Nelson, & Enna, 1978; Seligman, 1975) and to Piaget's (1952) characterization of the child as an active, information-processing organism. These writings converge in emphasizing the relationship between activity, feedback, effectance, and/or developing competence.

The recognition advanced here is that an active, experimental approach to the environment is facilitated to a greater extent in males than in females by their more frequent experiences with feedback and with contingent responding. By virtue of these sex-differentiated experiences with feedback and contingent responding, males are more likely than females to develop a premise system about the world that posits "actions have effects" and to develop a premise system about the self that posits efficacy and instrumentality. Data demonstrating the greater instrumentality of boys in barrier situations (Block, Block, & Harrington, 1975; Goldberg & Lewis, 1969) and in goal-directed situations (Yarrow, 1975) and their lesser "learned helplessness" (Dweck, et al., 1978) reflect a premise system—an expectancy—that includes instrumental competence.

These expectations of orderly effects resulting from effective actions serve to increase the salience of stimulus control differentially for males and females. Males appear to attach greater importance to the ability to control events originating in the environment as documented in two recent studies by Gunnar-Gnechten (1977, 1978). To summarize results of two studies deserving more extended discussion, Gunnar-Gnechten (1977, 1978) found that a potentially frightening toy was more distressing to boys who could not control its onset than it was to boys who had been taught to operate the toy themselves and thus to control the onset of a somewhat noxious, noisy stimulus. The relationship between fear and inability to control onset of an adversive event was found *only* in the sample of boys; fear was unrelated to the ability to control in the sample of girls. These results were replicated in a second study and Gunnar-Gnechten concludes that having control over external events is a more salient concern for 4-year-old boys than for girls. Bronson (1971) also demonstrated boys' greater interest in feedback in a study where, in each of three observed episodes, boys, more frequently than girls, acted upon stimuli in ways that produced contingent effects.

Although data on sex-differentiated parental contingency behaviors are suggestive, the studies are too few to permit strong conclusions. Few researchers have examined sex differences in maternal contingent responding and even fewer have assessed contingent responding on the part of the fathers. Because differences in the child's contingency experiences with parents and with toys appear to influence the psychological structures developed to process experience, more systematic, focused research on these questions is clearly required.

Sex-related Differences in Imitative Play

In discussing differences between boys' and girls' toys with respect to their feedback potential, it was noted also that the toys typically provided to girls, relative to those of boys, encourage more imitative play, play in which the child models maternal nurturing and caretaking behaviors and housekeeping tasks. Whereas many toys preferred by boys also elicit imitative play (e.g., vehicles, soldiers, arms), other toys preferred by boys (e.g., blocks, tools) elicit structural and manipulative play. The effects of providing girls with toys that predispose them toward imitative play at an early age may be reflected in their greater tendency toward imitation in other contexts as well.

Observations of children's play in nursery school settings indicate that girls engage more often in doll play, dance, and dress up like adults significantly more often than boys (Fagot, 1974, 1977). They have been observed to imitate and help the teacher more often in the nursery school setting (Etaugh, Collins, & Gerson, 1975) and to imitate primary human relationships in their group play activities (Lever, 1976); they also appear to be more prone to imitate the behaviors of an adult model (Bell, Weller, & Waldrop, 1971; Pederson & Bell, 1970; Portuges & Fesbach, 1972). This general conclusion about imitation must be qualified by considerations of setting and the nature of behaviors being modeled. Although imitation provides the child with a behavioral formula that can be applied in specific situations, imitation does not encourage active problem-solving attempts nor does it facilitate deutero-learning, "learning how to learn," of the sort discussed by Bateson (1942).

Additional perspective and implication accrues to the findings surrounding sex differences in the toys and play activities of males and females when the results of a recent study by Carpenter (1979) are considered. Carpenter analyzed the play activities of nursery school children with respect to their degree of structure, which was defined as the availability of a model performing given activities and by the amount of direction or instruction given. On the basis of composite measures of structuredness, Carpenter found that girls played significantly more often in high-structure activities, whereas boys played in low-structure activities. Independent measures of compliance and of innovative play in the activity settings revealed that compliance was significantly and positively associated with high-structure activities and that innovative play was significantly and positively associated with activity characterized as low in structure.

Carpenter's results are consistent with observations of differences in the formal characteristics of the games played by older boys and girls (Lever, 1976). On the playground, the games in which boys and girls spontaneously participate were found to differ on several dimensions. Of particular interest in the present context is Lever's observation that girls participated in highly structured, turn-taking games that are regulated by invariable procedural rules and do not involve contingent rules of strategy. Boys' games, although rule governed, reward initiative, improvisation, and extemporaneity. Lever's observations affirm Carpenter's findings with an older age group and suggest that more structured games, preferred by girls, demand prescriptive behaviors and discourage experimentation and innovation.

Although it is widely acknowledged that play is an important vehicle for children's learning about themselves and the world, the ways in which the *formal* characteristics of particular toys, play activities, and games differentially affect the developing psychological structures of males and females largely have been ignored until very recently. The specific qualities of child–object interactions elicited by particular toys or play situations and their implications for personality development and cognitive functioning are only now beginning to be explored systematically.

Sex-related Differences in Exploratory Behaviors

We turn now to the second set of psychological behaviors supported by sex-differentiated parental socialization practices and shaping behaviors that exert influence on organism–environment interactions and affect the child's developing psychological structures, namely, exploratory behaviors. Exploratory behaviors have been shown to relate to the child's perceived ability to control or to elicit response from the environment (Piaget, 1952; Watson & Ramey, 1972; White, 1959), sustaining the secondary circular reactions of the early sensorimotor period and ramifying at later ages to influence other cognitive strategies and problem-solving orientations.

Boys have been described by a number of investigators as engaging in more manipulation of objects than girls (Bell et al., 1971; Clarke-Stewart, 1973; Fagot, 1974, 1977: Pederson & Bell, 1970); as more curious (Daehler, 1970; Hutt, 1970; Smock & Holt, 1962), as engaging in more exploratory behavior (Goldberg & Lewis, 1969; Maccoby, 1966; Maccoby & Jacklin, 1974; Starr, 1969), and as participating more often in play activities characterized by low structure that fosters innovative, independent play (Carpenter, 1979). The further finding that the play of girls is more sedentary (Bell et al., 1971; Goldberg & Lewis, 1969; Pederson & Bell, 1970) again emphasizes the diverging characteristics of the play of boys and girls.

In seeking to identify parental behaviors that might promote more exploratory behavior on the part of males, the literature reveals a rather consistent pattern of male infants being given more physical stimulation by parents than female infants (Lewis, 1972; Moss, 1967, 1974; Parke & O'Leary, 1976; Yarrow, 1975). Male infants are held, aroused, and provided stimulation for gross motor behaviors more than female infants (Parke & Sawin, 1976). Yarrow (1975) found that mothers interacted more frequently with male infants, at higher levels of intensity, and with richer, more varied interactions than did mothers of female infants. Such stimulation is seen as encouraging greater responsiveness to the environment on the part of males. Boys also are given greater freedom to explore the neighborhood (Saegert & Hart, 1976).

In contrast to their male peers, girls are observed to play in greater proximity to their mothers both at home and in the laboratory (Fagot, 1977; Goldberg & Lewis, 1969; Lewis & Weintraub, 1974; Messer & Lewis, 1972), to be subjected to closer supervision of their activities (Block, 1979a; Newson & Newson, 1968), and to play closer to home (Saegert & Hart, 1976). These sex-differentiated socialization emphases discourage girls from venturing far from home or primary caretaker and may contribute to the greater timidity and lesser confidence noted in females at later ages.

In evaluating the specific features of sex-differentiated toys that may relate to greater exploratory behaviors on the part of males, boys' toys, according to the criteria used by Rheingold and Cook (1975) to classify toys, were found to direct them more into activities oriented away from the home. As noted earlier, boys' toys afford more inventive possibilities (Rosenfeld, 1975) and elicit less stereotyped play (Carpenter, 1979). In addition to the particular characteristics of masculine toys, males are given a greater variety of toys than are girls, thus promoting play engagement with a broader range of stimulus objects. Rheingold and Cook (1975) found twice as many *categories* of toys in the rooms of boys as in the rooms of girls, a finding consistent with the trend toward greater variety of toys for male infants found by Yarrow et al. (1972).

The differential assignment of household chores to boys and girls also supports the proximal–distal observations previously noted in that boys more often are given chores that take them out of the house and/or farther away from the home, whereas girls are assigned homebound chores such as cleaning and helping to baby-sit (Duncan, Schuman, & Duncan, 1973; Whiting & Edward, 1975). When we examine these seemingly inconsequential differences in chore assignments, it will be seen that they have rather substantial developmental implications. Not only do the chores permit boys the opportunity for more independent exploration of and commerce with the larger world, but Whiting and Edward (1975) note that differential chore assignments affect the interpersonal interactions of boys and girls as well. Because girls are more often assigned household chores, they interact more with adults and younger siblings than with peers. Boys, on the other hand, are given more errands and in some cultures are charged with the responsibility for taking animals to pasture and herding, chore assignments that permit more interaction with peers. According to the perspective being developed here, these different interactional contexts defined in part by chore assignment have diverging implications for the psychological development of boys and girls. The context of girls encourages social interactions focused on home and family, emphasizes imitation of adult behaviors and activities, fosters sensitivity to the needs of others, and often involves compromising one's own wishes for the welfare of the larger family or social group. In contrast, the chore assignments given boys encourage exploratory forays into the larger worlds, increasing their familiarity with the world outside the home, providing opportunities for experimentation, and promoting independent problem solving. The exploration permitted males at an early age may have long-term cognitive effects because improvisation, trial and error, and experimentation extend the behavioral repertoire and facilitate the development of alternative and flexibly sequenced cognitive strategies.

In summary, it is suggested that the nature of the toys, the sex-differentiated encouragement of proximity to the mother, and the kinds of chores assigned to males and to females function to shape different "world orientations" and environmental contexts for boys and girls. Together, these several sex-differentiated parental emphases and behaviors serve to define the home and family as the appropriate sphere of activity for girls and to define the world outside the home as the more salient sphere for boys.

Differential Exposure to Disequilibrating Experiences

Another area in which sex-differentiated parental behaviors and socialization practices influence the child's cognitive and personality development is the timing, frequency, and nature of the child's encounters with disequilibrating experiences. As proposed by Hunt (1961, 1964), Piaget (1952), Loevinger (1976), Perry (1968), Riegel (1976), and Sigel and Cocking (1976), the development and elaboration of cognitive and ego structures is mediated by a dialectical process that is catalyzed by confronting new inputs or experiences that cannot be incorporated into existing understandings or extant psychological structures. Exposure to such experiences forces reconsideration of previously established premises and, under optimal conditions, results in the restructuring of understanding and revision of ones premises. Within the average expectable environment, there appear to be important gender differences in the timing, intensity, and frequency with which disequilibrium is experienced by the two sexes.

The infant begins life in a psychologically undifferentiated and helpless state, depending on someone else to perform the many functions necessary for survival. Over the first several months of life and through a gradual process of learning to delay gratification and to tolerate minor frustrations, the infant begins to differentiate self from nonself and to develop attachment to the caring adult, an attachment similar for children of both sexes. Sometime during the second half of the first year of life, however, the male toddler in the average expectable environment experiences a massive discontinuity, one not shared by female toddlers. It is at this time that the mother, in the service of encouraging appropriate gender-role definition, begins actively to distance herself from her son. The distancing of the son is achieved by different stratagems. Male infants, more than female infants, receive proximal stimulation from their mothers in the first few months of life but the pattern appears to change at around 6 months of age, with proximal stimulation of males decreasing (Lewis, 1972; Lewis & Weintraub, 1974). Mothers report that boys are weaned earlier than girls (Block, 1979a; Sears, Maccoby, & Levin, 1957). The intriguing, but as yet empirically un-verified suggestion by pediatricians that mothers tend to hold their female infants *en face* while holding their male infants facing outward toward the external world also may be a manifestation of distancing behavior. In response to their child's distress, fear, or frustration, mothers appear to use different stratagems with males and females. Mothers are more likely to pick up a distressed female toddler, whereas they are more likely to dismiss signs of distress in male toddlers, encouraging them to resume play (Lewis, 1972). The earlier and greater emphasis on the development of sex-appropriate behaviors on the part of males may serve also to encourage mother–son disengagement (Lansky, 1967; Parke, 1978). Mother–son distancing behavior is a widely recognized phenomenon among primates where it has been observed that male infants are "peripheralized" at an earlier age than females, with the mother rejecting the male infant sooner, forcing the male into earlier contact with peers (Nash & Ransom, 1971).

It is suggested that males experience a discontinuity in the nature of the relationship with their mothers that is achieved by a set of distancing behaviors of the sort described. No such shift in maternal behavior is experienced by female toddlers, whose relationship with their mothers remains close and continuous over the childhood years. Although this discontinuity in the attachment relation-ship with the mother has been discussed by many theorists and developmentalists (Fenichel, 1945; Freud, 1943; Lynn, 1975; Maccoby & Jacklin, 1974), the discussion has been cast almost exclusively in terms of identification and the achievement of appropriate sex typing. It is suggested that this early experi-ence with discontinuity may have a consequential impact on cognitive develop-ment as well. The male child is forced to develop new schemata capable of encompassing the perception that mother is failing to respond in ways consistent with expectation. Not only does the male toddler's early experience with change in the nature of his mother's behaviors toward him challenge his developing premise system about the constancy of objects, but it is likely to affect his perceptions about the dependability of the social world as well. The early distanc-ing by the mother may be instrumental in directing the interactions of males more toward the physical world; it may, as demonstrated in primate studies (Nash & Ransom, 1971), encourage their pattern of extended peer relationships and may contribute also to caution and/or anxiety at later ages about investing themselves in intimate, sharing relationships.

For female toddlers, the nature of the relationship with both parents in the average expectable environment tends to remain relatively constant over the childhood period. Girls are not subjected to the disequilibrating experience of disruption in the relationship with their primary attachment figure. Unlike boys, girls at an early age are spared the task of revising understandings and restructuring their behaviors vis-à-vis their parents. Greater consistency in the quality of primary relationships, encouragement of proximity, emphasis on imitative behaviors, particularly maternal, nurturing behaviors, combine to insure a more predictable, constant world for girls than for boys.

Not only does the male child encounter major experiential discrepancies at an earlier age, but it is proposed that he encounters them more frequently over the years as well. Child-rearing orientations that encourage curiosity, independence, and exploration of the larger environment—more frequent among the parents of boys—increase the probability that the child will encounter new experiences challenging existing premises. Child-rearing orientations that encourage physical proximity as well as psychological closeness, emphasize supervision of the child's activities, discourage independence (Hoffman, 1972, 1977), encourage "ladylike" behaviors, and provide help, sometimes gratuitously, in problem-solving situations (Block, 1976b; Rothbart, 1971) lessen the opportunities for girls to engage in active, independent exploration of the environment, protect them against frequent encounters with discrepancy, and diminish their need to improvise alternative problem-solving strategies.

A series of research studies attest to the detrimental effects on achievement, self-confidence, and specific skill acquisition of excessive maternal help giving and overprotection (Bing, 1963; Gunnar-Gnechten, 1977; Harrington, Block, & Block, 1978; Hermans, terLaak & Maes, 1972; Hoffman, 1972; Kagan & Moss, 1962; Lynn, 1969; Sigel & Cocking, 1976). Indeed, this tendency toward overhelp appears to be a hazard of the mother–daughter relationship. Piaget (1970) underscores the importance of allowing the child to engage in independent trial-and-error learning by noting: "Remember that each time one prematurely teaches a child something he (*sic*) could have discovered for himself, that child is kept from inventing it and consequently from understanding it completely [p. 715]."

These parental protective behaviors, more frequent among parents of girls, motivated initially by a concern for the child's safety and well-being, have the unintended consequence of protecting the child from experiencing the discrepancies that encourage cognitive differentiation, facilitate alternative modes of problem solving, and contribute to feelings of efficacy (Sigel & Cocking, 1976).

DIFFERENTIAL STRATEGIES FOR COPING WITH NEW EXPERIENCES

Sex-differentiated parental socialization practices, many of which are reinforced by other socializing agents, contribute to the divergent strategies developed by boys and by girls to cope with discrepant experiences. The data from several sources cohere in suggesting that socialization behaviors manifested more frequently by parents of females tend to foster proximity, discourage independent problem solving, restrict exploration, minimize contingency experiences, and discourage active play and experimentation in the physical world. Because females are provided fewer opportunities for independent exploration and experimentation, because their toys encourage imitative play, because their play activities are more structured, and because proximity to mothers facilitates imitative behaviors, females are more likely to rely on existing structures in processing new inputs, finding it more difficult to modify premises, restructure experience, and forge new psychological structures.

In contrast, the socialization experiences of boys appear to be less constraining of activity and more encouraging of exploration. Because boys are given greater freedom to venture into the outside world, they more often are in a position to encounter situations that must be dealt with independently and improvisationally. Reliance on existing psychological structures may prove insufficient and new alternatives must be generated and tested. By virtue of the greater opportunity of males to encounter discrepancies, existing structures are, of necessity, more often subject to disequilibration that may provide the occasion for structure modification. These early experiences of boys, which demand reexamination of premises, restructuring of understandings, and the construction of new schemata, may serve to prepare males for the less predictable, less structured world they will inhabit in their adult lives.

CONCLUDING REMARKS

In an earlier article (Block, 1973), traditional sex-typed socialization emphases were considered in relation to gender-role definitions—agentic, communal, integrated, or androgynous (Bakan, 1966)—that were, in turn, related to stages of ego development. In the present chapter, the implications of sex-differentiated socialization emphases and practices for cognitive development have been emphasized.

As we move toward a new era in which equality of opportunity for the sexes is being emphasized, it is important that we examine closely existing socialization processes, noting their potential effects on the premise systems generated, the cognitive heuristics evolved, and the ego structures developed by males and females. According to the conceptualization offered here, differential socialization experiences of males and females consequentially affect the nature of the child's interactions with the environment. It is suggested that the greater experience of males with contingency relationships promotes development, in males more than females, of a premise system that includes feelings of efficacy. Further it is proposed that differences in the developmental contexts—the extended physical and the proximate social—of males and females affect differentially their emerging psychological structures. The nature of the toys given males engages them, to a greater extent than females, in the physical world of objects where feedback is more certain, consistent, and emphasizes qualities of the *object*. In addition, the greater opportunity accorded males to explore independently the larger environment outside the home places more demands for independent problem solving on them. The developmental context of females, in contrast, is more interpersonal. In the social world, feedback is less consistent and more often emphasizes qualities of the *subject*. The greater proximity of females to family members as well as the greater chaperonage given them over the childhood and adolescent years reduces the demand for independent problem solving. The greater exposure of males to disequilibrating, disconfirming experiences as a probabilistic function of the larger space of free movement granted them provides males, more than females, more opportunity to generate hypotheses, develop new premises, and restructure achieved understandings.

The characteristics of the environments experienced by males and females begin to diverge early in life and it is proposed that external socializing forces in conjunction with internal biological processes encourage boys and girls to begin to select for themselves different activities, games, and milieux. It has been suggested, and empirical evidence is admittedly sparse, that the environmental contexts experienced by males and females differ along dimensions such as structure, predictability, and need for improvisation. Differences in these environmental parameters are seen as affecting the nature of the premise systems developed by males and females and to predispose the two sexes toward the use of different cognitive heuristics, a greater tendency toward the use of conserving, fitting, assimilative strategies on the part of females, strategies consistent with Bakan's (1966) conception of communion and a greater tendency toward the use of innovative, structure-creating, accommodative strategies on the part of males, strategies consistent with Bakan's concept of agency. Just as socialization experiences that encourage the integration of communion and agency have been proposed to benefit ego development (Block, 1973), it is proposed that socialization practices encouraging the development of both assimilative and accommodative modes of problem solving and their application in context-responsive ways will benefit the problem-solving competencies of males and females alike.

ACKNOWLEDGMENTS

This chapter is an extended version of an Invited Address given at the meetings of the Western Regional Psychological Association, San Francisco, April 22, 1978. Preparation of this chapter was supported by a National Institute of Mental Health Research Scientist Award to the author and by a National Institute of Mental Health Research Grant, MH 16080, to Jack and Jeanne Block.

REFERENCES

Ainsworth, M., & Bell, S. Some contemporary patterns of mother–infant interaction in the feeding situation. In J. A. Ambrose (Ed.), *Stimulation in early infancy*. New York: Academic Press, 1969.

Bakan, D. *The duality of human existence*. Chicago: Rand McNally & Company, 1966.

Bateson, G. Social planning and the concept of deutero-learning. In *Science, philosophy and religion: Second symposium*. L. Bryson & L. Finklestein, (Eds.), New York: Harper & Row, 1942.

Bell, R. Q., Weller, G. M., & Waldrop, M. F. Newborn and preschooler: Organization of behavior and relations between periods. *Monographs of the Society for Research in Child Development*, 1971, *36* (Whole No. 142).

Bing, E. Effects of childrearing practices on development of differential cognitive abilities. *Child Development*, 1963, *34*, 631–648.

Block, J. Assimilation, accommodation, and the dynamics of personality development. Manuscript submitted for publication, 1980.

Block, J. H. Conceptions of sex-roles: Some cross-cultural and longitudinal perspectives. *American Psychologist*, 1973, *28*, 512–526.

Block, J. H. Debatable conclusions about sex differences. *Contemporary Psychology*, 1976, *21*, 517–522. (a)

Block, J. H. Issues, problems, and pitfalls in assessing sex differences: A critical review of *The Psychology of Sex Differences*. *Merrill–Palmer Quarterly*, 1976, *22*, 283–308. (b)

Block, J. H. Another look at sex differentiation in the socialization behaviors of mothers and fathers. In J. Sherman and F. L. Denmark (Eds.), *Psychology of women: Future directions of research*. New York: Psychological Dimensions, 1979. (a)

Block, J. H. *Socialization influences on personality development in males and females*. Washington, D.C.: American Psychological Association Audiotape, No. 15/11, 1979. (b)

Block, J. H., Block, J., & Harrington, D. *Sex role typing and instrumental behavior: A developmental study*. Paper presented at the meeting of the Society for Research in Child Development, Denver, Colorado, 1975.

Bronson, W. C. *Exploratory behavior of 15-month-old infants in a normal situation*. Paper presented at the meeting of the Society for Research in Child Development, Minneapolis, Minn., 1971.

Carpenter, C. J. *Relation of children's sex-typed behavior to classroom, and activity structure*. Paper presented at the meeting of the Society for Research in Child Development, San Francisco, March 1979.

Clarke-Stewart, A. Interaction between mothers and their young children: Characteristics and consequences. *Monographs of the Society for Research in Child Development*, 1973, *38* (No. 153).

Daehler, M. W. Children's manipulation of illusory and ambiguous stimuli, discriminative performance and implications for conceptual development. *Child Development*, 1970, *41*, 224–241.

Duncan, D., Schuman, H., & Duncan, B. *Social change in a metropolitan community*. New York: Russell Sage, 1973.

Dweck, C. S., Davidson, W., Nelson, S., & Enna, B. Sex differences in learned helplessness: II. The contingencies of evaluative feedback in the classroom and III. An experimental analysis. *Developmental Psychology*, 1978, *4*, 268–276.

Etaugh, C., Collins, G., & Gerson, A. Reinforcement of sex-typed behaviors of two-year-old children in a nursery school setting. *Developmental Psychology*, 1975, *11*, 255.

Fagot, B. I. Sex differences in toddler behavior and parental reaction. *Developmental Psychology*, 1974, *10*, 554–558.

Fagot, B. I. *Sex determined parental reinforcing contingencies in toddler children*. Paper presented at the meeting of the Society for Research in Child Development, New Orleans, 1977.

Fairweather, H. Sex differences in cognition. *Cognition*, 1976, *4*, 231–280.

Fein, G., Johnson, D., Kosson, N., Stork, L., & Wasserman, L. Sex stereotypes and preferences in the toy choices of 20-month-old boys and girls. *Developmental Psychology*, 1975, *11*, 527–528.

Felsenthal, H. Sex differences in teacher–pupil interaction in first grade reading instruction. *Proceedings of the American Education Research Association, 1970*.

Fenichel, O. *The psychoanalytic theory of neurosis*. New York: W. W. Norton, 1945.

Freud, S. *A general introduction to psychoanalysis*. Garden City, N.Y.: City Publishing Co., 1943.

Goldberg, S., & Lewis, M. Play behavior in the year-old infant: Early sex differences. *Child Development, 1969, 40*, 21–31.

Gough, H. E. An interpreter's syllabus for the California Psychological Inventory. In P. McReynold's (Ed.), *Advances in Psychological Assessment*. Palo Alto, Calif.: Science and Behavior Books, 1968.

Gunnar-Gnechten, M. R. *Control, predictability and fear in infancy: Differential effects as a function of the infant's sex*. Stanford University. In mimeo, 1977.

Gunnar-Gnechten, M. R. Changing a frightening toy into a pleasant one by allowing the infant to control it. *Developmental Psychology, 1978, 14*, 157–162.

Guttman, D. Woman and the conception of ego strength. *Merrill–Palmer Quarterly, 1965, 11*, 229–240.

Harrington, D., Block, J. H., & Block, J. Intolerance of ambiguity in preschool children: Psychometric considerations, behavioral manifestations, and parental correlates. *Developmental Psychology, 1978, 14*, 242–256.

Hermans, H. J., ter Laak, J. J., & Maes, P. C. Achievement motivation and fear of failure in family and school. *Developmental Psychology, 1972, 6*, 520–528.

Hoffman, L. Early childhood experiences and women's achievement motive. *Journal of Social Issues, 1972, 28*, 129–155.

Hoffman, L. W. Changes in family roles, socialization, and sex differences. *American Psychologist, 1977, 32*, 644–657.

Hoffman, M. L. Sex differences in empathy and related behaviors. *Psychological Bulletin, 1977, 84*, 712–722.

Hunt, J. McV. *Intelligence and Experience*. New York: Ronald Press, 1961.

Hunt, J. McV. The psychological basis for using preschool enrichment as an antidote for cultural deprivation. *Merrill–Palmer Quarterly, 1964, 10*, 209–248.

Hunt, J. McV. Intrinsic motivation and its role in psychological development. In D. Levine (Ed.) *Nebraska Symposium on Motivation*. Lincoln: University of Nebraska Press, 1965.

Hutt, C. Curiosity in young children. *Science Journal, 1970, 6*, 68–71.

Kagan, J., & Moss, H. A. *Birth to maturity*. New York: Wiley, 1962.

Lansky, L. M. The family structure also affects the model: Sex role attitudes in parents of preschool children. *Merrill–Palmer Quarterly, 1967, 13*, 139–150.

Lever, J. Sex differences in the games children play. *Social Problems, 1976, 23*, 478–487.

Lewis, M. Parents and children: Sex role development. *School Review, 1972, 80*, 229–240.

Lewis, M., & Freedle, R. Mother–infant dyad: The cradle of meaning. In P. Pliner, L. Krames, & T. Alloway (Eds.), *Communication and affect: Language and thought*. New York: Academic Press, 1973.

Lewis, M., & Goldberg, S. Perceptual–cognitive development in infancy: A generalized expectancy model as a function of the mother–infant relationship. *Merrill–Palmer Quarterly, 1969, 15*, 81–100.

Lewis, M., & Weintraub, M. Sex of parent and sex of child: Socioemotional development. In R. C. Friedman, R. M. Richard, and R. L. Van de Wiele (Eds.), *Sex differences in behavior*. New York: Wiley, 1974.

Loevinger, J. *Ego development: Conceptions and theories*. San Francisco: Jossey Bass, 1976.

Lynn, D. B. Curvilinear relation between cognitive functioning and distance of child from parent of the same sex. *Psychological Review, 1969, 76*, 236–240.

Lynn, D. B. A note on sex differences in the development of masculine and feminine identification. In R. K. Unger and F. L. Denmark (Eds.), *Women: Dependent or independent variable*. New York: Psychological Dimensions, Inc., 1975.

Maccoby, E. E. *The development of sex differences*. Stanford, Calif.: Stanford University Press, 1966.

Maccoby, E. E., & Jacklin, C. N. *The psychology of sex differences.* Stanford, Calif.: Stanford University Press, 1974.

Margolin, G., & Patterson, G. R. Differential consequences provided by mothers and fathers for their sons and daughters. *Developmental Psychology,* 1975, *11,* 537–538.

Messer, S. B., & Lewis, M. Social class and sex differences in the attachment and play behavior of the year-old infant. *Merrill-Palmer Quarterly,* 1972, *18,* 295–306.

Meyer, W., & Thompson, G. Sex differences in the distribution of teacher approval and disapproval among sixth grade children. *Journal of Educational Psychology,* 1956, *47,* 385–396.

Moss, H. A. Sex, age, and state as determinants of the mother–infant interaction. *Merrill-Palmer Quarterly,* 1967, *63,* 19–35.

Moss, H. A. Early sex differences and mother–infant interaction. In R. C. Friedman, R. M. Richard, and R. L. Van de Wiele (Eds.), *Sex differences in behavior.* New York: Wiley, 1974.

Murphy, L. B., & Moriarty, A. E. *Vulnerability, coping, and growth.* New Haven, Conn.: Yale University Press, 1976.

Nash, L., & Ransom, T. *Socialization in baboons at the Gombe Stream National Park, Tanzania.* Paper read at the meeting of the American Anthropological Association, New York, 1971.

Newson, V., & Newson, E. *Four years old in an urban community.* Hardmonworth, England: Pelican, 1968.

Parke, R. D. Perspectives on father–infant interaction. In J. D. Osofsky (Ed.) *Handbook of infancy.* New York: Wiley, 1978.

Parke, R. D., & O'Leary, S. E. Father–mother–infant interaction in the newborn period: Some findings, some observations, and some unresolved issues. In K. Riegel and J. Meacham (Eds.), *The developing individual in a changing world; Social and environmental issues* (Vol. 2). The Hague: Mouton, 1976.

Parke, R. D., & Sawin, D. B. The father's role in infancy. *The Family Coordinator,* 1976, *25,* 365–371.

Parsons, T., & Bales, R. F. *Family socialization and interaction process.* Glencoe, Ill.: Free Press, 1955.

Pederson, F. A., & Bell, R. Q. Sex differences in preschool children without history of complications of pregnancy and delivery. *Developmental Psychology,* 1970, *3,* 10–15.

Perry, W. G. *Patterns of development in thought and values of students in a liberal arts college.* Final report, Project No. 5-0825, Office of Education, April, 1968.

Piaget, J. *The origins of intelligence in children* (2nd ed.). New York: International Universities Press, 1952.

Piaget, J. Piaget's theory. In P. H. Mussen (Ed.), *Carmichael's Manual of Child Psychology.* New York: Wiley, 1970.

Portuges, S. H., & Feshbach, N. D. The influence of sex and socioethnic factors upon imitation of teachers by elementary school children. *Child Development,* 1972, *43,* 981–989.

Rheingold, H. L., & Cook, K. V. The contents of boys' and girls' rooms as an index of parents' behavior. *Child Development,* 1975, *46,* 459–463.

Riegel, K. The dialectics of human development. *American Psychologist,* 1976, *31,* 689–700.

Rosenfeld, E. F. *The relationship of sex-typed toys to the development of competency and sex-role identification in children.* Paper presented at the meeting of the Society for Research in Child Development, Denver, 1975.

Rothbart, M. K. Birth order and mother–child interaction in an achievement situation. *Journal of Personality and Social Psychology,* 1971, *17,* 113–120.

Saegert, S., & Hart, R. The development of sex differences in the environmental competence of children. In P. Burnett (Ed.), *Women in Society.* Chicago: Maaroufa Press, 1976.

Sander, L. W. Issues in early mother–child interaction. In N. S. Endler, L. R. Boulter, and H. Osser (Eds.), *Contemporary issues in developmental psychology.* New York: Holt, Rinehart & Winston, 1976.

Sears, R. R., Maccoby, E. E., & Levin, H. *Patterns of child rearing*. Evanston, Ill.: Row, Peterson, 1957.

Seligman, M. P. E. *Helplessness*. San Francisco: Freeman, 1975.

Serbin, L. A., O'Leary, K. D., Kent, R. N., & Tonick, I. S. A comparison of teacher response to the preacademic and problem behavior of boys and girls. *Child Development*, 1973, *44*, 796–804.

Sigel, I. E., & Cocking, R. R. Cognition and communication: A dialectic paradigm for development. In M. Lewis & L. Rosenblum (Eds.), *Communication and language: The origins of behavior* (Vol. 5). New York: Wiley, 1976.

Smith, M. B., Haan, N., & Block, J. H. Social-psychological aspects of student activism. *Youth and Society*, 1970, *1*, 262–288.

Smock, C. D., & Holt, B. G. Children's reactions to novelty: An experimental study of curiosity motivation. *Child Development*, 1962, *33*, 631–342.

Starr, R. H. Nurturance, dependence, and exploratory behavior in prekindergarteners. *Proceedings of the 77th Annual Convention of the American Psychological Association*, 1969, 253–254.

Terman, L. M., & Tyler, L. E. Psychological sex differences. In L. Carmichael (Ed.), *Manual of child psychology*. (2nd ed.). New York: Wiley, 1954.

Tyler, L. E. *The psychology of human differences*. New York: Appleton–Century–Crofts, 1965.

Walraven, M. *Mother and infant cardiac responses during breast and bottlefeeding*. Unpublished doctoral dissertation. Michigan State University, East Lansing, 1974.

Watson, J. The development and generalization of contingency awareness in early infancy: Some hypotheses. *Merrill–Palmer Quarterly*, 1966, *12*, 123–135.

Watson, J., & Ramey, C. Reactions to response-contingent stimulation in early infancy. *Merrill–Palmer Quarterly*, 1972, *18*, 219–228.

White, R. Motivation reconsidered: The concept of competence. *Psychological Review*, 1959, *66*, 297–333.

Whiting, B., & Edward, C. P. A cross-cultural analysis of sex differences in the behavior of children age three through 11. In S. Chess and Alexander Thomas (Eds.), *Annual progress in child psychiatry and child development*, 1974, New York: Brunner/Mazel, 1975.

Yarrow, L. J. *Infant and environment: Early cognitive and motivational development*. New York: Halsted, 1975.

Yarrow, L. J., Rubinstein, J. L., Pederson, F. A., & Jankowski, J. J. Dimensions of early stimulation and their differential effects on infant development. *Merrill–Palmer Quarterly*, 1972, *18*(3), 205–218.

10 The Child's Construction of Gender: Anatomy as Destiny

Dorothy Z. Ullian
Wheelock College

There is a good deal of evidence in the literature that suggests a pattern of sex differences organized around the issues of power and nurturance. Findings on male development cluster around such issues as aggression (Brodzinsky, Messer, & Tew, 1979; Erikson, 1950; Kagan, 1964), dominance (Rothbaum, 1977; Tiger & Shepher, 1975), achievement (Horner, 1972; McClelland, 1965), and anger (Goodenough, 1931), whereas the female personality has been viewed primarily in terms of emotionality (McClelland, 1965), interdependence (Chodorow, 1978), nurturance (Gilligan, 1979), and empathy (Miller, 1976). Despite the consistency of these findings from early childhood through adulthood, there is no general agreement about the source of these differences and the mechanisms that sustain them. Increasingly, the psychoanalytic position, with its emphasis on innate drives and anatomical differences, has been replaced by a psychological (and political) theory that stresses the role of social agents in shaping personality. In contrast to Freud's emphasis on sexual instincts, the social-learning approach focuses on external social influences as the primary determinants of masculinity and femininity. It assumes that there is a direct and decisive relationship between external social conditions and internal psychological events.

In this chapter, I review findings from the literature that suggest two distinct modes of male and female functioning—one organized around power, the other around nurturance—and I propose an alternative model for interpreting these data. Moving beyond the traditional nature–nurture debate that has dominated our thinking about the origin of sex differences, I offer a "constructivist" hypothesis that links many of the differences observed between males and females to early cognitive structures that shape and distort concepts in inevitable and predictable ways. Based on principles of cognitive development (Kohlberg,

1966; Piaget, 1950), this model locates a possible source of sex differences in the undifferentiated concepts of early childhood when "anatomy is destiny"; when global anatomical attributes such as size, strength, childbearing capacity, and the like are equated with such psychological attributes as power and nurturance.

I propose two major hypotheses regarding the development of a masculine or feminine identity. First, the heightened level of sex-role stereotypy consistently observed in children between 4 and 7 years of age represents a necessary developmental stage in which the child seeks to establish a clear sense of personal (including gender) identity. To achieve this, young children adopt concrete sex-typed personality attributes, games, interests, and activities that correspond to their concept of gender. Second, I suggest that the content of stereotypes exhibited by children is not merely the result of arbitrary or inequitable socialization practices. Rather, it is linked, through the preoperational child's interpretation of sex-related data, to visible anatomical attributes of adult men and women. Viewed from this perspective, sex differences in power and nurturance are seen as the inevitable result of cognitive judgments generated by children as they actively seek to interpret the psychological significance of biological gender.

EVIDENCE FOR A DISTINCT MODE OF MALE AND FEMALE FUNCTIONING

As noted earlier, research on sex differences yields a consistent pattern of findings that links masculinity to power and aggression, and femininity to issues of nurturance and interpersonal relationships. Viewed as a whole, these findings are interpreted to suggest that males typically respond to people and events in a more aggressive mode than females in order to maximize power and establish dominance. The search for power occurs within an impersonal system of rules and expectations that is presumed to govern relationships and adjudicate conflicts. Females, on the other hand, can be seen to adopt a nurturing orientation in order to enhance personal relationships and establish intimacy. Concern with the feelings of others, the need for close friendships, and the capacity for empathy are central themes that organize female experience. For the purpose of the present discussion, the male configuration of attributes is classified as an "impersonal power" orientation, whereas the female disposition is defined as "interpersonal nurturant."

In her chapter in this volume, Block refers to numerous studies of sex differences that support this distinction across broad social and cultural lines. The female's presumed "greater capacity for empathy, her desire for friendship, and her need for social approval" can readily be subsumed under the "interpersonal nurturant" dimension. Similarly, Block's characterization of males as competitive, dominant, and aggressive corresponds directly to the masculine mode I have labeled "impersonal power."

This pattern of findings around issues of personal and social functioning has found extensive support in the empirical literature. In the case of females, for example, Pitcher's (1974) open-ended conversations with children between 2 and 5 years of age reveal that girls tend to focus on people more vividly and more realistically than do boys, and that they identify more closely with the personalities and experiences of others. Boys speak with significantly greater frequency of material objects and their capacity for movement and manipulation.

Observational studies of children's play further demonstrate the young girl's tendency to care for others and to initiate social interaction. Domestic and familial themes repeatedly enacted in the household corner with dolls and small animals stress nurturance and protection of the young and helpless (Paley, 1973; Parten, 1933; Sutton-Smith, 1965) and the spatial configurations in the play of young girls has been characterized by Erikson (1950) as enclosed, static, safe, and peaceful. Furthermore, numerous studies demonstrate that aggression among girls is either controlled or deflected, rather than directly expressed (Brodzinsky et al., 1979).

In a similar vein, Feinberg's analysis (1976) of themes in children's art reveals a striking tendency for girls to perceive events in an interpersonal-dyadic mode. For example, when first-grade children are asked to draw pictures of "fighting" and "helping," the males portray these events in an organized, impersonal mode, whereas females consistently focus on familiar individuals in close intimate relationships (p. 67).

The theme of young girls' interpersonal sensitivity and caretaking behavior is seen clearly in Lever's (1976) study of the structure and organization of children's play during the middle school years. In an observational study of fifth-graders' games, Lever notes that the girls' behavior is directed less toward resolving problems and conflicts than toward maintaining the relationship among the players. Girls' play tends to occur in small, intimate groups, often in the best-friend dyad, and in private places. The organization of girls' play is more cooperative, focusing less on the development of an abstract rule system than on the development of empathy and sensitivity to the feelings of others.

Studies of women at later stages of development closely parallel the findings from early and middle childhood. Writing from a psychoanalytic perspective, Chodorow (1974) attributes sex differences to the fact that women, universally, are largely responsible for early child care and for later female socialization. As a result, Chodorow contends that the female personality inevitably develops in relation and in connection to other people more than the male does. In psychoanalytic terms, Chodorow contends that women are less individuated than men; they have more flexible ego boundaries.

Drawing from a clinical sample of female clients, Jean Baker Miller (1976) has also described the tendency of women "to participate in the development of others" through such behaviors as nurturing, helping, sharing, and empathy, behaviors that, she argues, have been repressed and undervalued in the wider male-dominated society. In the feminine mode, affiliation is valued more highly than self-enhancement, and intimacy more than personal achievement.

Concern with the welfare of others, the capacity for empathy, and caretaking are not merely aspects of personal relationships; they are also the major touchstones of women's moral philosophy. According to Gilligan (1979), the moral imperative that emerges repeatedly in interviews with women is "an injunction to care, a responsibility to alleviate the real and recognizable trouble of this world [p. 82]." From her perspective, the psychology of women, with its emphasis on interpersonal concerns and responsibility for caretaking, implies a more contextual mode of judgment and a different moral understanding. In contrast, the moral reasoning of males emphasizes the importance of autonomous judgment and action, free from interference and uninfluenced by the needs or opinions of others.

Taken together, the studies described above may be construed as a pattern of social "connectedness" among women, an interrelatedness of self with other people in close interpersonal relationships. The connection of self with others, responsibility for the welfare and safety of others, and concern with the consequences of interpersonal conflict are themes that apparently shape and define the female experience. As we have seen, it is manifest not only in work and play, but also in the conversations of young girls, their games and their artistic creations, and even in their moral judgments.

In contrast to this view of females, the studies of male development point to a preponderance of aggressive, often power-seeking behaviors that occur in an abstract depersonalized context. Striving toward autonomy, independence, and achievement, males participate in a social structure that permits the pursuit of individual goals unimpeded by the particular claims or needs of others.

Studies with young children indicate that boys in all cultures are more apt to engage in rough-and-tumble play (Maccoby & Jacklin, 1974) and to exhibit more aggressive themes in their play and fantasy (Brodzinsky et al., 1979). The young boys' preoccupation with guns and instruments of war (Feinberg, 1976), their choice of dramatic roles stressing danger and conflict and heroes of gigantic proportions (Cramer & Hogan, 1975) reiterate the fantasies of expulsion, protrusion, destruction, and conflict originally described by Erikson (1950).

This behavioral evidence is further supported by parents' perceptions of the differences in expressions of anger between sons and daughters. In an early interview study with mothers of young children, Goodenough (1931) reported:

Parents' comments about aggression or activity in their children seem to imply in boys a force barely held under control, "dynamic," "a bomb shell," "bold," "belligerent." Those mothers felt that the cup was running over; "a great deal to do, so much energy, he can't use it all up." (p. 132)

The evidence further suggests that the striving aggressive features of young boys' play and fantasy occur within the context of a depersonalized system of rules and interpersonal relations. Paralleling Piaget's original observations of the rule-bound nature of young boys' games, Lever's (1976) work referred to earlier indicates that boys participate with greater frequency in depersonalized events and in the adjudication of disputes. They gain experience in controlled and socially approved competitive games in which they must learn to deal with interpersonal competition in a relatively direct manner, playing with their enemies and competing against their friends, as is required in play governed by rules.

Feinberg's (1976) data on children's representations of helping and fighting further substantiate this hypothesis. In contrast to the girls' concern with interpersonal relations, boys depict helping and fighting as abstract depersonalized events in which organized groups of individuals either come to the rescue or battle against equally nonspecific masses of individuals. Persisting into adult life, these typical male characteristics have been described in terms of the adult male's unwillingness to engage in close, emotional relationships (Miller, 1976), or his inability to provide nurturance and caretaking without fear of jeopardizing his masculinity (Chodorow, 1974). The rule-bound nature of his social universe is further reflected in his abstract notions of justice, which generate "principled" moral judgments involving hypothetical individuals in a generalizable context (Gilligan, 1977).

In sum, the findings on male development reveal a more aggressive pattern of activity in which power is sought and the rules of social organization and principles of ethical behavior are presumed to govern and sustain interpersonal relationships.

THE SOCIALIZATION MODEL

In this section I review the major features of the social learning model, and also some findings that force us to reconsider that position. Classical psychoanalytic theory has been vigorously challenged in recent years by the focus on environmental forces that presumably shape behavior and influence the course of male and female development. Based on a theory of social transmission, a major assumption of socialization theory is that incremental changes in sex-role stereotypes occur as a linear function of increased exposure to sex-differentiated socialization practices (Kagan, 1964; Thompson, 1975). Greater conformity to conventional standards of masculinity and femininity is viewed as a direct result of increased exposure to social models and cultural expectations.

Numerous studies derived from this perspective have been designed to investigate the effects of inequitable socialization experiences on the development of masculine and feminine traits. For example, studies with children as young as 1 week to 2 years (Goldberg & Lewis, 1972; Kuhn, Nash, & Brucker, 1978; Thompson, 1975) have examined the relationship between early parental behaviors and the development of sex-typed behaviors, whereas others have sought to demonstrate the growing internalization of norms with increasing age (Block, 1976; Lever, 1976; Best, Williams, Cloud, Davis & Robertson, 1977).

With regard to the dimensions of power and nurturance, theorists (as well as social activists) have argued forcefully that male dominance and female subordination are primarily the result of pervasive and inequitable social standards. Working from a sociological model of psychological development, they have focused on the ways in which the structures of family (Chodorow, 1978), school (Serbin, O'Leary, Kent, & Tonick, 1973), media (Frueh & McGhee, 1975), work (Kanter, 1976), and general social expectations (Kagan, 1964; Rosenkrantz, Vogel, Bee, Broverman, & Broverman, 1968) all contribute to the development and maintenance of sex differences.

This theoretical position, put forth in the scientific literature and reinforced by popular belief, must be considered in the light of three strands of conflicting evidence. First, it should be noted that no significant correlations have been found to exist between such predicted antecedent variables as social class (Thompson, 1975), cultural background (Best et al., 1977), maternal employment (Guttentag & Bray, 1974; Paley, 1973), father absence (Smith, 1966), parental ideology (Barnett, in press), and the degree of sex-role stereotypy. Studies with young children (especially between 4 and 7 years) reveal a tendency toward heightened stereotypy in their choice of games, play, interests, and vocational aspirations that is independent of previous experience (Kohlberg, 1966). In fact, Maccoby and Jacklin (1974) were forced to conclude from their extensive review of the literature that factors other than imitation or social learning must account for the acquisition of sex-typed behaviors.

The puzzling questions raised by these studies have been further compounded by the lack of success encountered by numerous intervention projects. One of the most curious aspects of efforts to sensitize school age children to cultural and sex-role inequities has been their resistance to change. Guttentag and Bray's (1974) ambitious study with kindergarten, fifth- and ninth-grade students yielded few significant results. In fact, the adolescent males exposed to "liberating" influences exhibited even more stereotypy after the intervention than before it. More modest efforts to influence the sterotypic play, interests, and aspirations of young children at the classroom level have also yielded unimpressive findings (Bjerke, 1978; Paley, 1973). In addition, studies designed to measure changes in attitudes as a result of the women's liberation movement reveal few discernible shifts in the personal preferences of young girls (Barry & Barry, 1976; Scheresky, 1976). Such findings cannot be adequately explained through social-learning principles, and they suggest that a developmental process more complex than social conditioning is needed to account for the persistence and pervasiveness of sex-typed attitudes.

A third source of data that makes a linear model of sex-role development implausible is the decrease in stereotypy found beyond 7 or 8 years of age. Ullian's (1975; 1976) developmental analysis of sex-role concepts indicates that by 8 years of age, children's judgments tend to be more flexible or "liberated." This shift is attributed to the awareness of the permanence of gender, despite apparent changes in dress, physical appearance, games, and other visible signs of gender.

Developmental studies of children's sex-role concepts have yielded similar findings that suggest a ceiling of sex-role stereotypy at 7 or 8 years, followed by a decline at 8 or 9 years (Emmerich, Goldman, Kirsch, & Sharabary, 1977; Marcus & Overton, 1978; Rothbaum, 1977). Clearly, the principles dictated by social learning theory would suggest precisely the opposite; that is, one would expect incremental shifts with age as a linear function of increased exposure to social norms and expectations.

Thus, the universality of sex-role stereotypes in young children, their persistence despite educational and social interventions, and the decrease in stereotypy at 8 or 9 years force us to reexamine the assumptions of the social-learning model. In the remainder of this chapter, I propose a "constructivist" position that suggests that there are age-related cognitive perceptions that lead children to attach particular psychological significance to biological and social reality in universal and predictable ways.

THE CONSTRUCTIVIST PERSPECTIVE

The "constructivist" model of sex-role development has its origins in the cognitive–developmental framework originally described by Piaget (1928; 1950), and later elaborated by Kohlberg in the domain of sex roles (1966). Through the application of Piagetian concepts such as conservation and object constancy, Kohlberg generated a model that links children's conceptions of the physical universe to the development of conceptions of sexual gender.

According to Kohlberg's model, sex-role development begins at approximately 3 to 5 years of age with a simple cognitive judgment about gender. After this initial self-identification as boy or girl, the child engages in and values those activities, objects, and attributes that are seen as consonant with and representative of his or her own sex. Kohlberg specifies that in the case of boys, the adoption of such masculine attributes as strength or dominance is motivated directly by the desire for power and competence.

Noting the tendency for females to adopt a less prestigious role, as defined by power and competence, Kohlberg is forced to assume that there is sufficient value in "niceness" and "attractiveness" to prevent the female from renouncing her femininity. In a formulation reminiscent of Freud's account of feminine development, Kohlberg simply suggests that girls adopt the feminine nurturing style as compensation for their basic lack of power. However, why such attributes as niceness and helpfulness come to be associated with adult femininity, and why they should seem attractive to the young girl remain unexplained.

The constructivist position differs from Kohlberg's analysis in several important respects. First, it offers a parallel model of male and female development. It proposes that *both* the male and female personality develop from the child's tendency to behave in gender-related ways. This tendency, which reflects the child's need to establish a permanent identity, is especially heightened in children up to 7 or 8 years of age, when gender is still experienced as potentially shifting and changeable. In contrast to Kohlberg's emphasis on the motivating role of power or competence, this approach views male and female development simply as a function of the child's need to give concrete expression to his or her gender identity.

Second, this approach proposes that the development of male dominance and female nurturance is rooted in the concepts children generate about the nature of men and women. Because gender distinctions in personality are linked to concrete bodily differences such as size, childbearing capacity, bodily hair, and the like, it is postulated that "toughness" and aggression inhere in the young child's concept of masculinity to the same extent that niceness or helpfulness are presumed to inhere in femininity. With regard to female development, then, this position suggests that such attributes as nurturance and interpersonal sensitivity do not reflect a displaced need for power and competence, as Kohlberg suggests; rather, they represent the young girl's effort to give psychological expression to her perceived gender attributes.

The theoretical principles and empirical data that I have reported [Ullian, 1975; 1976 & in press] lead to three major hypotheses regarding the development of sex differences. The first hypothesis suggests that there is a distinct developmental stage of gender consolidation, coinciding with preoperational thought, during which children seek out and exhibit concrete visible attributes of masculinity and femininity. This is manifested in the heightened level of sex-role stereotypy observed in children between 4 and 7 years of age. The second hypothesis posits a predetermined correspondence, mediated by the child's cognitive structures, between observable physical attributes of adult men and women and the subsequent sex-role orientations adopted by young boys and girls. This correspondence is demonstrated in the typical male concern with power and aggression, in contrast to the female tendency toward nurturance and interpersonal relations. The third hypothesis suggests that those attitudinal and behavioral dispositions acquired in the phase of gender consolidation (4 to 7 years) establish a pattern for the subsequent development of male and female attributes. This hypothesis is supported by the consistent findings of sex differences that persist from childhood through adolescence and adulthood.

From the constructivist point of view, then, it is the child's interpretation of masculinity and femininity, coupled with his or her need to behave in gender-specific ways, and not just biological or social influences, that is presumed to shape the substance and direction of male and female development. Obviously, social and cultural influences reinforce these distinctions and often perpetuate early manifestations of gender into adult sex differences. However, the central feature of this position is that particular male–female distinctions, especially those organized around power and nurturance, originate in the primitive cognitive constructions that children use to differentiate the sexes.

Let us consider the specific features of the constructivist hypothesis. Developmental studies of sex-role concepts have shown that the characteristics used by preoperational children to differentiate the sexes tend to be concrete attributes that can be easily recognized and understood at the young child's level of cognitive functioning. A developmental study of children's sex-role concepts revealed that children between the ages of 5 and 7 distinguish masculinity and femininity along such physical dimensions as depth of voice, body and facial hair, and the capacity for bearing children, as well as size and strength (Kohlberg & Ullian, 1974; Ullian, 1975). In a series of open-ended interviews, 5- to 7-year-old children described men as bigger, stronger, and hairier than women, with deeper voices, whereas women were perceived as smaller, weaker, with gentler voices and smoother skin, and able to bear children.

Unable to distinguish physical from psychological attributes, these children concluded that women were "nicer," "softer," cried more easily, and were more capable of caring for children. When asked to explain why, both boys and girls relied on physical or anatomical distinctions to justify their responses. Thus, women were viewed as nicer than men because "their skin is softer," or "their voices are nice," whereas men were viewed as more powerful because "they have tougher skin." The author concluded from this study that children between the ages of 5 and 7 years are led, by the nature of their structuring of sex-related data, to equate physical and psychological attributes. Focusing on concrete perceptible cues such as size, strength, childbearing capacity, voice, and body characteristics, young children conclude that men are powerful, dominating, scary, and tough, whereas women are kinder, gentler, and more fragile.

In accordance with the 5- to 7-year-old's focus on the external visible differences that distinguish the sexes, conformity to sex-role stereotypes is deemed necessary to maintain clear gender distinctions. Even as late as 7 years of age, deviation from conventional standards of dress, appearance, toys, and activities is viewed as a violation of the laws of physical reality as well as a threat to one's gender identity (Emmerich et al., 1977; Marcus & Overton, 1978). The preoperational child, bound by concrete perceptual cues, relies on observable physical evidence to generate a correct judgment about his or her own identity.

On the basis of these findings, it is proposed that the development of sex differences in power and nurturance are cognitively linked to the child's beliefs about his or her gender characteristics. Males are seen as tough, aggressive, and dangerous as a result of their superior size, their tough skin, and their deep voices, whereas females are seen as nice and caring as a result of their childbearing capacity and their soft skin. In accordance with these physical distinctions, young children of both sexes are inclined to adopt the corresponding behavioral and psychological attributes in order to ensure a stable and irreversible identity.

The sequence of female development may be conceptualized by the following example: (1) she perceives a set of physical attributes that distinguish adult women (e.g., childbearing capacity); (2) she assumes that she too possesses a set of traits identical to those of the adult women (she believes that she, too, has a baby); (3) she proceeds to behave in ways that are consistent with those attributes (e.g., taking care of babies, in doll play perhaps); and (4) simultaneously, and as a result of these behaviors, she adopts beliefs and attitudes that are consistent with her self-perception (e.g., she prefers doll play over blocks and values nurturing).

Based on her beliefs about herself as physically vulnerable and relatively powerless, she is also more apt to adopt a set of beliefs and values that emphasize people, gentleness, caretaking, and nurturance. This would inevitably be reflected, as indeed the data indicate, in her conversations, her artistic creations, her doll play, her moral judgments, her work, her vocational interests, and, probably, on any other dimension one might examine in this way.

In the case of boys, it is also postulated that many of the "male" behaviors reported in the literature arise from their need to adopt and exhibit those attributes that they associate with the male role. Striving to be large, powerful, dominant, and scary, the young male child is apt to select those games, roles, and activities that promote and reflect such attributes. The sequence of male development may be summarized in the following way: (1) he perceives a set of attributes that define the male gender (e.g., superior size, strength); (2) he perceives that he does not possess many of the characteristics that distinguish men (e.g., he is small, relatively powerless); (3) he proceeds to behave in ways that resemble or correspond to those aspects of the male role (he acts "big," adopting aggressive behaviors of "superhero" proportions); and (4) simultaneously, and as a result of these these behaviors, he adopts the skills, beliefs, and attitudes that are consistent with his self-perception (e.g., he prefers to do things that reflect power and aggression). With regard to such male characteristics as a deep voice and a hairy body and face, the young boy is also more apt to stress the correspondingly "tough," "scary," and dangerous features of the male role.

The analysis outlined here raises a further developmental issue with potentially important psychological consequences. With regard to the female child, we see that on all the dimensions of significance to young children, young girls resemble adult women. Like their mothers, they are small and relatively powerless; they have high-pitched voices and relatively little hair on their faces and bodies. Most important, perhaps, they believe they are capable of bearing children. (In fact, studies indicate that young girls believe there is already a baby in them, and that it is merely a matter of time before the child will be born (Bernstein & Cowan, 1975). Thus, on all the physical characteristics that define her gender, the young girl is like the woman she will become.

However, if we consider the young male child's physical traits and those that he is expected to acquire, a different picture emerges. The young boy of 5 or 6 is small relative to the general population, he is physically powerless, he is relatively hairless on his face and body, and he has a high-pitched voice. In contrast to the adult male, the young boy's small stature and his voice and body characteristics are obviously discrepant from those attributes he uses to define his gender. On none of the traits of significance to him—except perhaps the possession of a penis (which may explain the young child's preoccupation with it and its subsequent importance in theories of psychosexual development)—is he like the man he wants and is expected to become. If the male child experiences a discontinuity between existing attributes and those he must acquire to confirm his masculinity, it is likely that he must strive to exhibit the "appropriate," if not exaggerated masculine behaviors, and that these choices will be consistent with the adult male attributes of strength, size, and physical prowess. Thus, expressions of power, aggression, dominance, and grandiosity in the child's behavior reflect his need to exhibit those attributes that define his sexual gender. In contrast to the young girl, whose more flexible expressions of femininity emerge from her belief that she is already like other women (Bettelheim, 1975; Paley, 1973), the young boy is forced to confirm his sexual identity through a narrow range of behaviors that represent a clear and unambiguous masculine identity.

From the constructivist perspective, then, the source of sex differences does not lie primarily outside the individual in the organization of social institutions or the members who inhabit them. Rather, this model suggests that particular stereotypes of masculinity and femininity are inevitable at certain stages; they are constructed by children as they seek out recognizable cues to define and express their identities. The puzzled and often exasperated reactions of parents or teachers to their previously "liberated" young girl's requests for nailpolish, earrings, and the like testify to the child's spontaneous need to exhibit such distinct gender-related signs. I would venture to hypothesize that if we removed all external observable cues that distinguish the sexes, children would invent or construct similarly obvious distinctions as a means of securing a stable gender identity.

Second, the constructivist hypothesis proposes that there is an actual correspondence, mediated by the child's cognitive interpretations, between the stereotypes adopted by children and the nature of the anatomical differences that actually exist between men and women. In other words, the organization of male experience around issues of power and aggression is dictated by the early cognitive structures that link those traits to such tangible criteria as size, strength, depth of voice, and facial and body hair. Correspondingly, the young girl is naturally inclined to link nurturing and interpersonal skill with such female attributes as smallness, softness, and childbearing capacity.

Although the connections established in childhood are subject to later structural transformations that moderate the effects of this early stereotypy (Ullian, in press), the literature also suggests that many of the skills, interests, and personality traits established in the formative years from 4 to 7 influence the subsequent course of male and female development. The tendency for early patterns of male-female behavior to shape or limit subsequent development would account for the persistence of such differences into adolescence and adult life. It might also provide an explanation for the resistance to change of sex-role stereotypes, even after continuing efforts at educational intervention.

The perspective outlined here suggests that many of the sex differences reported in the literature, as well as those posited by Block (this volume), represent separate domains of functioning generated by children as they order their experience in gender-specific ways.

The position offered here also suggests an alternative paradigm from which to examine the development of sex differences. Implicit in much of the literature on sex differences is the notion of deficit—the assumption that female development is deviant or immature when compared with males along a variety of dimensions. Whereas males are thought to proceed in the direction of independence, autonomy, principled morality, and achievement, females assessed against these standards are inevitably viewed as dependent, undifferentiated, and steeped in interpersonal concerns. Block's assumption that males are inclined to accommodate, whereas females assimilate reality, implies greater structural complexity in the cognitive-affective functioning of males, an assumption with no empirical support in the research literature. More recently, studies that are methodologically sensitive to these biases have yielded important findings that support the notion of separate domains of experience. For example, Gilligan's (1977) developmental analysis of the moral judgments of women has led to a reformulation of Kohlberg's theory in ways that account for qualitative differences in male and female reasoning. In contrast to Kohlberg, Gilligan has identified a distinct sequence in the moral stages of women that culminates in their concern for intimacy and attachment, as opposed to autonomy and independence. The results of her study cast serious doubt on the previously accepted, yet unsubstantiated, view of women as morally inferior or deficient—an inevitable conclusion when female responses on any dimension are assessed against a standard of male development.

The constructivist perspective provides an alternative theoretical framework from which additional data on male and female differences may be examined and assessed. Rather than assigning relative values to male and female attributes on the basis of predetermined categories of mental health, psychological maturity, or cognitive complexity, the present model seeks to examine the development of sex differences in terms of the categories generated by males and females themselves as they organize and interpret their experience in gender-specific ways.

REFERENCES

Barnett, R. Parental sex-role attitudes & child rearing values. *Sex-Roles*, in press.
Barry, R., & Barry, A. *Psychological Reports*, 1976, *38*, 948–950.
Bernstein, A., & Cowan, B. Children's concept of how people get babies. *Child Development*, 1975, *46*, 77–91.

Best, D. L., Williams, J. E., Cloud, J. M., Davis, S. W., & Robertson, L. S. Development of sex-trait stereotypes among young children in the United States, England, and Ireland. *Child Development,* 1977, *48,* 1375-1384.

Bettleheim, B. Some further thoughts on the doll corner. *School Review,* 1975, *83,* 363-368.

Bjerke, K. A study of attitude change in fifth graders generated by a direct teaching strategy to promote conscious awareness of sex-role stereotyping. *Dissertation Abstracts,* 1978, *38*:5234.

Block, J. H. Issues, problems, and pitfalls in assessing sex differences: A critical review of *The Psychology of sex differences. Merrill-Palmer Quarterly,* 1976, *22,* 283-308.

Brodzinsky, D. M., Messer, S. B., & Tew, J. D. Sex differences in children's expression and control of fantasy and overt aggression. *Child Development,* 1979, *50,* 372-379.

Chodorow, N. Family structure and feminine personality. In M. Rosaldo and L. Lamphere (Eds.), *Women, culture and society.* Stanford, Calif.: Stanford University Press, 1974.

Chodorow, N. *The reproduction of mothering.* Berkeley: University of California Press, 1978.

Cramer, P., & Hogan, K. Sex differences in verbal and play fantasy. *Developmental Psychology,* 1975, *11,* 145-154.

Emmerich, E., Goldman, K., Kirsch, B., & Sharabary, R. Evidence for a transitional phase in the development of gender constancy. *Child Development,* 1977, *48,* 930-939.

Erikson, E. *Childhood and society.* New York: Norton, 1950.

Feinberg, S. Conceptual concept and spatial characteristics in boys' and girls' drawings of fighting and helping. *Studies in Art Education,* 1976, *18,* 63-72.

Frueh, T., & McGhee, P. E. Traditional sex role development and amount of time spent watching television. *Developmental Psychology,* 1975, *11,* 109.

Gilligan, C. In a different voice: Women's conceptions of the self and of morality. *Harvard Educational Review,* 1977, *47,* 481-517.

Gilligan, C. Women's place in man's life cycle. *Harvard Educational Review,* 1979, *49,* 431-445.

Goldberg, S., & Lewis, M. Play behavior in the year old infant: Early sex differences. In Bardwick (Ed.), *The Development of Sex Differences.* New York: Harper & Row, 1972.

Goodenough, F. L. *Anger in young children.* Minneapolis: University of Minnesota Press, 1931.

Guttentag, M., & Bray, H. *Undoing sexual stereotypes: Resources for educators.* New York: McGraw Hill, 1974.

Horner, M. Toward an understanding of achievement related conflicts in women. *Journal of Social Issues,* 1972, *28,* 157-174.

Kagan, J. Acquisition and significance of sex-typing and sex-role identity. In M. Hoffman & L. Hoffman (Eds.), *Review of Child Development Research I.* New York: Russell Sage, 1964.

Kanter, R. The impact of hierarchical structures on the work behavior of men and women. *Social Problems,* 1976, *33,* 415-430.

Kohlberg, L. A cognitive developmental analysis of children's sex-role concepts and attitudes. In E. Maccoby (Ed.), *The development of sex differences.* Stanford, Calif.: Stanford University Press, 1966.

Kohlberg, L., & Ullian, D. Stages in the development of psycho-sexual concepts and attitudes. In R. Friedman, R. Richart, & R. Vande Wiele (Eds.), *Sex differences in behavior.* New York: Wiley, 1974.

Kuhn, D., Nash, S., & Brucken, L. Sex role concepts of two and three year olds. *Child Development,* 1978, *49,* 445-451.

Lever, J. Sex differences in the games children play. *Social Problems,* 1976, *23,* 478-487.

Maccoby, E., & Jacklin, C. *The development of sex differences.* Stanford, Calif.: Stanford University Press, 1974.

Marcus, D., & Overton, W. The development of cognitive gender constancy and sex-role preferences. *Child Development,* 1978, *49,* 434-444.

McClelland, D. C. Wanted: A new self-image for women. In Robert Jay Lifton (Ed.), *The Woman in America.* Boston: American Academy of Arts and Sciences, 1965.

Miller, J. B. *Toward a new psychology of women.* Boston: Beacon, 1976.

Paley, V. Is the doll corner a sexist institution? *School Review*, 1973, *81*, 569–576.

Parten, M. B. Social play among preschool children. *Journal of Abnormal Psychology*, 1933, *28*, 136–147.

Piaget, J. *The child's conception of the world*. Paterson, N.J.: Littlefield, Adams & Co., 1950. (Originally published, 1928.)

Piaget, J. *The psychology of intelligence*. New York: Harcourt Brace, 1950.

Pitcher, E. Male and female. In J. Stacey, S. Bereaud and J. Daniels (Eds.), *And Jill Came Tumbling After: Sexism in American Education*. New York: Dell Publishing Co., 1974.

Rosenkrantz, P., Vogel, S., Bee, H., Broverman, I., & Broverman, D. M. Sex-role stereotypes and self concepts in college students. *Journal of Counseling and Clinical Psychology*, 1968, *32*, 287–295.

Rothbaum, F. Developmental and gender differences in the sex stereotyping of nurturance and dominance. *Developmental Psychology*, 1977, *13*, 531–532.

Scheresky, R. Occupational roles are sex-typed by six to ten year old children. *Psychological Reports*, 1976, *38*, 1207–1210.

Serbin, L. A., O'Leary, K. D., Kent, R. N., & Tonick, I. J. A comparison of teacher response to the pre-academic and problem behavior of boys and girls. *Child Development*, 1973, *44*, 796–804.

Smith, C. *The development of sex-role concepts and attitudes in father-absent boys*. Unpublished master's thesis, University of Chicago, 1966.

Sutton-Smith, B. Play preference and play behavior: A validity study. *Psychological Reports*, 1965, *16*, 65–66.

Thompson, S. K. Gender labels and early sex-role development. *Child Development*, 1975, *46*, 339–347.

Tiger, L., & Shepher, J. *Women in the kibbutz*. New York: Harcourt, Brace, Jovanovich, 1975.

Ullian, D. The development of conceptions of masculinity and femininity. In B. Lloyd and J. Archer (Eds.), *Exploring sex differences*. New York: Academic Press, 1975.

Ullian, D. *A developmental study of conceptions of masculinity and femininity*. Unpublished doctoral dissertation, Harvard University, 1976.

Ullian, D. Why boys will be boys: A structural analysis. *American Journal of Orthopsychiatry*. (in press.)

VI

The Development of Children's Awareness of Intrapsychic Processes

Much of our knowledge of children's cognitive development has concerned the child's developing understanding of concepts, processes, and relationships in the material world. The effort to extend cognitive developmental methods of inquiry to the child's construction of knowledge about social and psychological phenomena is exemplified by Robert Selman's work. In this chapter Selman examines the growth of understanding of salient aspects of inner feelings: Can one have two feelings at the same time? Can one fool oneself? What is personality, and how can one change? Selman describes an approach to research on subjective experiences and offers data that conform to a sequential analysis. His interpretation of the development of reflective understanding is informed by and in turn illuminates a clinical as well as a developmental perspective on thinking about feelings.

11 What Children Understand of Intrapsychic Processes: The Child as a Budding Personality Theorist

Robert L. Selman
Harvard University

The figures in fairy tales are not ambivalent—not good and bad at the same time, as we all are in reality. But since polarization dominates the child's mind, it also dominates fairy tales. A person is either good or bad, nothing in between. One brother is stupid, the other is clever. One sister is virtuous and industrious, the others are vile and lazy. One is beautiful, the others are ugly. One parent is all good, the other evil. The juxtaposition of opposite characters is not for the purposes of stressing right behavior. . . . Presenting the polarities of character permits the child to comprehend easily the differences between the two, which he could not do as readily were the figures drawn more true to life, with all the complexities that characterize real people. Ambiguities must wait until a relatively firm personality has been established on the basis of positive identifications. Then the child has a basis for understanding that there are great differences between people, and that therefore one has to make choices about who one wants to be.

Bruno Bettelheim, *The Uses of Enchantment,* 1976, p. 9

INTRODUCTION: THE COGNITIVE-DEVELOPMENTAL APPROACH

Does concrete polarization dominate the mind of the child? Are feelings recognized by adults as intangible so poorly differentiated by the child from tangible matter that having two feelings at the same time is viewed akin to being in Chicago and New York simultaneously—a physical impossibility? If so, when, how, and in what ways do children gain the more "realistic" understanding of the nature of each person's inner life that characterizes adult insight? And must

187

the child's understanding of the ambiguity of human character and the potentially ambivalent nature of human feelings await further personality development alone, as Bettelheim suggests, or are there cognitive mechanisms that are also involved? Indeed, is adult understanding of these phenomena consistently qualitatively different from the child's understanding never reverting to polarization, isolation, stereotype, and oversimplification in making psychological judgments about the motives and attitudes of the self or others?

These are but a few of the questions about children's understanding of inner experience that have for a long time been of concern to those working clinically with children. Now these questions are becoming the focus of systematic attention by developmental psychologists interested in normal growth and development (Broughton, 1978; Chandler, Paget, & Koch, 1978; Harter, 1977; Selman, 1980). But although there is a long history of child development research in related areas such as self-concept and the psychological attributions children make about others, until fairly recently there has been very little systematic developmental research oriented toward the child's naturally developing conceptions of the human capacity for reflection on inner experience. In fact, most of what we actually do know of children's ideas of how human beings internally experience social reality comes from the writings of astute clinicians like Axline (1964), Moustakis (1971), or Bettelheim (1976). Their experience with the complexities of the minds of children comes from working with troubled children, who within the security of the therapeutic relationship have felt enough trust to share some of the content of their sacred thoughts and feelings.

Obviously, when dealing with the child's understanding of inner experiences, by their very nature intangible and confusing phenomena, so-called "clinical methods" have certain advantages over those usually available to the developmental psychologist, who feels a greater pressure to abide by constraints imposed by issues of reliability of measurement and consensus in observation. In trying to reach out to larger samples and to use fairly standardized measures and procedures, developmental psychologists, guided more by empirical than by clinical methods, generally have failed to capture the richness potentially available; children simply will not easily share their own understanding about experiences they view as personal or difficult to articulate. What one usually gleans from these more cautious-qua-scientific studies is the somewhat general and pallid conclusion that children's thinking about human inner workings gets more complex, psychological, systematized, and abstract with age (Lively & Bromley, 1973; Peevers & Secord, 1973), a conclusion that only begins to do justice to the phenomena under examination.

But, as most of us are aware, the generalizations obtained from clinical experience also suffer in their own way. For example, the message the clinician often sends us as to what the young child is capable of truly understanding of the reality of inner life is often inherently contradictory, a message that at once claims for early childhood both naivete and precocious insight. For example, several pages after cogently articulating the ideas quoted in the introduction to this chapter, Bettelheim (1976) goes on to say:

> Just as important for the young child's well-being as feeling that his parents share his emotions . . . is the child's feeling that his inner thoughts are not known to his parent until he decides to reveal them. If the parent indicates that he knows them already, the child is prevented from making the most precious gift to his parent of sharing with him what until then was secret and private to the child [p. 11].

Are we to believe that the child who is hardly capable of looking into persons, much less of seeing in them anything beyond the achromatic simplicity of all good or all evil, is the same child who is capable of knowing not only that he or she has complex inner thoughts and feelings, but that parents have them also, that theirs may or may not be the same, that they do not know his or hers and he or she does not know theirs, and even that he or she can have control over these thoughts and feelings and keep them unrevealed from the parents until the appropriate time? How does one sort out this apparent contradiction?

Generating precise and consistent knowledge about the sequential patterns of children's growing capacity to understand their world has long been a challenge to psychologists interested in cognitive processes and concept development (Flavell, 1977; Piaget, 1954). More recently, a group of researchers has begun to apply cognitive developmental methods and models to the description of the growth of knowledge and conceptions about social and psychological experience as well (Broughton, 1978; Damon, 1977; Elkind, 1976; Furth, 1976; Selman, 1976; Turiel, 1975; Youniss and Volpe, 1978). It should be stressed that beyond their concern for the accurate description of the growth of *what* the child knows (his or her social knowledge), developmental psychologists are interested in *how* a child knows, the ways he or she thinks about social and psychological relations and how these change with experience. This concern with the changing structures of the child's psychological understanding rather than with the specific content acquired is a key difference in orientation between developmental and clinical approaches.

For example, consider the dream as viewed from clinical and developmental perspectives. The difference between a psychoanalytic and a developmental approach clarifies general differences between so-called affective and cognitive perspectives. From a psychoanalytic or dynamic perspective, dreams are important because the manifest, surface content of any particular dream masks a latent content representative of some relatively general emotional issue or interpersonal conflict (e.g., separation, dependency, competition, or rivalry). If a 3-year-old is having recurrent nightmares about large angry monsters chasing him or her out of the house, one of a number of possible interpretations might be that the monster–child relationship is a manifest symbol of a frightening, perhaps repressed, latent, deeper conflict around feelings of competition in another relationship, perhaps with a father or authority figure. A 6-year-old having the same dream might well be seen as dealing with the same underlying theme, for the latent content of conflicts that the dream process plays out is timeless and universal. Thus when looking at the latent *content* of the dreams children have, the age of the child or the way he or she actually experienced the dream itself would not be of central importance.

However, for a developmentalist, whose major focus is on the growth of children's understanding of natural interpersonal and intrapsychic phenomena such as friendships or feelings, the major focus in this case would be the way the 6- and the 3-year-old, upon awakening, differ in their *understanding* of the dream as a phenomenological experience. The developmentalist would expect that the 6-year-old might readily understand that "it was just a dream" and "the monster was not real," whereas the 3-year-old might be afraid to look in the closet, where he might well assume the monster is still hiding. In other words, the Piagetian focuses on the development of the understanding of dreams, beginning by defining a dream's intrinsic qualities: the nature of its tangibility, locus, and origin. The Piagetian then tries to discover the developmental sequence of conceptions of dreams through which all children progress in coming to understand the basic properties that adults usually take for granted in their own thinking about dreams.

In addition, stages in conceptions of dreams are seen as a particular instance of more general cognitive stages through which children pass. For example, we have already alluded to the difficulty the young child has differentiating between the nature of physical and psychological phenomena. Parallel to a confusion of the physical and psychological nature of dreams is the quasi-physicalistic conception of feelings we spoke of earlier. For young children, dreams are typically considered material, or "real," rather than immaterial, or "not real" (e.g., an actual monster is chasing the 3-year-old). They are considered externally located, outside the body (e.g., "Can your parents see you dream?" "Yes, if they come in my room."). And its origins are also considered to be outside the self (e.g., "Where did your dream come from?" "It came from the zoo with the monster.").

The developmental claim is that there is a logic to the emerging sequence of conceptions of dreams, each step or stage of which depends on the discoveries or conceptual differentations made at the prior stage. For example, the child must first differentiate between material (physical) and immaterial (thoughts, feelings) phenomena before he or she can understand that a dream is internally located (that no one else can "see" it). This sequence is logical and universal; at an early age the child knows that two tangible bodies cannot be located in the same space at the same time. Not until dreams can be clearly understood as intangible (psychological) can they be located within a tangible self. For the child who conceptualizes dreams as "real" or tangible, their locus will most likely remain external, although children may not always be so illogically logical.

Although the clinical focus on the symbolic meaning of the content of experience and the developmental focus on structure[1] of understanding are not inherently contradictory, they can lead to different "explanations" of specific instances of behavior. For example, the 3-year-old might be scared both because the monster seemed "real" from his or her developmentally immature perspective *and* because it symbolized an important and frightening conflict within his or her own psyche—literally a "double whammy." It is therefore important to remember that both cognitive *and* affective factors are critical determinants of the psychological meaning of the experience.

THE DEVELOPMENTAL STUDY OF INTRAPSYCHIC UNDERSTANDING

As practitioners, we in our project are concerned with both aspects of intrapsychic phenomena: the symbolic meaning of intrapsychic content in affective or dynamic terms as well as the developmental meaning of how the child organizes and understands these intrapsychic phenomena. As researchers, however, our aim has been to look from the developmental point of view at the growth of understanding about certain important aspects or qualities of both inner and interpersonal life. It is our belief that this outlook on child development adds an important perspective to the comprehension of a child's social behavior and social relations, in the same way that an understanding of how a child experiences or theorizes about the nature of dreams in general adds an important factor to our understanding of the child's reaction to any particular dream.

Our research includes the study of other related aspects of social–cognitive development, in particular the level and quality of concepts of interpersonal relationships—about friendship, about peer group relations, and about parent–child relationships—as well as of concepts of intrapsychic relationships. Working back and forth between the theoretical cognitive–developmental model and the data collected from hundreds of interviews with subjects aged 3 to 43, our research has described a stage sequence of children's developing concepts in each of these four interpersonal and intrapsychic domains. (Table 11.1)

Within this model, the basic theoretical assumption is that although in each domain, at any given stage, there are unique and different characteristics, there are also certain basic cross-domain commonalities. In the domain of intrapsychic understanding, we have examined how the child sequentially develops more sophisticated and integrated understandings of four intrapsychic phenomena:

---

[1]Clinical theories also use the term *structure,* usually to refer to personality structures, such as id, ego, superego. Here, however, we are using the term "structure" in the cognitive–developmental sense, to refer to the way conceptions are organized, as opposed to the term *content,* or the objects of thinking.

TABLE 11.1

Developmental Sequence of Stages Across Domains of Intrapsychic (Individuals) and Interpersonal (Friendship, Peer Group, and Parent/Child) Relations

	Intrapsychic	Interpersonal		
Stage	Individuals	Friendship	Peer Group	Parent/Child
0	Physical entity	Momentary physical playmate	Physical connections	Boss/servant relationship
1	Intentional subject	One-way assistance	Unilateral relations	Caretaker/helper relationship
2	Introspective self	Fair-weather cooperation	Bilateral partnership	Guidance Counselor/need-satisfier relationship
3	Stable personality	Intimate–mutual sharing	Homogeneous community	Tolerance/respect relationship
4	Complex self-systems	Autonomous interdependence	Pluralistic organization	Communicative system

subjectivity (understanding of how thoughts, feelings, and motives may relate to or conflict with one another); *self-awareness* (understanding of the relation between the self as an observer and the self observed); *personality* (understanding of how inner attitudes, beliefs, and values may coalesce to form a coherent system); and *personality change* (understanding of the nature of transformations in the basic nature of the self).

As with the cognitive–developmental analysis of the various aspects of the dream concept, the four issues within the domain of intrapsychic understanding that we have examined do not develop independently of one another. In fact, each subsequent stage in the development of intrapsychic understanding can be depicted as the further differentiation of one of these issues from an initially undifferentiated matrix within the mind of the child (Table 11.2). For example, just as the concept of immateriality of the *substance* of dreams is logically necessary for the concept of internality in the child's understanding of the *locus* of the dreams, so, too, the child's understanding that individuals can have more than one feeling or motive toward a person or social event at the same time (*subjectivity*) is logically necessary for understanding that the self can present an outward appearance indicating one feeling while actually holding an opposite belief or feeling (*self-awareness*). It is the aim of this chapter to specify in greater detail how these concepts differentiate and subsequently integrate with each other with development. With this kind of developmental analysis, we can better assess the validity of claims by clinical observers, such as Bettelheim's statements that the young child can understand that complex inner feelings or experiences may be kept from outer expression or observation but that he or she cannot view people as possibly holding mixed feelings or motives.

Methods for Constructing Stages of Intrapsychic Understanding

Because we could not establish a truly intimate or therapeutic relationship with each child or adult in our initial sample, and because we wanted to explore thinking on aspects of human nature that adults seldom ask children about and that children seldom reflect upon unless asked to do so, our first methodological aim was to recruit the child as a coinvestigator, to encourage him or her to consider what he or she understood of the nature of inner experience. Using a technique common in developmental descriptive research, we devised dilemmas that directly involved the child's conceptions of intrapsychic processes and questions that tapped his or her reflections on experience with these phenomena. In constructing the research, the interview method is largely open-ended; it is akin to a clinical interview, following trails in the child's mind within the broad constraints of the topic under examination. However, because it is difficult for subjects in general and the young child in particular to think about hypothetical situations and even more difficult to think about intangibles such as feelings,

TABLE 11.2
Concepts of Intrapsychic Issues at Each Developmental Stage*

	Subjectivity	Self-Awareness	Personality	Personality Change
Stage 0	All Categories of Intrapsychic Phenomena Undifferentiated from Physicalistic (Nonpsychological) Phenomena			
1	Differentiation of subjective (inner) experiences from objective (outer) experiences.	Actions will reveal intentions.	Personality as a particular motive.	Growth as change in likes or dislikes.
2	Differing subjective responses (e.g., feelings) to one object or event can occur, but only in sequence.	Differentiation of inner experience from reflection on that experience.	Personality as context-specific mood.	Growth as change through trying hard.
3	Conflicting feelings about the same object or event can be simultaneous.	Self is aware of the interaction between self as subject and self as object.	Differentiation of generalized personality traits from specific inner states.	Personality change; a stable system, difficult to change in part.
4	Conflicting subjective experiences can yield new qualitatively subjective states.	Self understands certain aspects of self's behavior are unavailable to self-awareness (unconscious).	Personality as integration of complementary and conflicting systems.	Differentiation of personality change as a restructuring of system, but maintaining identity.

*Adapted from Jurkovic, G. J. and Selman, R. L. A developmental analysis of intrapsychic understanding: Treating emotional disturbances in children. In Selman, R. L. and Yando, R., *New Directions For Child Development: Clinical-Developmental Psychology*. San Francisco: Jossey-Bass, 1980.

thoughts, and motives without some concrete problem to which to apply their conceptions, we developed our dilemmas into sound filmstrip dramas using young actors and actresses. Our expectation was that the dramas would be gripping enough to facilitate the observing subjects' thinking about the problems we were exploring. To investigate, for example, the general topic of intrapsychic understanding, the following dilemma was often used:

Eight-year-old Tom is trying to decide what to buy his friend Mike for his surprise birthday party. By chance, he meets Mike on the street and learns that Mike is extremely upset because his dog, Pepper, has been lost for two weeks. In fact, Mike is so upset that he tells Tom, "I miss Pepper so much I never want to look at another dog again. No other dog would be the same.'' Tom goes off, only to pass a store with a sale on puppies; only two are left and these will soon be gone.

The dilemma for the child is whether to buy the puppy for Mike. Insofar as the child's decision is based on a determination of Mike's possible psychological reaction, the dilemma allows the interviewer to tap the child's understanding of intrapsychic issues. The interview questions following this dilemma cover each of the four issues basic to our definition of the child's developing intrapsychic concepts (Table 11.2). Each issue has a basic orienting question followed by a series of probing questions designed to elicit further explanation and clarification of the child's reasoning. Based on previous pilot work, the questions for each issue are ordered developmentally. That is, they sequentially "test the developmental limits" of the child's conceptions. For example, to explore the child's understanding of *subjective experience* (thoughts, feelings, motives) and their relation to one another within an individual, we ask questions such as: "If Mike is smiling, could he still be sad? How is that possible? Could he feel happy and sad at the same time? Has there ever been a time when *you* have felt more than one way about something? Tell me about it if you want to.'' To explore the issue of *self-awareness* we ask questions such as: "Mike said he never wants to see another puppy again. Why did he say that? Did he mean what he said? Can someone say something and not mean it? How? Is it possible that Mike doesn't know how he feels? How is that possible? Did you ever think you'd feel one way and then find out you felt another? How could that happen? Can you ever fool (deceive) yourself? How? What's the difference between fooling yourself and fooling someone else?''[2]

Using these response data in a developmental analysis, we have constructed the following five stages of conceptions of each of the four intrapsychic issues. It is important to keep in mind that during the initial constructive phase of this type of developmental research, one does not seek to attach absolute age norms to the initial emergence of given concepts. We recognize that methods can influence data, and that a stage of understanding *may* be understood by a child before he or she can put it into words or "theories" in an interview. But because the primary aim at this phase is to describe the *sequence* of logical transformations through which concepts develop, age norms are rough indicators of when most children express their theories of psychological development under reflective interview conditions.

---

[2]A second filmstrip (or story) using older actors is oriented toward adults and older children; in it a boy (or girl) who defeats an older child in Ping-Pong for the first time after many defeats finds out that the older opponent may have "thrown the game." The erstwhile winner claims that he (she) did not really care about winning anyway, and the interviewer probes the child's speculations about the validity of that statement, using questions similar in structure to those used for the Lost Puppy Dilemma.

A Developmental Analysis of Four Intrapsychic Issues[3]

Subjective Experiences. In general terms, the development of children's verbally expressed conceptions of subjectivity starts with an initial confusion between overt actions and underlying psychological experience (Stage 0). For instance, as noted earlier, because the child does not clearly differentiate physical and psychological states, he or she appears to believe that a person can hold (be in) only one psychological orientation (state) at a time. From this point, the child moves to a recognition of the unique and covert nature of each individual's thoughts, feelings, and motives and to an understanding that an individual may hold more than one feeling at the same time (Stage 1). However, the belief appears to be that these pluralistic feelings must be directed toward distinctly different situations or objects, as in the following example:

DO YOU THINK MIKE COULD BE BOTH HAPPY AND SAD AT THE SAME TIME IF HE GETS A NEW PUPPY? A little.
WHY WOULD HE BE A LITTLE HAPPY? Because he got a dog for a present.
WHY WOULD HE BE SAD? Because he lost his dog.
COULD HE FEEL BOTH HAPPY AND SAD ABOUT GETTING THE NEW PUPPY? No. He'd be happy about that.

(8:1)

At Stage 2, it appears the child understands that one may possess multiple but still isolated feelings toward a single object, or that conflicting feelings toward the same object may occur in temporal succession. The following are examples of each:

IS IT POSSIBLE TO FEEL TWO WAYS ABOUT SOMETHING? DID THAT EVER HAPPEN TO YOU? Yes.
HOW IS THAT POSSIBLE TO FEEL HAPPY AND SAD?
If you borrowed some money from your friend and you feel happy you have it, and sad that you have to pay him back.
IF HERE IS THE INSIDE OF YOUR MIND (interviewer draws a circle in pencil on a white sheet of paper), HOW CAN YOU HAVE TWO FEELINGS? CAN YOU DRAW IT?
One can be in the back and one in the front.

(9:2)

---

[3]The examples and stage descriptions in this section are adopted from a manual developed by the Harvard–Judge Baker Social Reasoning Project (Assessing Interpersonal Understanding, 1979). Numbers in parentheses refer in years and months to the age of the subject whose responses are excerpted. Because of the constraints of space I provide more extensive examples of the first two issues, subjectivity and self-awareness, and less extensive excerpts from the issues of personality and personality change.

SO, YOU SAY, IF HALF YOUR BRAIN IS HAPPY AND HALF YOUR BRAIN IS SAD, HOW DO YOU FEEL OVERALL? CAN YOU FEEL BOTH HAPPY AND SAD AT THE SAME TIME? No. I would change my attitude once I thought about it. YOU WOULD CHANGE YOUR ATTITUDE ABOUT WHAT? You think you are happy that the guy fell in the mud, but all of a sudden you really feel sorry for him. And it just sticks that way. Once you feel one way. I don't really feel both ways at the same time. One comes and then the next. YOU MEAN ONE FOLLOWS THE OTHER, FIRST YOU FEEL HAPPY AND THEN SAD? Yes. WHY CAN'T THEY BE AT THE SAME TIME? I don't know.

(8:3)

Stage 3 is characterized by an understanding of the potential for having mixed feelings or motives about the same object or situation, and Stage 4 by an understanding that the process of coming to have mixed feelings toward a particular event or person can lead to a subjective internal state or affect qualitatively distinct from either of its component parts. For instance, categorized as a Stage 3 understanding is the idea that feelings come in phases. Unlike Stage 2, where each ensuing feeling is thought to bump the temporally prior feeling out from within the self (and from awareness), at Stage 3, each ensuing phase or wave of feelings is seen to mix with the old phase in a state that is viewed as often confusing and conflicted. One form this mixing takes is the domination of one feeling by the next:

YOU SAY HE SAID, I DON'T CARE THAT I LOST AND HE BELIEVES THAT AT ONE LEVEL, BUT IN ANOTHER WAY, HE REALLY DOES CARE THAT HE LOST? Yah, you have levels in your system, really, the brain system. YOU WERE SAYING THERE ARE LEVELS IN THE BRAIN. One level, two levels (drawing), five levels. The top level is don't care. Second level, uncertain, might be; that means beginning to care a little. It's like the turning point of a play, where somebody dies and it all turns back again. It is the turning point where in the middle of it it happens, like he begins to care. The fourth level he cares, and then he really cares. If you look at that. This is him, Jerry, he wins the game, he loses, he doesn't care, it is like an elevator, you lift, taking you down to different stages. Your brain is like little people working on it. But like number 5 becomes the most important.

(13:11)

And at Stage 4:

HOW WOULD MIKE FEEL IF TOM GAVE THE PUPPY TO HIM? He could feel, he could immediately look at it and say this is so cute. He could look at it and say this will never be Pepper and reject it, and eventually love or reject it always. CAN YOU FEEL BOTH HAPPY AND SAD? Yes. EXPLAIN THAT TO ME, OR

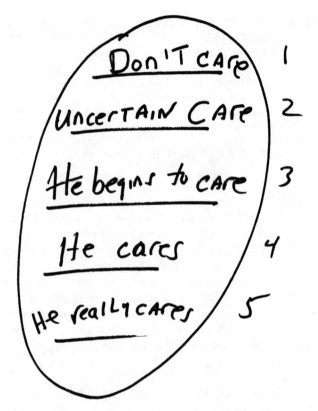

FIG. 11.1 A thirteen-year-old boy's conception of conflicting feelings.

GIVE ME A SITUATION WHERE YOU CAN FEEL BOTH HAPPY AND SAD?
A new friend is moving away, you are happy that they are going somewhere where
they really like it, but you are unhappy that you won't be able to see them so much.
You can write to them, but you won't be able to see them. SO DO YOU FEEL
MORE HAPPY OR MORE SAD? You feel both. Or maybe you feel something
that's a mixture of both—maybe you have a mixed emotion, not just happy and sad
together.

(14)

Self-awareness.   This issue concerns the child's growing knowledge of
thoughts, feelings, and motives as objects of thought and of the kinds of insights
that individuals are capable of having into their own understanding of these
subjective experiences.

There are two aspects of children's responses that characterize the earliest
(Stage 0) reflective conception of self-awareness. First, as with subjective experiences, the child does not appear to view psychological, inner experience as

different from material, outer experience. Second, although very young children can articulate an awareness of a self, that self seems to have a quasi-physical quality.

WHEN YOU THINK, WHERE DO YOU THINK? In my mouth.
HOW DO YOU THINK? My words tell me.

(3)

This developing sense of self-communication as one part of the body telling another part of the body something appears equivalent in a syncretic sense to the child's notions of thinking and of will or intention.

I am the boss of myself.
HOW DO YOU KNOW?
My mouth told my arm and my arm does what my mouth tells it to do.

(3)

There are three interesting aspects to the quality of thinking about conceptions of self-awareness coded as Stage 1. First, young children do not realize that people can hide their inner or "true" feelings. Of course, young children know how to lie (i.e., they are well aware they can hide *facts* from or deny their actions to others). For example, the child who eats a forbidden cookie is capable, at quite an early age, of denying the reality of the situation and being aware that he or she is doing so. Despite this, however, we have drawn the inference from our interviews that the young child does not yet seem cognizant that one can *purposefully* misrepresent one's *inner* experiences (thoughts, feelings, or motives) to either another or to the self. The following interview provides some insight into the immature form of awareness we are talking about:

MIKE SAYS HE NEVER WANTS TO SEE ANOTHER PUPPY AGAIN. WHY DID HE SAY THAT? Because he lost his dog Pepper.
DID HE MEAN WHAT HE SAID? Yes.
HOW DO YOU KNOW? Because he said it.
CAN HE SAY IT AND NOT MEAN IT? He could be lying.
WHY WOULD HE DO THAT? I don't know. His dog may not be lost.
COULD HE THINK HE DIDN'T WANT A DOG BUT REALLY WANTED ONE? Nope.
WHY NOT? Because he said he wanted one.
IS IT POSSIBLE THAT MIKE DOESN'T REALLY KNOW HOW HE FEELS? He said he was sad.

(9)

When the interviewer first asks the child whether Mike meant what he said, in the interviewer's mind the question is whether Mike was being true to himself (i.e., in touch with his own feelings). The first thing the interviewed child responds, "He meant what he said because he said it," is fairly typical of young children's analyses of inner experience. People do not seem to be credited with the ability to distort purposefully inward-looking observations.

In further probing, the child is asked, "Can he say it and not mean it?" This question may become more understandable when the child has a better sense of self-awareness. Here the particular response, "He could be lying," is an indication of this child's confusion, for although he seems to know that objective actions can be distorted in their presentation to others, he doesn't seem to understand that the same principle can apply to subjective feelings. Thus, while the child in this excerpt indicates that he is aware of Mike's depressed subjective state, he responds to a question about self-deception ("Can he say it and not mean it?") as if it were a question of the factuality of Mike's comment that he feels sad because his dog is lost and responds in kind ("He could be lying; his dog may not be lost.")[4]

A second and related aspect of self-awareness concepts at Stage 1 is that although now covert attitudes (intentions) and their overt representations (actions) are seen as separate, children using this level of awareness still seem to believe that a person's overt actions will eventually belie one's inner attitude, that if one is a careful observer of another's outside, then one can begin to make a good guess about how the person feels inside.

HOW DOES MIKE FEEL INSIDE? Sad.
HOW DO YOU KNOW? Because of the way he looks.
COULD HE LOOK SAD AND BE HAPPY INSIDE? He could but you would be able to tell if you watched him long enough, he'd show you he was happy.

(8)

Although there is validity to this assertion—we do know something of inner feeling from observation—when the child's thinking appears to be limited to this Sherlock Holmesian conception of keeness of material observation, his or her responses are coded at Stage 1.

Third, the young child's conception of "fooling oneself," or the "awareness of unawareness" is qualitatively different from that of older children and adults. Because Stage 1 is not yet truly a self-reflective perspective on the self's inner life, the young child seems to view "fooling oneself" as a *shift* or *change* in one's beliefs, feelings, or motives rather than *unawareness* of feelings, etc.

WHAT DOES IT MEAN TO FOOL THE SELF? You do something and then you disagree with it. You find out you didn't want to do it.

(8:5)

---

[4]I should stress that it is probably more accurate to say that the child reinterprets or understands the question at a lower level than to say that the child does not understand the question at all.

According to Stage 1 theorizing, one does not fool oneself in the sense of being actively self-deceptive; one simply discovers there has been a shift in one's subjective concerns. One may have been wrong about what one thought one wanted originally, but now one knows.

Conceptions of self-awareness coded as Stage 2 incorporate the further understanding that the individual can take a clear perspective on the inner life, which life was distinguished from outer experiences at the previous stage. As a result of the self's ability to take the perspective of a second person and look back toward the self's inner states, at least three new developments in the child's understanding of the nature of self-awareness occur.

First, the ability to take a "second person" social perspective allows the child to rethink the relative importance of outer appearance and inner reality. Whereas at Stage 1 the child responds as if he or she believes that the inner can be ascertained from the outer (and in a sense this is a valid if incomplete insight maintained through life), at Stage 2 the child favors the theory that inner experience acts as reality and outer actions are only an appearance or one manifestation of that reality. In other words, there appears to develop an articulated sense of the *priority* of inner experience (how one "really feels" about social events or interactions) over outer appearance (what one chooses to demonstrate to others).

HOW IS IT YOU CAN HIDE THE WAY YOU FEEL? If he felt sad and stuff, you put a smile on your face and you go with everyone else and try to be regular, but sometimes you can really be sad.
IS THERE A KIND OF INSIDE AND OUTSIDE TO A PERSON? Yes.
WHAT WOULD THAT MEAN? If there was a brother and a sister, like the brother always says I can't stand you, but really inside, he really likes her.
REALLY DEEP INSIDE. WHAT IS THAT INSIDE, CAN YOU DESCRIBE IT? Yah, I guess so, really what you really feel about something.

(10:11)

Second, Stage 2 marks the emergence of a working belief in the self's ability to constantly monitor the self's thoughts and actions. How does the shift manifest itself in beliefs about the ways in which the self can fool the self? How is it different from the Stage 1 "changing one's opinion?" The following interview excerpts may give us some ideas.

IS IT POSSIBLE TO FOOL YOURSELF? Yes, sometimes.
HOW CAN YOU FOOL YOURSELF? You can say to yourself, I didn't really care and keep on saying I didn't really care and sometimes it works and you don't really care about it.
DO YOU THINK DEEP DOWN INSIDE YOU THINK YOU REALLY DON'T CARE, OR DO YOU THINK YOU ACTUALLY DO CARE, DEEP DOWN INSIDE? You really care.
WHEN YOU SAY THAT, CAN YOU TRY TO FOOL YOURSELF INSIDE? No.

WHY NOT? If you are really upset about something, you don't really forget about it that easy.
WHY NOT, WHY IS IT HARD TO FORGET ABOUT THINGS THAT UPSET YOU? It is hard, you are thinking about that thing most of the time. So it is real hard to forget about it.
SO YOU THOUGHT IT ISN'T POSSIBLE TO FOOL YOURSELF? No.

(12:4)

Whereas at the previous level, self-deception was understood to occur due to external events or forces, at Stage 2 we repeatedly see a new theme, that through mechanistic force of habit or repetition, a belief can be changed by the self's effort.

There is another way that "fooling the self" is understood in a Stage 2 framework—in the manner of "forgetting." The term forgetting, in this context, usually means to the average 10-year-old that the "observing ego" has had a lapse in vigilance or is attending to other matters at the time and cannot be bothered to review the particular issue at hand.

WHAT'S THE DIFFERENCE BETWEEN FOOLING YOURSELF AND FOOL-ING SOMEONE ELSE? When you fool yourself, you kind of don't know that you fooled yourself sometimes, but when you are fooling another person, you know that you are doing it.
WHY IS IT YOU DON'T KNOW YOU ARE FOOLING YOURSELF WHEN YOU ARE FOOLING YOURSELF, HOW IS THAT POSSIBLE? DOESN'T YOUR MIND ALWAYS KNOW WHAT IS GOING ON? Yah, but sometimes you forget you are thinking about a different thing when you are fooling yourself. And you are thinking you are not fooling yourself.

(9:2)

Although this conception still defines self-deception as a passive reaction, it is becoming understood, apparently, as being to a greater extent under the self's control; to restore the state of "accurate awareness," what is needed is to reattend to or refocus on the particular problem at hand.

Third, the child realizes at Stage 2 that the individual, the self included, can consciously and often deceptively put on a facade that is meant to mislead other individuals with respect to what is "really" going on internally. The idea of "fronting" or putting on an appearance is understood by the child as a useful way for people to cover up their inner feelings, for example, to save the self from embarrassment or ridicule.

SUPPOSE THAT JERRY FINDS OUT KEITH LET HIM WIN AND HE SAYS TO KEITH I NEVER REALLY CARED ABOUT PING-PONG ANYWAY. WHY WOULD HE SAY SOMETHING LIKE THAT? Because he wants to make it like he didn't really care if he lost or not, it doesn't matter to him.

WHY WOULD HE TRY TO DO THAT? To cover up his feelings.
WHAT KIND OF FEELINGS IS HE COVERING UP? Sad ones.

(13:6)

The Stage 2 conception of subjective duality, the inner or true versus the outer or apparent, is transformed at Stage 3 into a deeper, more dynamic, and simultaneous understanding of the relation between self as subject and self as object. At Stage 3, the older child conceives of mind as serving a dual role, not only as an organ where mental processes are located (Broughton, 1978), but also as a *monitor,* deciding which thoughts get into the domain of awareness and which are kept out.

IS IT POSSIBLE TO HIDE YOUR FEELINGS FROM YOURSELF? Yes, you just don't tell it to anybody. You put it out of your mind.
IS IT POSSIBLE TO REALLY SUCCEED IN HIDING IT FROM YOURSELF? Yah, you just put it out of your mind and you don't want to know about it.
DO YOU THEN NOT KNOW ABOUT IT, OR INSIDE, DO YOU STILL KNOW ABOUT IT? You still know about it, but you don't think about it or talk about it.

(12:10)

WHAT IF YOU FORGET ABOUT SOMETHING, IS THAT FOOLING YOURSELF? Yes, that might be fooling yourself but now it is sort of like a mixture.
WHAT WOULD IT BE A MIXTURE OF? It might be sort of forgetfulness and trying to put it out of your mind.
IS THERE A DIFFERENCE BETWEEN FORGETTING SOMETHING AND PUTTING IT OUT OF YOUR MIND? Yes. (WHAT?) When you forget something you can forget something like your keys or something like that, but you can't put keys out of your mind or put it in your mind.

(12:11)

The last two examples show how lower stage concepts are often either rejected or integrated into higher levels of understanding. This second youngster seems to be going through a transition, one that takes into consideration the earlier stage explanation, but that also includes the higher level explanation as well. "It is sort of like a mixture . . . it might be sort of forgetfulness and trying to put it out of mind." To him brainwashing is almost literal, a forceful washing of the thought from the brain. However, at Stage 3, no matter how long one is not aware of inner experience, accurate self-awareness still always appears to be seen as potentially available "if one tries hard enough," "thinks about it long enough," or "pays more attention." It is now a matter of will.

Perhaps the most striking change from Stage 2 to Stage 3 conceptions of self-awareness is the shift from viewing the self as passive observer (keeper of secrets, hider of ideas, forgetter of unpleasant feelings) to seeing the self as an active psychological manipulator of inner life (forceful remover of painful ideas).

What appears new and striking at Stage 3 is the belief in the observing ego—the self-aware self—as an active agent. This concept of active agency strikes us as critical for a child's feeling of having some control over his or her own thoughts and feelings. For the "Stage 3" child, the mind (or ego) is now seen as playing an active moderating role between inner feelings and outer actions.

Stage 4 understanding is distinguished by the realization that no matter how vigilant the conscious mind is, no matter how hard the mind works, there are still internal experiences not readily available to awareness. At this stage, an adolescent sees that individuals can and do have thoughts, feelings, and motivations that are resistant to self-analysis by even the most introspective mind. There are two aspects to this discovery that are not often articulated until well into adolescence. First, there is the understanding of the existence of unconscious *processes*, an understanding seen in the child's own growing natural theory of psychic phenomena such as coping and defending as autonomic processes. Second, there is the concept of unconscious psychological *causes* of behavior, that below inner reality there may be an even deeper reality. The development of the concept-in-theory of the unconscious emerges out of a need to explain observed aspects of social behavior and experience that previous conceptions of intrapsychic phenomena were inadequately structured to explain.

It is not necessary for the adolescent to use psychological terminology to demonstrate reflective understanding of these psychological processes. As the following interview demonstrates, an understanding that persons can behave on the basis of motives or needs of which they themselves are not aware, and that no purposive act of conscious effort or will can yield a total understanding of certain self-actions, can be expressed without ever using the term "unconscious."

IF MIKE SAYS HE NEVER WANTS TO SEE ANOTHER PUPPY AGAIN, WHY DOES HE SAY THAT? Because he doesn't think that any puppy could take the place of Pepper.
DOES HE REALLY MEAN THAT, THAT HE NEVER WANTS TO SEE ANOTHER PUPPY AGAIN? No.
CAN YOU SAY SOMETHING AND NOT MEAN IT? That is something right off the top of his head, like when you are really upset, you might say get out of here I never want to see you again. But you are really going to see them tomorrow and you are not going to be mad at them.
SO MIKE MAYBE DOESN'T KNOW HOW HE FEELS? He is just talking out of emotions. He may think that at that instant he doesn't want to see another puppy, but he will get over the initial loss.
IF MIKE THINKS ABOUT WHAT HE SAID, WILL HE REALIZE THAT HE REALLY WOULD LIKE ANOTHER DOG? Maybe, but maybe not. He might not be aware of his deeper feelings.
HOW IS THAT POSSIBLE? He may not want to admit to himself that another dog could take Pepper's place. He might feel at some level that would be unloyal to

Pepper to just go out and replace the dog. He may feel guilty about it. He doesn't want to face these feelings, so he says, no new dog.
IS HE AWARE OF THIS? Probably not.

(16)

Personality. This issue covers changing conceptions of individuality in persons—what constitutes it, what factors coalesce into integrated forms of attitudes, values, and beliefs. Just as a key aspect of conceptions of self-awareness, the duality of inner experience and outer appearance, does not become a salient concept for the child until he or she can differentiate among multiple subjective reactions to events, a key aspect of conceptions of personality, the description of an individual in general and psychological rather than context specific terms, does not become salient until the child understands that individuals can take a third-person perspective on the feelings and actions of selves (at Stage 3, see Table 11.2). Nevertheless, lower stages can be described, as with other issues, by analyzing those aspects of personality upon which the child does focus when asked to give a general description of an individual.

Not surprisingly, when persons are described in purely physical appearance terms alone, these responses are characterized as Stage 0:

WHAT KIND OF PERSON IS YOUR FRIEND TOMMY? Kind of old, 7 or 8. A colored person.

(7:3) (6:2)

At Stage 1, although conceptions include concern with individual's actions as well as their physical appearance, nevertheless, these actions are still unelaborated, devoid of in-depth psychological motives and often equated with having good or bad skills.

WHAT KIND OF PERSON DO YOU THINK JERRY IS? Rotten.
WHAT DO YOU THINK, DO YOU THINK HE IS A ROTTEN PERSON? I don't know, yah.
WHY IS HE A ROTTEN PERSON? Because he stinks.
IN WHAT WAY? He can't play Ping-Pong.

SO THAT MAKES HIM A ROTTEN PERSON? Yah.

(11:2)

Whereas at Stage 0, the book on an individual's personality is literally judged by its cover, at Stage 1, a person *is* what a person *does*. The concept of personality is equated with the overt behavioral skills the child can perceive in self or in another.

Two personality conceptions coded as Stage 2 are of particular interest. The first is the equation of a person's personality with a specific underlying motive; the second is its equation with a specific mood. Below is an example of each.

YOU SAID HE COULD BE MORE THAN ONE PERSONALITY. HOW IS THAT POSSIBLE? Like Christmas, he might be boring, but before Christmas, or at his birthday or something like that, he could be great. Wow, he could be a mean old thing and then not.
BUT ON HOLIDAYS HE MIGHT GET TO BE NICE? Yah, I know someone who is.
WHAT MAKES THEM CHANGE: The holidays are very near.

(11)

WHAT KIND OF PERSONALITY DO YOU THINK MIKE HAS? Lousy.
WHY DO YOU THINK HE HAS A LOUSY PERSONALITY? Because he lost his dog and he don't feel so good.

(8:3)

At Stage 2 a child has a clearer understanding of the relation of inner states to outer actions and appearances. Now, the term personality is understood to signify an emotional reaction to some immediate event ("If they lost they start not liking the sport"), which in turn produces a more general mood ("You get mad."). However, the child does not yet construct personality as a system that shapes or interprets events in a predictable, characteristic way. Rather, it is the specific events that shape a specific mood. Changes in that personality–mood are brought about through changes in the situation ("Once you get older, you stop being a poor sport, you hardly play games."). The child believes that fundamental characteristics of personality (e.g., "being a sore loser") are like moods, dependent on and altered by specific activities ("winning") that change these superficial feelings. Personality within the self can be in conflict in the sense that specific feelings can be in conflict.

DO YOU THINK JERRY MIGHT BE A SORE LOSER? WHAT DOES THAT MEAN? You get mad and you don't like to lose and if you lose you get really mad at the other person. And you are not a very good sport about losing.
COULD JERRY BE A SORE LOSER SOMETIMES AND OTHER TIMES BE AN OKAY GUY? Yah, in some games he could just have not tried and in other games he tries and he gets mad because he lost.

(8:4)

I have described the development of the child's personality conceptions from the context-specific subjective description of actions (Stage 1) to the consideration of context-specific actions or feelings as they are meant to impress or be considered by others (Stage 2). At the third Stage, simple generalizations or characterizations about persons or selves are drawn from their diverse actions or attitudes. Such characterizations require as a prerequisite or corequisite a concept of a self on which to cast a descriptive psychological analysis. This is the third person or self-reflective self we see being constructed at Stage 3 in the domain of self-awareness (Table 11.2). Often the Stage 3 (or early adolescent) personality analysis seems oversimplified and stereotypical from an adult point of view. However, from a developmental perspective, it represents an advance over the previous stages.

WHEN YOU ARE TRYING TO FIGURE OUT WHAT KIND OF PERSON SOMEONE IS, HOW DO YOU DO IT? There are three kinds of people in this world. There is the crazy people that don't know it, there is the crazy people that do know it, that's me—that is what keeps me from going to a mental institution. WHAT DOES? That I know I am insane, I am really crazy, but I know it so that keeps me from going anywhere. WHY DOES IT HELP TO KNOW IT? It is just good. Everyone is crazy in a way, nuts. And then there are the people who think they are absolutely every way perfect, and they are really gooey ones. YOU THINK THEY ARE THE GOOEY ONES? They need help. YOU THINK SO, BUT THEY DON'T KNOW IT? Yah. HOW CAN YOU TELL? That means they have a superiority complex. And the reason they got the superiority complex is because if they think they are inferior, that is one reason. They think they are not as good as other people, so they always talk about doing things good, that is one reason. Other reasons is that they just might have a little more money or something, so they might be better, so they might speak two languages. They are snobbish people, snobs.

(12:10)

In an adolescent passing from Stage 3 to 4, it is not uncommon to find the idea of persons as a particular type (the same) conflicting in part with the idea of persons as different in different contexts ("You could be different, like at home you are all grouchy and then when you come into school you would be friends."). Here the adolescent begins to realize there are both normative (nomothetic) and particular (ideographic) natures of persons, but has not yet put the two together in a coherent conception or "theory of personality." Making this integration is the work of Stage 4.

WHAT KIND OF PERSON IS TOM, THE BOY WHO HAD TO DECIDE WHETHER OR NOT TO GET MIKE THE PUPPY? I don't know. It's hard to tell from the story. He seems like a pretty nice kid, but just a little bit selfish. CAN SOMEONE BE BOTH NICE AND SELFISH? Sure. People are not always consistent in the way they act. If you really want something, if it really means a lot to you, you might do anything to get it, even if it means stepping on someone else. The next minute you may turn around and give a lot of dough to some charity.

HOW DO YOU EXPLAIN SOMEONE LIKE THAT? Well, people have different
values. They may need something for their own self-esteem, or they may want
power, but in a calmer moment, they may be very generous.

(18)

Personality Change.   Developing conceptions of personality change follow a
similar sequence. Personality Change at Stage 0 is conceived of in physical
terms, equated with size change, activity choice change, or changes in other
perceptually apparent qualities ("You get bigger."). At Stage 1, Personality
change is seen as increasing physical skills ("You get better.") and at Stage 2 as
increasing mental abilities ("You get smarter.") or as change in specific habits.

Stage 3 preadolescents begin to recognize the stability of character beyond
specific "habits" or "attitudes"; personality becomes a predictable set of
character traits that are not easily changed, because they represent one's particular individuality. Superficial changes in one's behavior can occur but there is
recognition of the qualitative difference between changing personality and changing "habits."

DO YOU THINK THERE IS ANYTHING THAT CAN CHANGE IN A PERSON
BESIDES THEIR FEELINGS? Yah, but I don't think you would be able to change
your personality, but you could probably change your attitudes, like if you are a
real brat, you could probably change that.
WHY IS IT SO HARD TO CHANGE PERSONALITIES? Because you are with
your own self and if you were going to try to change yourself it would be sort of a
little—not so good.
WHAT IS A PERSONALITY ANYWAY? A personality is something inside you.
Like if you had a habit, and you keep on doing that, that is part of your personality.
And it can be how you act around other people and how you act around the house.

(11:5)

Ideas of individual "style" or "stable personality" characterize this stage of
conceptions of personality change. Personality change is seen to occur around
broad areas such as maturation ("Don't act like a kid anymore."), or around
broad environmental influences ("It depends on how you were brought up."). In
coming to understand the processes that form and change personality, the child
now becomes the clinician. The past shapes the present, which in turn shapes the
future. The hallmark of this conceptual level is the ability to distinguish short
term environmental effects, which shape one's immediate feelings or behaviors,
from long term environmental forces, which go into shaping one's personality.

At Stage 4, however, the subject is concerned with not merely change or
stability but also with the relationship between the obvious changes with age and
the sometimes more subtle changes that may occur in ordinarily stable characteristics. One of the resulting concepts is that of *temperament,* a core or underlying set of tendencies that undergoes various changes throughout development but

that maintains an essential identity and integrity. At Stage 3, there is the concept
of stability, but it refers to personality as a simple trait. At Stage 4, there is a
complex system with many facets or personalities. Believing there is a need to
ground these personalities in a more elemental core tendency, the adolescent
searches to identify that identity.

> IN WHAT WAYS DOES A PERSON CHANGE AND WHAT WAYS DO THEY
> STAY THE SAME? I can speak from personal experience. A lot of the things that
> you had thought were important in your life you find out aren't important. You find
> it easier to make trade-offs. I find it easier to make trade-offs in the last couple of
> years, something for something else. You find that the pursuit of certain goals is no
> longer as important as you thought they were, they are no longer as important to
> you as they were.
> WHAT PARTS OF YOU HAVE STAYED THE SAME? WHAT PARTS OF A
> PERSON'S MAKEUP STAY THE SAME? OR DOES EVERYTHING
> CHANGE? No. A lot of things stay the same. But in my own particular case in the
> last 5 or 6 years there have been a lot of changes in my personality. I suppose that I
> still suffer from the same inferiority complex that I had, and I need people to push
> me. I still have some of the values that I always had, ever since I can remember. I
> value certain people's friendship, I don't value certain material things, and I never
> did.
>
> (41)

These last examples demonstrate a phenomenon that applies to the developmental analysis of all social and intrapsychic issues. As individuals grow up, they not
only change their conceptions of intrapsychic experiences, but also their actual
inner experiences (the content or object of experience). For example, not only do
children's ideas about personality develop with age and experience, but so do
their personalities. Six-year-olds do not maintain or seek the same kind of identity within themselves that 16-year-olds do because their personalities do not
require it, not because it is there, fully developed, but they simply do not fully
understand it.

Validation of the Model: A Return to Our Initial Question

The result of the constructive phase of research, exemplified by our description
of stages of each of the four intrapsychic issues, is a formal stage-by-issue model
of understanding derived from both empirical research and logical analysis.
Intrapsychic understanding is but one domain of four, and the four issues described are but a part of 22 in our descriptive system (Table 11.3). One goal of
the phase of research that follows developmental descriptions is to evaluate
whether children's developing social (interpersonal and intrapsychic) conceptions across the 22 issues actually fit this stage model (and to establish age
norms). To do this, new interview data are gathered and evaluated to determine

TABLE 11.3

Issues of Interpersonal Understanding Related To Conceptions of the Individual, Close Friendships, Peer-Group Organizations, and Parent–Child Relations

(adapted from Selman, 1980)

Individual (Intrapsychic)	Friendship	Peer Group	Parent–Child Relations
Subjectivity: covert properties of persons (thoughts, feelings, motives); conflicts between thoughts or feelings within the person	1. *Formation:* why (motives) and how (mechanisms) friendships are made; the ideal friend	1. *Formation:* why (motives) and how (mechanisms) groups are formed; the ideal member	1. *Formation:* motives for having children and why children need parents
Self-awareness: awareness of the self's ability to observe its own thoughts and actions	2. *Closeness:* types of friendship, ideal friendship, intimacy	2. *Cohesion/loyalty:* group unity	2. *Love and emotional ties:* between parents and children
Personality: stable or predictive character traits (a shy person, etc.)	3. *Trust:* doing things for friends; reciprocity	3. *Conformity:* range and rationale	3. *Obedience:* why children do as their parents tell them
Personality change: how and why people change (growing up, etc.)	4. *Jealousy:* feelings about intrusions into new or established friendships	4. *Rules/norms:* types of rules, and reasons for them	4. *Punishment:* the function of punishment from the parent's and the child's perspective
	5. *Conflict resolution:* how friends resolve problems	5. *Decision-making:* setting goals, resolving problems, working together	5. *Conflict resolution:* optimal ways for parents and children to resolve their differences
	6. *Termination:* how friendships break up	6. *Leadership:* qualities, and function to the group	
		7. *Termination:* why groups break up or members are excluded	

whether or how well reasoning in these areas actually meets the stage criteria of structured wholeness, invariant sequence, and universality, and to document normal patterns of development.

If valid, the five stages of intrapsychic and interpersonal understanding should emerge at about the same age across issues, in only the prescribed order, under a variety of circumstances, and in the lives of all children interviewed. Taking appropriate methodological safeguards, children would be expected to express an optimal level of understanding that is relatively homogeneous across issues (i.e., at roughly the same stage). This does not mean that children might not use lower levels of expression under stress or about an issue where their experience has been less extensive. Nevertheless, at some point we would expect to find some consolidation of understanding and be surprised to find wide gaps in level of development across issues at this point (e.g., gaps of two or more stages). To determine the model's validity according to these criteria, once the descriptive map was composed, we interviewed a second sample of 149 subjects aged 3 through 40. Evidence speaking to the validity of the model is summarized in a recently published book, *The Growth of Interpersonal Understanding* (Selman, 1980).

However, a different but nevertheless important question of validity needs to be addressed here. Early in this chapter, I questioned clinical claims such as Bettelheim's that a young child of 3 or 4 may wish to withhold his or her private and personal inner thoughts from his or her parents until such a time as he or she chooses to reveal them and may experience disappointment if parents are found to know these inner thoughts already. Our own interview data suggest that the young child does not begin to reflect clearly on the distinction between his or her own affective or psychological perspective and another's, much less reflect on how inner (or private) thoughts differ from outer (or public) expressions of these thoughts, until 6 to 8 (Stage 1). And we have seen that the child does not appear to realize that such thoughts can be hidden from others until roughly age 8 to 10 (Stage 2).

One possible explanation for the conflict between our data and these clinical claims is the thought that children may be more likely to express their highest level of understanding in the presence of familiar adults such as parents or therapists and in familiar contexts such as their own homes, rather than with strange interviewers in strange places. Even considering this possible effect, the roughly 6-year disparity, from age 4 to 10, between a clinical assertion and empirical evidence, still seems difficult to reconcile. Our age norms, as we have carefully stressed, are not rigid, but they *are* based on numerous interviews with preschool children, and in no case did a child of 3 or 4 express understanding even approaching that which would seem logically requisite to the reactions Bettelheim claims occur.

Perhaps clinical age norms are vague or inaccurate. If one can reinterpret Bettelheim's or other statements so that the reaction described is valid but occurs only in older children, beginning at age 8 or 9, then the conflicts are neutralized. But if one does not exempt younger children from the claims made on their behalf, then the conflicts remain. If all the possible explanations we have tendered are considered together, there still remains an impasse of sorts.

However perhaps an explanation of a different sort, and of theoretically greater significance, could come from making a distinction between what we (researchers *or* clinicians) mean when we say, on the one hand, that the child must *feel* his or her inner thoughts are not known, and on the other hand, what we mean when we say that the child *understands* that his or her inner thoughts can be concealed. The former may be considered an unreflective or intuitive kind of knowledge, whereas the latter may be considered a reflective or conceptual form of understanding. This distinction in psychology is by no means new. As early as the turn of the century, James Mark Baldwin (1906) argued that expressions of socioemotional understanding in the young child could be seen to have developmental forms, an initial organic form and a later reflective form. For instance, in his discussion of the growth of sympathetic understanding, Baldwin noted that even the young infant shows an organic form of understanding; for example, when a baby's sister falls down or when its father feigns crying, the baby will cry, too. Although Baldwin claimed these organic forms of understanding remain present throughout life, he maintained that reflective forms of understanding do not begin to emerge until a period he called the "Stage of Intelligence" (roughly ages 5 to 6), that is, to paraphrase Baldwin, until there arises in the child the notion of the self. And, according to Baldwin (1906), the rise of the concept of self is possible only through the dialectical process of *reflectively understanding* relations between the self (ego) and other (alter). "Reflective [intrapsychic] understanding . . . therefore is distinctly a social outcome. It is the inevitable result of the growth of reflection, and reflection is just a relation of separateness created between the ego self and the alter self. If there were no alter thought, there could be no reflection and with it no [intrapsychic] . . . understanding [p. 22]."

In other words, the rise of reflective modes of intrapsychic understanding is a function of the emerging cognitive construction of the nature of the relation of self to other, and this in turn leads to new levels of understanding of the self (intrapsychic understanding). The work described in this chapter can be viewed as an attempt to specify the pattern that levels of reflective understanding take in the intrapsychic domain.

Furthermore, if Baldwin's distinction between organic (or affective) and reflective (or theoretical) understanding is valid, then it is less difficult to understand how young children can appear to be both as precocious in their psychological insight as clinicians might claim and as naive as cognitive psychology suggests. However, rather than simply stating that this distinction exists and letting the two forms of understanding go their separate affective and reflective ways, researchers must accept the challenge and study the ways in which these two forms of knowing inner life relate to one another. In very young children, the organic form appears to dominate. Children cannot easily verbalize, let alone reflect upon their own nascent, often intuitive knowledge of human nature. Therefore it is not surprising that researchers working with toddlers or preschoolers have used largely observational and naturalistic methods to infer what young children know of intra- and interpersonal relations (Mueller & Lucas, 1975). Results have generally demonstrated the precocity of the child's organic understanding; for instance, children as young as 2 years of age modify their communications according to the ages of their listeners (Shatz & Gelman, 1973).

On the other hand, the approach described in this chapter demonstrates an attempt to describe the developmental sequence of *reflective* social understanding and also a rationale for the interview method that is typical of that approach. At this point, studies are needed to examine how reflective and organic expressions of understanding interact. In young children this kind of research might be focused on how children transform their astute organic or "feeling" knowledge into reflective thought. In older children one interesting question is how organic and reflective knowledge interact in the way children express their feelings.

As noted, research into developmental aspects of what and how children know about intrapsychic events and processes usually has focused exclusively on one or the other of various forms or modes of knowing but seldom on these forms in conjunction with one another. In "real life," these forms are not expressed in mutually exclusive fashion, but it is hard for psychologists to find real-life situations that have enough contextual information to study both together. There is, however, one context where each of these forms can be simultaneously studied with some validity; that is during the process of individual child psychotherapy. During this process children are often asked to express their intrapsychic understanding in both forms. For instance, when asked to talk to the therapist about personal problems, or feelings, the child is essentially being asked to reflect upon and put into words notions about subjective personal experience and feelings—their relation to one another, to actions, and to social reality as perceived and defined by others. The child's ability to do this is closely related to his or her level of reflective understanding. At other times, the structure of one-to-one psychotherapy, with its availability of art materials and toys, encourages the child to express what he knows organically, through nonverbal media such as drawings or doll play. Through each of these forms of expression, the clinician attempts to put together a more complete and textured picture of what the child knows, understands, and means. But this is no simple task.

Take for an example a 6-year-old girl who announces to her therapist (with a devilish grin) that she will not attend their next scheduled session "because she has to go to the dentist." When the therapist shows some surprise and inquires more deeply for details, the child laughingly admits, "I was just fooling." The therapist is unsure of what to make of this statement. Does his young client understand, affectively or reflectively, that her therapist is invested in her coming to the session and does she demonstrate this understanding through a deliberately teasing remark? Focusing on an alternative but not necessarily incompatible meaning to the statement, the therapist inquires whether there is something about therapy that the child doesn't like. She responds, ''I want to come and I don't.'' How does he interpret this? Does her statement reflect a comprehension of the possibility of psychological ambivalence or a simple inability or unwillingness to articulate her own feelings?

Clearly, it is at this point that the stage-descriptive analysis in this paper has something to contribute, for it alerts us that there can be a range of different levels of understanding implied by the statement, ''I want to come and I don't.'' This analysis suggests it would be inappropriate for a therapist working with a 6-year-old child to go into a didactic discourse about how sometimes when individuals have negative or anxious feelings about some course of action (such as going to therapy) they ''act them out,'' for example, by ''forgetting,'' or by making conflicting appointments. Such theoretical insights into the idea of ''acting out,'' even if valid, are conceptually too sophisticated for most 6 year olds to comprehend. On the other hand, some discussion of how it is natural for people to have two different kinds of feelings about some person or activity seems reasonable from a developmental point of view and is therapeutically appropriate as well.

In suggesting that youngsters have difficulty grasping confusing inner states that Anna Freud noted (1965): ''as such are not incapable of consciousness but have not yet suceeded in achieving ego status, consciousness, and secondary elaboration,'' I am further suggesting that the child psychotherapy process with its frequent (weekly or biweekly) meetings and long-term process (sometimes over several years) is an extremely appropriate environment to observe the development of intrapsychic understanding in each of its forms of expression. Understanding how a child's consciousness of intrapsychic processes is raised to a higher level of reflective understanding is a worthwhile goal in both cognitively oriented developmental psychology and affectively oriented psychotherapy.

REFERENCES

Axline, V. *Dibs in search of self.* New York: Ballentine, 1964.

Baldwin, J. M. *Social and ethical interpretations in mental development.* London: MacMillan, 1906.

Bettelheim, B. *The uses of enchantment: The meaning and importance of fairy tales.* New York: Knopf, 1977.

Broughton, J. The development of concepts of self, mind, reality and knowledge. *New Directions for Child Development,* 1978, *1,* 75–100.

Chandler, M., Paget, K., & Koch, D. The child's demystification of psychological defense mechanisms: A structural and developmental analysis. *Developmental Psychology,* 1978, *14,* 197–206.

Damon, W. *The social world of the child*. San Francisco: Jossey-Bass, 1977.

Elkind, D. Cognitive development and psychopathology. Observations on egocentrism and ego defense. In E. Schopler & R. Reichler (Eds.), *Psychopathology and child development: Research and treatment*. New York: Plenum, 1976.

Flavell, J. *Cognitive development*. Englewood Cliffs, N.J.: Prentice-Hall, 1977.

Freud, A. *The psychoanalytical treatment of children*. Translated by N. Proctor-Gregg. New York: Schocken, 1964. (Originally published, 1946.)

Furth, H. Children's conception of social institutions: A Piagetian framework. *Human Development*, 1976, *19*, 351-374.

Harter, S. A cognitive-developmental approach to children's expression of conflicting feelings and a technique to facilitate such expression in play therapy. *Journal of Consulting and Clinical Psychology*, 1977, *45*, 417-432.

Livesley, W. J., & Bromley, D. B. *Person perception in childhood and adolescence*. London: Wiley, 1973.

Moustakis, C. (Ed.). *Existential child therapy: The child's discovery of himself*. New York: Avon, 1971.

Mueller, E., & Lucas, J. A developmental analysis of peer interaction among toddlers. In M. Lewis, & L. A. Rosenblum (Eds.), *Friendship and peer relations*. New York: Wiley, 1975.

Peevers, B. H., & Secord, P. F. Developmental changes in attribution of descriptive concepts to persons. *Journal of Personality and Social Psychology*, 1973, *27*, 120-128.

Piaget, J. *The construction of reality in the child*. New York: Basic Books, 1954.

Selman, R. L. Toward a structural analysis of developing interpersonal relations concepts: Research with normal and disturbed preadolescent boys. In A. Pick (Ed.), *Tenth Annual Minnesota Symposium on Child Psychology*. Minneapolis: University of Minnesota Press, 1976.

Selman, R. L. *The growth of interpersonal understanding: Developmental and clinical analyses*. New York: Academic Press, 1980.

Shatz, M., & Gelman, R. The development of communication skills: Modifications in the speech of young children as a function of listener. *Monographs of the Society for Research in Child Development*. Chicago: University of Chicago Press, 1973.

Turiel, E. The development of social concepts. In D. DePalma and J. Foley (Eds.), *Moral development*. Hillsdale, New Jersey: Lawrence Erlbaum Associates, 1975.

Youniss, J., & Volpe, J. A relational analysis of children's friendships. In W. Damon (Ed.), *New Directions for Child Development*, 1978, *1*, 1-22.

Author Index

Numbers in italics indicate the page on which the complete reference appears.

A

Abrams, M., 67, *82*
Adcock, C., 24, *30*
Adorno, T. W., 50, *62*
Ainsworth, M., 156, *165*
Allport, F. H., 50, 55, *62*
Allport, G. W., *62,* 74, *82*
Almy, M., 141, *142*
Anderson, B. J., 107, *108*
Anthony, E. J., *214*
Apple, M. W., 138, *142*
Asch, S. E., 49, *62*
Ashton, P. J., 115, 116, *128*
Ausubel, D., 135, *142*
Axline, V., 188, *214*

B

Bakan, D., 151, 164, 165, *166*
Baldwin, J. M., 212, *214*
Bales, R. F., 151, *168*
Barker, R. D., 134, *142*
Barnett, R., 176, *182*
Barrett, P. H., 78, *83*
Barron, F., 23, 26, 27, *28*
Barry, A., 176, *182*
Barry, R., 176, *182*
Barten, S., 69, *82, 83*
Bateson, G., 158, *166*

Bee, H., 176, *184*
Bell, R. Q., 107, *107, 128,* 158, 159, *166*
Bell, S., 156, *165*
Bergman, A., 39, *46,* 89, *95*
Berlyne, D. E., 55, *62*
Berman, L. M., 136, 141, *142*
Bernstein, A., 180, *182*
Bernstein, R. J., 82, *82*
Best, D. L., 176, *183*
Bettleheim, B., 181, *183,* 187, 188, 189, *214*
Biber, B., 9, 10, 11, 12, 13, 14, 17, 21, 23, 24, *28, 29,* 40, *45,* 65, 66, 71, 77, *82, 83, 84,* 123, *129*
Bing, E., 163, *166*
Birch, H. G., 101, *108,* 122, *129*
Bjerke, K., 176, *183*
Black, I. S., 66, 77, *82*
Black, M., *82*
Block, J., 151, 157, 163, *166, 167*
Block, J. H., 60, *62,* 148, 149, 150, 151, 157, 160, 161, 162, 163, 164, 165, *166, 167, 169,* 176, *183*
Bloom, B. S., 134, *142*
Bower, T. G. R., 100, *107*
Bray, H., 176, *183*
Brazelton, T. B., 102, *107*
Brodzinsky, D. M., 171, 173, 174, *183*
Bromley, D. B., 188, *215*
Bronfenbrenner, U., 134, *142*
Bronson, W. C., 157, *166*

Broughton, J., 188, 189, *214*
Broverman, D. M., 176, *184*
Broverman, I., 176, *184*
Brucken, L., 175, *183*
Bruner, J. S., 21, 25, *28*, 50, *62*
Burke, K., 77, *82*

C

Cairns, R. B., 107, *107*
Carpenter, C. J., 158, 159, 160, *166*
Cassirer, E., 66, *82*
Chandler, M. J., 59, *62*, 122, 127, *129*, 188, *215*
Chess, S., 101, *108*, 122, *129*
Chesterton, G. K., 41, *45*
Chodrow, N., 171, 173, 175, 177, *183*
Chomsky, N., 79, *82*
Clarke-Stewart, A., 159, *166*
Cloud, J. M., 176, *183*
Cocking, R. R., 161, 163, *169*
Cohen, D., 9, *28*
Cohen, S. B., 75, *83, 84*, 135, *143*
Cole, M., 115, *128*
Collins, G., 158, *166*
Cook, K. V., 155, 156, 160, *168*
Copans, S., 102, *108*
Corman, H. H., 122, *128*
Counts, G. S., 15, *28*
Cowan, B., 180, *182*
Cramer, P., 174, *183*

D

Daehler, M. W., 159, *166*
Damon, W., 118, 120, *128*, 189, *215*
Dasen, P. R., 115, 116, *128*
Davidson, W., 157, *166*
Davis, S. W., 176, *183*
deHirsch, K., 53, *62*
Deming, L., 19, *29*
de Riviera, J., 43, 45, *45*
DeVries, R., 24, *29*, 133, *142*
Dewey, J., 15, *28*
Dollard, J., 49, 51, 62, *63, 81, 82*
Doyle, C., 43, *45*
Drucker, J., 43, *45*, 81, *82*
Duchowny, M., 102, *108*
Duckworth, E., 125, *128*
Duncan, B., 160, *166*
Duncan, D., 160, *166*

Dweck, C. S., 157, *166*
Dyk, R. B., 58, *63, 84*

E

Eggleston, V. H., 70, *96*
Edward, C. P., 160, *169*
Eisner, E. W., 139, *142*
Elkind, W., 189, *215*
Emde, R., 100, *107*
Emmerich, E., 177, 179, *183*
Engels, F., 37, *46*
Enna, B., 157, *166*
Erikson, E. H., 23, 26, *28, 89, 95,* 121, *128,* 171, 173, 174, *183*
Escalona, S. K., 41, *46, 57, 62,* 95, *95,* 101, *107,* 122, *128*
Etaugh, C., 158, *166*
Evans, E. D., 24, *29*

F

Fagot, B. I., 155, 158, 159, 160, *166*
Fairweather, H., 147, *166*
Faris, E., 18, *29*
Fein, G., 155, *166*
Feinburg, S., 173, 174, 175, *183*
Feldman, D. H., 128, *128*
Felsenthal, H., 154, *166*
Fenichel, O., 162, *166*
Feshbach, N. D., 158, *168*
Flavell, J., 189, *215*
Foster, J. C., 132, *142*
Fox, N., 115, *129*
Fraisse, P., 35, *46*
Frank, L. K., 50, *62*
Franklin, M. B., 9, 14, 23, *29,* 40, 43, *45, 46,* 65, 69, *83*
Freedle, R., 153, *167*
Frenkel-Brunswick, E., 50, *62*
Freud, A., 214, *215*
Freud, S., 162, *167*
Freuh, T., 176, *183*
Furth, H., 189, *215*

G

Gardner, J., 100, *107*
Gay, J., 115, *128*
Gelman, R., 213, *215*

Gerson, A., 158, *166*
Gesell, A., 131, *142*
Giddens, A., 82, *83*
Gill, M. M., 49, 53, *62, 63*
Gilligan, C., 171, 174, 175, 182, *183*
Glick, J., 115, *128*
Goldberg, S., 99, *107,* 155, 157, 159, 160, *167,* 175, *183*
Goldman, K., 177, 179, *183*
Goldstein, K., 74, *83*
Goodenough, D. R., 58, *63, 84*
Goodenough, F. L., 171, 174, *183*
Goodlad, J. I., 138, 141, *142*
Goodman, N., 66, *83*
Gough, H. E., 151, *167*
Greenfield, P., 115, *128*
Gruber, H. E., 68, 78, *83,* 114, 128, *129*
Gunnar-Gnechten, M. R., 157, 163, *167*
Guthrie, W. K. C., 36, *46*
Guttentag, M., 176, *183*
Guttman, D., 151, *167*

H

Haan, N., 57, *62,* 150, *169*
Hall, G. S., 131, *142*
Hardesty, F. P., 74, *83*
Harlow, H. F., 55, *62*
Hartmann, H., 23, 26, *29,* 81, *83*
Harmon, R., 100, *107*
Harper, L. V., 107, *107*
Harrington, D., 157, 163, *166, 167*
Hart, R., 160, *168*
Harter, S., 188, *215*
Headley, N. E., 132, *142*
Heider, G. M., 57, *62,* 122, *128*
Hermans, H. J., 163, *167*
Hertzig, M. D., 101, *108,* 122, *129*
Hertzman, M. D., 58, *63*
Hill, K. T., 49, *63*
Hoffman, L. W., 151, 163, *167*
Hoffman, M. L., 59, *62,* 150, *167*
Hogan, K., 174, *183*
Holt, B. G., 159, *169*
Holt, R. R., 49, *62*
Horner, M., 171, *183*
Hovland, C. I., 49, *62*
Huebner, D., 137, *142*
Hull, C. L., 72, *83*
Hunt, J. McY., 157, 161, *167*
Hutt, C., 159, *167*

I

Ilg, F. L., 131, *142*
Issacs, S., 23, 25, *29*

J

Jacklin, C. N., 148, 149, 154, 159, 162, *168,* 174, 176, *183*
Jackson, P. W., 138, *142*
Jahoda, M., 57, *62,* 114, *129*
Jankowski, J. J., 155, 156, 157, 160, *169*
Jersild, A. T., 132, *142*
Johnson, D., 155, *166*
Johnson, H. M., 16, *29*
Johnson, M., 18, *29*
Johnson, T. H., *46*
Jones, R. M., 21, 23, 25, *29*

K

Kagan, J., 122, 127, *129,* 163, *167,* 171, 175, 176, *183*
Kamii, C., 23, 24, *29,* 133, *142*
Kanter, R., 176, *183*
Kaplan, B., 67, 68, 73, 75, 77, 81, *83, 84,* 91, *95,* 135, *143*
Karp, S. A., 58, *63, 84*
Kelly, G. A., 55, *62*
Keniston, K., 134,
Kent, R. N., 154, *169,* 176, *184*
Kessen, W., 114, *129,* 140, *142*
King, N. R., 138, *142*
Kirsh, B., 177, 179, *183*
Klein, M. F., 138, *142*
Koch, D., 188, *215*
Kogan, N., 127, *129*
Kohlberg, L., 13, 24, *29,* 171, 172, 176, 177, 179, *183*
Konstadt, N., 53, *63*
Korn, S., 101, *108,* 122, *129*
Kosson, N., 155, *166*
Krown, S., 9, *29*
Kuhn, D., 126, *129,* 175, *183*
Kuhn, T. S., 66, 78, *83*

L

Ladd, H., 52, *63*
Langer, J., 68, *83*

Lansky, L. M., 162, *167*
Laurendean, M., 118, *129*
Lavatelli, C. S., 23, 24, *29*
Lever, J., 158, 159, *167*, 173, 175, 176, *183*
Levin, H., 162, *169*
Levinger, L., 20, *29*
Levinson, D. J., 50, *62*
Lewin, K., 75, 77, *83*, 126, 127, *129*
Lewis, H. B., 58, *63*
Lewis, M., 99, *107*, 153, 155, 157, 159, 160, *167*, *168*, *183*
Livesley, W. J., 188, *215*
Loevinger, J., 57, *63*, 114, *129*, 161, *167*
Lucas, J., 213, *215*
Lynn, D. B., 162, 163, *167*

M

Maccoby, E. E., 148, 149, 154, 159, 162, *167*, *168*, *169*, 174, 176, *183*
Macdonald, J. B., 136, *142*
Machover, K., 58, *63*
Mackinnon, D. W., 23, 26, *29*
Maes, P. C., *167*
Mahler, M. S., 39, *46*, 89, *95*
Marcus, D., 177, 179, *184*
Margolin, G., 154, *168*
Maw, E. W., 55, *63*
Maw, W. H., 55, *63*
Mayer, R., 24, *29*
McCall, R., 127, *129*
McClelland, D., 24, *30*, 171, *184*
McGhee, P. E., 176, *183*
McKeon, R., 36, *46*
McLaughlin, J. T., 35, *46*
Mead, G. H., *215*
Meissner, P. B., 58, *63*
Messer, S. B., 160, *168*, 171, 173, 174, *183*
Messick, S., 58, *63*
Meyer, W., 154, *168*
Miller, J. B., 171, 173, 175, *184*
Miller, N. E., 49, 51, *62*, *63*, 81, *82*
Minuchin, P., 9, *29*, 55, *63*, 77, *83*
Mischel, W., 72, *83*
Mitchell, L. S., 17, 20, 21, *29*
Moss, H. A., 122, *129*, 160, 163, *167*, *168*
Moriarty, A. E., 41, *46*, 57, *63*, 141, *142*, 153, 156, *168*
Moustakis, C., 188, *215*
Mueller, E., 213, *215*
Murphy, G., 23, 26, *29*

Murphy, L. B., 41, *46*, 52, 57, *63*, 77, *82*, 141, *142*, 153, 156, *168*

N

Nash, L., 162, *168*
Nash, S., 175, *183*
Naumberg, M., 18, *29*
Neisser, V., 51, *63*
Nelson, S., 157, *166*
Neugarten, B. L., 114, *129*
Newson, E., 160, *168*
Newson, V., 160, *168*
Novikoff, A. B., 72, *83*, 117, *129*
Noy, P., 44, *46*

O

O'Leary, K. D., 154, *169*, 176, *184*
O'Leary, S. E., 160, *168*
Olesker, W., 42, *46*
Ollman, B., 34, *46*
Osgood, C. E., 81, *83*
Overton, W. F., 27, *29*, 68, 70, *83*, 140, *142*, 177, 179, *184*

P

Paget, K., 188, *215*
Paley, V., 173, 176, 181, *184*
Parke, R. D., 153, 160, 162, *168*
Parsons, T., 151, *168*
Parten, M. B., 173, *184*
Pascal, B., *46*
Patterson, G. R., 154, *168*
Paterson, H. F., 58, *63*, *84*
Pedersen, F. A., 104, *108*, 155, 156, 157, 158, 159, 160, *168*, *169*
Peevers, B. H., 188, *215*
Pepper, S., 66, 67, 68, *83*
Perry, R., 39, *46*
Perry, W. G., 152, 161, *168*
Phenix, P. H., 137, *142*
Piaget, J., 23, 24, *29*, 35, 42, *46*, 69, *83*, 90, *95*, 100, *107*, 113, 114, 116, *129*, 152, 157, 159, 161, 163, *168*, 172, 177, *184*, 189, *215*
Pinard, A., 118, *129*
Pine, F., 39, 40, *46*, 89, *95*
Pirotta, S., 115, *129*
Pitcher, E., 173, *184*
Pope, A., 36, *46*

Postman, L., 50, *62*
Portuges, S. H., 158, *168*
Pratt, C., 19, *29*

R

Ramey, C., 157, 159, *169*
Ransom, T., 162, *168*
Rapoport, D., 23, 26, *29*, 43, *46*, 53, *63*
Reese, H. W., 27, *29*, 68, 70, *83*, 140, *142*
Rheingold, H. L., 155, 156, 160, *168*
Riegel, K. F., 38, *46*, 119, *129*, 161, *168*
Robertson, L. S., 176, *183*
Roderick, J. A., 136, *142*
Rogers, L., 24, *30*
Rogoff, B., 115, *129*
Rosenfeld, E. F., 156, 160, *168*
Rosenkrantz, P., 176, *184*
Rothbart, M. K., 163, *168*
Rothbaum, F., 171, 177, *184*
Rubinstein, J. L., 104, *108*, 155, 156, 157, 160, *169*

S

Sackett, G. P., 107, *107*
Saegert, S., 160, *168*
Sameroff, A., 122, 127, *129*
Sander, L. W., 156, *168*
Sanders, S., *133, 143*
Sanford, N., 23, 25, *29*
Sanford, R. N., 50, *62*
Sarason, S. B., 49, *63*
Sawin, D. B., 153, 160, *168*
Schachtel, E. G., 49, *63*, 118, *129*
Schafer, R., 53, *63*
Scheresky, R., 176, *184*
Schludermann, E. H., 112, *129*
Schludermann, S., 112, *129*
Schneirla, T. C., 72, *83, 84*
Schuman, H., 160, *166*
Schur, M., 43, *46*
Scribner, S., 115, *129*
Sears, R. R., 162, *169*
Secord, P. F., 188, *215*
Seligman, M. P. E., 157, *169*
Sellers, M. J., 115, *129*
Selman, R. L., 188, 189, 211, *215*
Senn, M. J. E., 65, *84*
Serbin, L. A., 154, *169*, 176, *184*
Shantz, C. U., 59, *63*

Shapiro, E. K., 9, 11, *29*, 65, 77, *83, 84*, 123, *129*
Shapiro, T., 39, *46*
Sharabary, R., 177, 179, *183*
Sharp, D. W., 115, *128*
Shatz, M., 213, *215*
Shepher, J., 171, *184*
Sherif, M., 49, *63*
Sigel, I. E., 134, *143*, 161, 163, *169*
Skinner, B. F., 72, *84*
Smart, M., *133, 143*
Smith, C., 176, *184*
Smith, M. B., 57, *63*, 150, *169*
Smock, C. D., 159, *169*
Soule, B., 102, *108*
Spence, K. W., 49, 54, *63*
Spitz, R. A., 100, *107*
Standley, K., 102, *108*
Stan, R. H., 159, *169*
Stork, L., 155, *166*
Sutton-Smith, B., 173, *184*

T

Taylor, J. A., 49, 54, *63*
terLaak, J. J., *167*
Terman, L. M., 148, 149, *169*
Tew, J. D., 171, 173, 174, *183*
Thomas, A., 101, *108*, 122, *129*
Thompson, G., 154, *168*
Thompson, S. K., 175, 176, *184*
Tiger, L., 171, *184*
Tonick, I. S., 154, *169*
Tonick, I. J., 176, *184*
Turiel, E., 13, *29*, 118, *129*, 189, *215*
Tyler, L. E., 148, 149, *169*
Tyler, R. W., 138, *143*

U

Ullian, D., 176, 178, 179, 181, *183, 184*

V

Vonéche, 114
Volpe, J., 189, *215*
Vogel, S., 176, *184*
Vygotsky, L., 81, *84*

W

Waldrop, M. F., 158, 159, *166*
Walraven, M., 153, *169*
Wapner, S., 48, 58, *63,* 73, 75, *83, 84,* 135, *143*
Washburn, S. L., 125, *130*
Washburn, C., 18, *29*
Wasserman, L., 155, *166*
Watson, J. S., 99, *108,* 157, 159, *169*
Weikart, D., 23, 24, *30*
Weintraub, M., 160, 162, *167*
Weisz, J. R., 127, *130*
Weller, G. M., 158, 159, *166*
Werner, H., 23, 27, *30,* 43, *46,* 48, *63,* 69, 70, 72, 73, 74, 75, 77, 81, *84,* 91, *95,* 120, *130*
White, R. W., 23, 26, *30,* 57, *63,* 157, 159, *169*

White, S. H., 115, *129, 130*
Whiting, B., 160, *169*
Williams, J. E., 176, *183*
Winsor, C. B., 20, *30*
Witkin, H. A., 58, *63,* 74, *84*
Wohlwill, J., 127, *129*
Wolff, P., 81, *84*
Woodcock, L., 77, *82*
Wozniak, R. H., 81, *84*

Y,Z

Yarrow, L. J., 100, 102, 104, 107, *108,* 153, 155, 156, 157, 160, *169*
Youniss, J., 59, *63,* 189, *215*
Zigler, E., 23, 25, *30*
Zimbardo, P. G., *63*
Zimiles, H., 53, 58, *63,* 77, *83*

Subject Index

A

Adolescence
  understanding of intrapsychic processes in, 204-205
  understanding of personality in, 207-208
Affect, *see also* Emotion
  as driving force, 51-52
  influence on thought processes, 49-50
  interaction with cognition, 42-44
  Werner's emphasis on, 69-70
Age, stage theory and, 114
Altruism, development of, 59-60
Anger, sex differences in expression of, 174
Art, sex differences in, 173
Attitudes, overt actions and, 200
Authority, resistance to, 53-54

B

Behavior, personality conception based on, 205
Behaviorism, 47-48, 49, 72, 75
Bias, in sex difference studies, 148-149

C

Caretakers, *see* Father; Mother; Parents; Socialization
Child, interaction with environment, 121-123
Child-rearing orientation, sex differences and, 163

Chores, exploratory behaviors and, sex differences in, 160-161
Cognition, *see also* Learning
  interaction with affect, 42-44
  social, 59-60
Cognitive-affective interaction
  historical overview of, 47-51
  methodological problems and, 60-62
Cognitive development, interaction with emotional development, 99-101
Cognitive dispositions, 58-59
Cognitive perceptions, sex-role development and, 177-183
Cognitive processing, sex differences in, 149-152
  socialization and, 152-163
Cognitive style, 57-59
College curriculum, developmental stages and, 133
Communication gestures, walking and, 90, 94
Concept formation, 91
  impulse control and, 91-94
Concrete operations stage, universality of, 115
Consolability, 103
Constructionist hypothesis, gender differences, 177-182
Contingent responding, sex differences and, 153-154, 156-158
Coping mechanisms, 57
Coping strategies, sex differences in, 163-164

223

Creativity, Werner's view of, 70
Culture, developmental stages and, 115, 140
Curiosity, correlates of, 55
Curriculum, developmental stages and, 132–134
    problems in, 135–141

D

Deepening, in theory development, 79–81.
Defensive interactions, parent-infant interactions
    and, 101–102
Development
    differentiation in, 38–41
    integrated view of, 38, 41–44
    research directions in, 40–41
Developmental-interaction
    definition of, 9, 87–88
    evolution of, 80–81
    examples of, 88–95
    integrative nature of, 70–71
    prototypical forms of theory and, 77
Developmental lacks, instruction geared to, 135
Developmental stages, 114, 131–132
    curriculum and, 132–134
        problems in, 135–141
    discontinuity versus continuity of, 117–120
    invariant sequence of, 116–117
    in Piagetian theory, 114
    unevenness of, 120–121
    universality of, 115–116
Developmental theory, 72, 73, 74
    differences between Piaget and Werner and,
        69–70
    gestalt theory compared with, 69
    psychoanalytic theory compared with, 69
Differentiation in development, 38, 40
    of self-environment, 100
Discipline, impulse control and, 93–94
Discontinuities, developmental, 117–118
Discrimination, emotional development and, 99
Distancing, maternal, sex differences and,
    161–162
Dreams, differing perspectives on, 189–190
    dramatic play, 19, 20
Drive, role in learning, 51

E

Eclecticism, 70–71
    dangers of, 68
Ecological psychology, 134–135

Ego control, 54
Ego-functioning, 26–27, 56–57, 70
Emotion, see also Affect
    disabling effect on learning, 52–54
    experience of, 45
Emotional development
    cognitive development and, 99–101
    interaction with motor development, 98–99
Emotional reaction, personality conception
    based on, 206
Environment, see also Socialization
    characteristics of, 121–122
    child's interaction with, 121–123
    curriculum and, 136–139
    developmental stages and, 116
    differentiation of self from, 100
    in Freudian and Piagetian theories, 113
    influence of infant on, 101–107
Existentialism, curriculum and, 136–139
Experience(s), disequilibrating, sex differences
    and, 161–163
Experimental method, limitations of, 61
Exploratory behavior
    motivation for, 55
    sex differences in, 159–161
Extension, of theories, 79–80

F

Family of theories, 27, 67–68
Father, see Parents
Feedback, from toys, sex differences and, 155–
    156, 158–159
Friendship, conception of, 192, 210
Freudian theory, environment in, 113
Function, of behavior or process, 43

G

Gender, see also Sex
Gender consolidation, 178
Generalizability, of theories, 112, 127–128
Gestalt psychology, 48
    developmental theory compared with, 69
Gestalt theory, 72–73
Gestures, walking and, 90, 94
Group, psychologies of, 74n
Group influence, 49

H

Helplessness, learned, contingent responding
    and, 157

Historical perspectives, 2
Humanist values, 10-15

I

Imitative play, sex differences in, 158-159
Impulse control, concept formation and, 91-94
Individual
    curriculum based on stage theory and, 136-137
    relationship of theory to, 124-125
    theoretical lack of emphasis on, 111-112
Individuality, in psychology of person, 73-74
Infant, see also Maternal behavior
    influence on environment, 101-107
Innate behaviors, in psychologies of the mind, 71
Integrationist approach, to development, 38, 41-44
Interaction
    among motor, cognitive, social, and emotional development, 98-101
    sex differences in chore assignments and, 160-161
Internal development, of theories, 79
    developmental interactionism, 81
Intrapsychic processes
    children's understanding of, 187-188
    developmental study of, 191-209
    methodological issues in, 188-191, 193-195
    validation of model for, 209-214
    reflective understanding of, 212-213
I-valve relationships, 137

L

Language, role in organizing experience, 44
Language development, interaction with motor development, 98
Learning
    disabling effect of emotion on, 52-54
    role of drive in, 51-52
    interaction with emotional development, 99
Learning disabilities, influence of emotion on, 53
Lewinian theory, 75, 126, 127

M

Maternal behavior, infant characteristics and, 102-106

Maternal relationship, walking and, 89-90, 94
Measurement, limited perspective on, 61
Memory, discontinuities in, 117-118
Mental processes, "primitive," Werner's emphasis on, 70
Metaawareness, 41
Metatheorizing, 82
Methodology
    for sex difference studies, 148
    study of cognitive-affective interaction and, 60-62
Mind, psychologies of, 71-72
Mind-body relationship, 34-35
    integrated view of, 37-39
    reason and passion and, 35-37
Models, continuum of, 66-67
Mother, see also Parents
    distancing of, sex differences and, 161-162
Motor development
    interaction with cognitive, social, and emotional development, 98-99, 100-101
    interaction with language development, 98

N

Need(s)
    to know, 54-55
    role in learning, 51-52
Nurturance
    sex-role identity and, 171-172
    cognitive perceptions and, 177-183
    evidence for, 172-175
    socialization and, 175-177

O

Object permanence, development of, 100
Organism, psychologies of, 72-73
Organismic psychology, 48
Organization, developmental stages and, 140
Overprotection, consequences of, 163

P

Parents, see also Mother
    contingent responding of, sex differences and, 153-154, 156-158
    protective behaviors of, consequences of, 163
    sex differences and, in exploratory behaviors, 159-161
Parent-child interaction, reciprocity of, 122
Passion, mind-body relationship and, 35-37

Perception
   autocentric and allocentric, 49
   cognitive, sex-role development and, 177–183
   factors influencing, 50
   interaction with emotional development, 99
Person, psychologies of, 73–74
Personality, 193
   interaction with environment, 122
   sex differences in, 150, 173, 174
   understanding of, 205–208
Personality change, 193
   developmental analysis of understanding of, 208–209
Philosophy, sex differences in, 174, 175
Physical attributes, sex-role identity and, 179–182
Piagetian theory, see also Developmental stages
   environment in, 113
   reexamination of, 50–51
   stages in, 114
Play
   imitative, sex differences in, 158–159
   sex differences in, 173, 174–175
Power
   sex-role identity and, 171–172
      cognitive perceptions and, 177–183
      evidence for, 172–175
      socialization and, 175–177
Premise systems, sex differences in, 153
   contingent responding and, 153–154, 157, 161–163
Protective behaviors, consequences of, 163
Psychoanalytic approach, cognition-affect relationship and, 44
Psychoanalytic theory, 48–49, 72, 74
   developmental theory compared with, 69
Psychology(ies)
   of group, 74n
   of mind, 71–72
   of organism, 72–73
   of person, 73–74
   as a science, 66
   of situations, 74–77

R

Readiness, problems with, 135–136
Reason, mind-body relationship and, 35–37
Reductionism, limitations of, 97
Reflective awareness, development of, 212–213

Reinforcement, sex differences and, 154
Research
   ecological psychology and, 134–135
   implications of integrated view for, 42
   methodological problems in, 60–62
   relationship to theory, 126
Response(s), competing, 54
Responsiveness, of toys, sex differences and, 155, 156
Rigidity, curricular, 135
"Root-metaphor method," 67
   theory families and, 67–69

S

School, role of, 15–18
Self
   development of feelings about, 99, 100–101
   differentiation from environment, 100
Self-awareness, 193
   developmental analysis of, 198–205
   study of, 195
Self-concept, 55–56
   shaping of, 56
Self-deception, children's understanding of, 200–203
Self-esteem, 54
Sex, of infant, maternal behavior and, 103–104
Sex differences
   bases of, 149
   in cognitive functioning, 60
   cognitive perceptions and, 177–183
   in cognitive processing, 149–152
      socialization and, 152–163
   development of, hypotheses regarding, 178
   historical background, 147–149
   in personality, 150
   power versus nurturance and, 171–172
      evidence for, 172–175
      socialization and, 175–177
   sex-role stereotyping, 172
   socialization and, 164–165, 171–172
Situations, psychologies of, 74–77
Social interaction
   integration of feelings about, 59–60
   reciprocity of, 121
Socialization
   sex differences and, 60, 152–153, 164–165
      in coping strategies, 163–164
      disequilibrating experiences and, 161–163
      exploratory behaviors and, 159–161

feedback from toys and, 155–156, 158–159
imitative play and, 158–159
power versus nurturance and, 175–177
premise system and, 153–154, 157, 161–163
Social psychology, 49–50
Spatial comprehension, walking and, 90, 94
Spelling, resistance to authority and, 53–54
Stage theory, *see* Developmental stages
Stimulus control, sex differences in, 157
Structuralization, 40
Structure, in play, sex differences in, 158–159
Subjectivity, 193
developmental analysis of, 196–198
study of, 195

T

Teachers, contingent responding of, sex differences and, 154
Temperament
concept of, 208–209
parent-infant interactions and, 101–107
Theory(ies)
construction of, 66
development of, 78–81
generality of, 112, 127–128
lack of emphasis on individual, 111–112
metaphors in, 67
prototypical forms of, 71–78
relationships among, 67–71
relationship to practice, 3–4, 122–127
relationship to research, 126

Theory combination, 79
in evolution of developmental interactionism, 80–81
Thought
influence by affect, 49–50
role in organizing experience, 44
Toys
differential experience with, sex differences and, 155–156, 158–159
exploratory behaviors and, sex differences in, 160
Types, theories of, 74

V

Values, 4
curriculum and, 136, 141–142
Variables, definition of, 148
Variation, in psychology of person, 73

W

Walking
communication gestures and, 90, 94
maternal relationship and, 89–90, 94
spatial comprehension and, 90, 94
"Whole child" concept, 77
development of, 80–81
evolution of, 71
Widening, in theory development, 79–81
developmental interactionism, 81
Women's liberation movement, sex-role stereotype and, 2, 176
World hypotheses, 67